OPEN HOUSE

PATRICK CREAN EDITIONS

HarperCollins*Publishers*Ltd

OPEN HOUSE

A Life in Thirty-Two Moves

Jane Christmas

Published by Patrick Crean Editions, an imprint of HarperCollins Publishers Ltd

First edition

HarperCollins Publishers Ltd
Bay Adelaide Centre, East Tower
22 Adelaide Street West, 41st Floor
Toronto, Ontario, Canada
M5H 4E3

www.harpercollins.ca

Library and Archives Canada Cataloguing in Publication

Title: Open house : a life in thirty-two moves / Jane Christmas.
Names: Christmas, Jane, 1954- author.
Identifiers: Canadiana (print) 20190168706 | Canadiana (ebook) 20190168714 |
ISBN 9781443458764 (softcover) | ISBN 9781443458771 (ebook)
Subjects: LCSH: Christmas, Jane, 1954-—Homes and haunts. |
LCSH: Travel writers—Canada—Biography. |
LCSH: Dwellings—Remodeling—Canada. | LCSH: Moving, Household—Canada.
Classification: LCC TH4816 .C57 2020 | DDC 643.7092—dc23

Printed and bound in the United States of America

LSC/C   10 9 8 7 6 5 4 3 2 1

I would keep my place if I knew my place;
things have never been that neat.
—Graffiti on the wall of a Toronto home

CONTENTS

OPEN HOUSE

1

The Acknowledged Catalyst

I cannot live in our home anymore. We have to move.

The Husband and I face one another at the security cordon of London's Gatwick Airport. These words have not yet sprung from my lips; they remain in my head, though they have also spilled onto a missive, crafted in careful language, which is folded and tucked under my husband's pillow at home. It awaits his patient reading and will demand his complete understanding and action. I am asking a lot of him, because unlike me he is a creature of routine and stability. He does not like change. He does not like moving. Less than two years earlier, I had promised him that this was it; that we would not move again for a very, very long time. But now that promise must be broken.

Back when the promise was made it had been a reasonable, heart-felt one. We had just endured a level of home-buying stress that had all the bewildering confusion of a pantomime and none of the hilarity. England's convoluted system of buying and selling houses is not built for gentle constitutions, which goes some way in explaining why Britons are one of the least mobile and most risk-averse cultures on earth.

As a Canadian, I am made of hardier stuff: I enjoy moving house. No, let me rephrase that: I *love* moving house. I love the search for a new home, the packing up and the subsequent assessment and de-cluttering of all that I own, when old and new face off in a fight to survive the charity shop box. I love planning a new space, designing and styling the interior, thumbing through stacks of paint and fabric swatches. I love the ruminating, the budgeting, the logistical organization, the legal details involved in a title search. I have even grown to enjoy (with the exception of our last move) the chaos that is part and parcel of the moving experience.

Statistics reveal that Britons move on average three times in a lifetime, Canadians about seven times, and Americans about eleven times. I, however, have moved thirty-two times.

To some people, thirty-two house moves looks like recklessness; to me, thirty-two moves looks like life. And life is one big open house.

A track record like that does not come without personal stock-taking. Here is one: I have had more homes than lovers, by a long shot. A virtuous statement, and one that I wear proudly. Thirty-two homes in sixty-three years works out to one home every second year. Would I trade that for a new lover every second year? Are you crazy? I could never maintain a sex life like that—I would be too bored. But while I am not sexually promiscuous, when it comes to homes I am a shameless, serial adulterer. I have cast a covetous eye over other homes in my neighbourhood. I have brassily walked up to a new neighbour and drawn him or her into such intimate conversation, twirling the ends of my hair around a painted fingernail, that within seconds I am purring my way into their home just to check the lay-out and decor. I have sat on the sofa in a home I have just moved into and immediately started swiping left and right on Rightmove or MLS. Sex toys? Forget it. But give me a pencil and a floor plan and, oh, baby, I can reach ecstasy before you can say "stud wall."

Second fact: I fall in love faster with a house than I do with a person. This I am not so proud of, because it probably puts me at the wrong end of the Asperger's spectrum. Nevertheless, it is the God's honest truth: I get more excited about meeting a new house than I do about meeting a new person. Perhaps that is true of most introverts. No tedious or awkward conversation required, no probing questions to circumvent. Does that make me cold-hearted? Indicate intimacy issues? Does it mean I relate better to buildings than humans? Does it look like I care?

For their part, houses are not as obviously discriminating as peo-ple, but they size you up—oh yes, they do. They absolutely pass judg-ment on you. For that reason, I am always on my best behaviour when I meet a new house, especially one that is for sale. A house can smell desperation on a potential buyer as surely as you can smell damp on it. There have been times when I have been actually flustered, almost on a crush level, about visiting a particular house. I think a home can smell that, too. Where I draw the line about lusting after a house is when it is a friend's: I never flirt with or fantasize about their homes. I will cheer their own plans, and gush about their decorating exper-tise, but I will not so much as tamper with the placement of a sofa cushion. Unless, that is, I am asked.

Like lovers, houses can and do disappoint; on the outside they can be as sleek as a runway model, but on the inside they are vapid—a few radiators short of a heating system, if you know what I mean. The seasoned homebuyer deftly learns to separate the pretentious from the practical.

That is not to say that I can't easily be seduced by a house. My pulse quickens when my eyes land on something that I know was built for me. There are some that I have actually stalked—online and in person—and I have occupied pleasant hours gazing at photos of its interior online or in a realtor's brochure, imagining the place decorated and arranged with my furniture, and me cuddled into it with the sort of happy contentment that puts an end to my roving eye. When the object of my affection falls into the hands of a real buyer, I have been known to become distraught and to tumble into a period of deep mourning.

Buying a home has never frightened me or kept me up late at night; buying a car, yes; perhaps an item of clothing; but never a house. I am completely at home with homes in the same way people are at home with horses or recreational drugs. Nothing scares me about them. If a house intrigues me, and as long as a murder has not taken place in it, I can work with anything. Actually, if a murder has taken place in it, I will still look at the floor plan. I have been in houses where the layout was not appealing or where the scope and the result of a renovation would not produce enough of a satisfactory buzz, but I can pretty much look at anything and envision a spotless transformation. No floors? No problem. Leaky roof? Whatever. Dated and ugly bathroom? Piece of cake. My fantasies extend into that semi-masochist stratosphere of buying and renovating a home in a country where I do not speak the language. What a delicious thrill that would be. But I am not there yet, and I have accepted the fact that it is unlikely to happen. Not in this lifetime, anyway.

The only time I have come close to swearing off houses is when the experience has been a nightmare, such as our last move. It was so nerve-racking that I vowed never to go through it again. More specifically, I vowed never again to put my husband through it. As The Husband will read in the note that lies waiting for him beneath his pillow: "I do not relish the idea of moving, either, but I am prepared to take it on because I am desperate. The combination of unbearable noise and lack of natural light hampers my concentration. All the ideas and dreams I have when I am outside the house are crushed the moment I walk through the front door. This house is suffocating me."

Of course, he does not know any of that right now because we are at the airport. I am about to fly across the ocean for three weeks of work, which will give him time to digest my note and acclimatize to the idea of boxes, house hunts, and unforeseen costs. Of uprooting a settled life and starting over.

It is only when he kisses me goodbye at the security gate that I tell him about the note under his pillow. I do not tell him about its contents.

His face falls.

"Don't be upset," I say. "You know me—I have to write out my thoughts in order to express myself clearly. I get tongue-tied when I try to talk to you about emotional things."

"Can you give me a hint what it's about?" he asks, searching my face for clues concealed beneath a practised smile.

I give him another kiss goodbye. "Just read it. We'll talk about it when I return."

Now he looks on the verge of panic, eyes wide, jaw trembling ever so slightly.

I reassure him with a wink. "Don't worry, sweetheart. I'm not leaving you."

Once he reads that note he will wish I was.

IF I HAD HAD AN INKLING during our seven-year transatlantic courtship of The Husband's reticence about moving and about change in general, I would never have married him. It would not have been fair to either of us. I see moving as a natural, exciting adventure; he sees moving as a high-ranked indicator in the Holmes-Rahe Stress Inventory.

The Husband is English through and through. He likes his Sunday roast, football, and tea or a pint in front of the fire. He likes the quiet life. His calm, easygoing demeanour belies the cautious, worrying type who lives behind the facade. He does not court chaos. He judges things by how they appear in front of him, not by what they can become. His approach veers toward the pessimistic, weighing the probability of disaster especially if he is about to purchase something big.

He had lived in the same two-bedroom flat in northeast London for twenty-five years. It was the upper flat of a double-bayed Victorian semi-detached house on a tree-lined street of similar homes. It always frustrated me that the house was divided into upper and lower flats, and I often wondered how it might have looked had we bought the lower flat and returned the house to a single-family home.

Until I arrived in his life, he had never had anything done to update his place. It looked like bad student digs, with mismatched charity furniture, faded magnolia walls, and bare bulbs hanging from the ceiling, unsuccessfully masked with flimsy paper shades. I do not know where one even buys that sort of thing. The original state of the bathroom and kitchen do not merit description, but once renovated they looked very smart.

When we married and I moved to England, it was a given that we would move to a larger place once he retired. He was keen to move, though in hindsight he might not have been keen to move away from Walthamstow. However, as London property prices soared and it became glaringly obvious that we were priced out of the market, he was as relieved as I was to leave the city.

We could have moved anywhere in Britain, but we chose south-west England for its more reasonable weather and rugged coastal scenery. Our intensive weekend searches of Devon and Cornwall eventually brought us to the coastal town of Brixham, a place that attracted us. "Attracted" is not an entirely honest term. "Became infatuated to the point of obsession and losing all sense of the practical" is more like it, at least from my standpoint.

Brixham lured us with its relaxed coastal vibe and its authenticity. It was a proper working fishing port, with fleets of trawlers chugging out to sea early each morning and returning by mid-afternoon, hulls heaving with mackerel, conger, whiting, cod, black bream, bass, mussels. Neither The Husband nor I was *au fait* with seafood, but we were eager to try it. Besides, there was more than fish here: there was the gentle whoosh of the surf; the parade of shops, pubs, restaurants, and ice cream kiosks; the replica of the Golden Hind. There were cheerfully painted terraced homes draped like strung beads in a multi-strand necklace around the collar of the harbour, where skiffs and sailboats bobbed in watery glitter. We had walked into a cliché and fallen for it hook, line, and sinker.

The British seaside has long held an appeal for a certain type of retiree, but were we that certain type? Are you, dear reader? If, like me, you are a fan of cultural diversity, of year-round arts and street scenes, of cinemas, libraries, museums, art galleries, bookshops, live theatre, and fast trains to the city, then heed my words: avoid the seaside. It was only when we had finally moved to the Devon countryside that I detected a subtle but insidious campaign by social planners to nudge older people out of the cities and decant them to coastal geriatric ghettos. But by then, I was so high on love for Brixham that I did not care if such an edict had been mandated by a Russian oligarch.

Usually, my well-honed intuition will kick in to save me from making a huge error in judgment, but it did not this time. Or if there was a kick, I likely misread it as a sign to buy the early nineteenth-century double-fronted stucco cottage we eventually fell for. It was the type of place where you expected to find Poldark leaning against the mantel with a glass of port, smouldering with lust. And I am not even a fan of Poldark.

The front door opened into a small vestibule that in turn opened to a spacious room—to one side was the living area; to the other, separated by whitewashed beam work, was the dining area. It was all bleached wood, white walls, and tawny sisal carpeting. Behind this area was a kitchen that spanned the width of the house, and that came equipped with a Belfast sink and a large five-burner, three-oven range. A stable door led to a tiny courtyard that was dominated by what would have made an excellent climbing wall had we been rock climbers. From there, thirty-three precarious flagstone steps led up to the garden and its panoramic view of the town and harbour. We could see right across the bay to Torquay. Back inside the house, the two upper levels held four double-size bedrooms, two beautifully appointed and spacious bathrooms, and a storage room. It had more room than we needed, and aside from a bit of tweaking it required no work. A bonus was that the house was all of fifteen seconds from the harbour, the shops, pubs, and restaurants, and a fifteen-minute walk to the gorgeous, undulating Devonian coastline.

I felt a sudden connection to the house, convinced that we had "lucked out." The Husband had agreed only because he saw the joy it gave me: "Happy Wife, Happy Life," as the saying goes. If he voiced any objection, I did not hear it. I was too smitten. The house had the trifecta of English charm: quaint, quirky, and cozy—catnip to anglophiles like me. I was the one who had anointed it the "perfect home," the one who upon entering it for the first time had squealed, "Let's put in an offer." And the price? This beautiful, spacious house cost less than the cramped two-bedroom, gardenless flat we had just sold in London.

Unusually—and prophetically—the estate agent for the property tried to talk us out of it, or at least tried to quell my enthusiasm. He had prudently suggested we look at nearby towns, where the culture and amenities were more suited to our personalities. I paid him no heed; did not even bother to visit the places he suggested, so confident was I in my heart's desire. But I was wrong; he was right. There are times when other people—strangers, especially—can read you better than you can read yourself. Not long after we moved in, we visited the towns the estate agent had recommended, and I immediately regretted not having listened to him. To this day, I still troll property websites for homes in those same towns. As the adage goes, it really is about "location, location, location," because on the days when your house wears you down, there is no place like town.

We bought the Brixham house and moved in. It took our furniture easily. We painted, redid the kitchen; put in bookcases and a wood-burning stove in the living room. The house was entirely comfortable.

When I would mention to friends that we had moved to Devon, their mouths would drop, their shoulders would relax, their eyes would glaze with envy. "You lucky bastards," they would say. When they visited us, their envy was confirmed: the house was "chocolate box," the town's laid-back lifestyle was idyllic. Even the weekend pirates who descended on the town in full Johnny Depp and growling "Arrrr" gave a bit of cheesy charm to the place. A walk up the high street, where I did my grocery shopping at the butcher's and the green grocer's, guaranteed a wave back from the merchants. I felt like the reborn Scrooge who became a friend to all. I got involved in my local church. Our neighbours were lovely. There were days when I had to pinch myself that I was living in this little slice of heaven.

As for the house, it was like a rambunctious, eager-to-please Labrador, happy to be teased with paint colours and furniture arrangements, anything to save it from holiday-home hell and restore it to a permanent family home. Our talk became inclusive of the house, as in: "The house would look nice in this colour." Or, "This would look great in the house." Or, "Should we do this to the house?" Or, "If we go away, what should we do with the house?" In fact, the house became The House, as if it were an animated entity. When a gutter leaked like a dripping nose, we rushed to tend to it. Each month the window cleaner would arrive, and you could feel The House perk up as it welcomed the pampering. In the evenings, when The Husband and I snuggled on our sofa in front of the roaring fire, I could not help thinking that The House was relaxing, too, smiling benignly at its wonderful owners who coddled and loved it. It was like the third person in our marriage, and we were absolutely fine with that. I adored The House.

And then I did not.

Never have I fallen so completely and irrevocably out of love with a home as I did with this one. This loss of affection had nothing to do with The House itself: I would have happily picked it up and moved it elsewhere had that been possible. The problem was where it had been planted, and when the issue involves location, there is no option but to move. The pluses of the location, the ones of convenience that had seduced me, were many, but the few negatives carried more weight. We had viewed the house in February, which gave no clue to the tourist traffic nightmare that awaited us. At the first whiff of summer, cars and trucks whizzing past our front door became intolerable. Impatient drivers, caught up in the traffic-clotted narrow street, would lean on their horns and swear. Not the nice swearing, either, the sort done under the breath, but the bullying kind that spews the worst possible language at full bray. If it wasn't the cars and their drivers, it was the motorbikes. From April to November, the town's drug trade shifted into full gear, and numerous times an hour we endured the razor-like rip and whine of motorbikes gunning it back and forth as the dealers delivered their wares. A writer requires a certain level of quiet, though in my case not necessarily absolute silence: I can write with power drills and jackhammers in the background, but not with people swearing and motorbikes screaming.

Then there were the seagulls. No one had warned us about the seagulls.

Our first memory of Brixham was of driving into the town and watching masses of gulls wheel and dip against a steel-wool sky, white feathers lit by a single shard of sun that had penetrated dense stratocumulus clouds. We could not hear them—our car windows were rolled up tightly against the threat of rain—but even with the windows down I doubt we would have noticed. Their languid arabesques muted all our other senses and transported us to imaginary childhood memories of seaside holidays. This was Famous Five territory. Enid Blyton awaited us with sand pail and shovel in hand.

How quickly seagulls go from being the siren of playful days at the beach to the siren that drives you to consider self-harm or murder. Noisy, dirty scavengers. By night they kept us awake; by day they terrorized us in our garden.

I had decided to turn the shed at the top of our garden into a writing studio, but this did not sit well with the seagulls. As I repainted the shed and stocked it with my supplies and writing totems, a pair of gulls perched on a nearby roof, monitoring my movements like Gestapo agents, screaming their disapproval to their brethren, who seconds later swooped in and joined the squawk of displeasure. I persisted. But hunched over my laptop, working up my thoughts, I could hear the seagulls land on the shed roof with a great thud and stomp back and forth, their gnarly talons scraping the abrasive asphalt felting like fingernails on a chalkboard. I would emerge from the shed and yell and shake my fist at them; they would step up their assault, dive-bombing and pelting me with their guano. Eventually, I surrendered. I packed up my laptop, files, writing materials, and carried them back down the perilous steps, into the house and up two flights of stairs, where I set up camp in a spare bedroom. Which faced the road with the bumper-to-bumper traffic and the swearing drivers.

Moving my study inside did not silence the seagulls. They were particularly vociferous during their breeding and nesting seasons, but even in the off-season they made an unholy racket. At 3 a.m. one morning, they inexplicably erupted into a wild round of screeching that sounded like a party of toddlers having a go at one another with baseball bats and knives in the ball pool at Ikea. The Husband, who is a friend to nature and is so gentlemanly that his face winces and his body jerks when he hears profanity, shot up in bed and shouted, "WHEN THE FUCK ARE THEY GOING TO SHUT UP?" The seagulls were turning us into ugly versions of ourselves, driving us away as quickly as they had ensnared us.

Another big negative was that natural light was an infrequent visitor in our home. The narrow road we lived on was bordered on both sides by towering terraced homes that blocked virtually all available light and sense of the outdoors from the ground level of our home. We had to climb two flights of stairs to view the sky and get a true picture of the weather conditions. Something had to give.

Surreptitiously at first, I began to troll the property websites. As desperation mounted, I called estate agents and arranged for viewings of other homes. We would return from these outings and slink in the front door, not wanting to offend The House, not wanting it to know what we had been up to. But The House knew. It could tell we had been out admiring another house; it could smell the cleaning products of a rival on our clothes; it could read our distracted expressions, our lost affection as we wrestled with how to break the news to it. I sensed it glowering at us, hands on hips, scolding, "You've been seeing other houses. I know you have. You shameful two-timers!"

The House was all wrong for me for other reasons. I thought I would be happy living a small-town life, but I was not. I felt cut off from the wider world. I wanted more: more culture, more discourse, more diversity, nicer shops, galleries, a cinema, more anonymity, and I began to not only resent the absence of these things but mourn them like the loss of oxygen. Each time we drove back into town after being away for a few hours or a few days I could feel a part of me dying inside.

I DO NOT KNOW WHAT went through The Husband's head that day when we parted at Gatwick's security cordon, or his first reaction upon reading the note that lay under his pillow. For me, I adopted a fearless, stoic resolution that you only see on the faces of veterans of war. I marched resolutely through security, sat patiently in the departures lounge while flipping through property websites, and then boarded the flight. Settled into my window seat, I stared tight jawed at the tarmac beyond and took a deep breath. "We have to move," I finally said aloud to no one in particular, after having repeated the phrase so many times to myself.

CARKFIELD DRIVE

2

The Foundation Is Set

Moving has been in my blood, has been my way of life since my earliest years, but the crucial support framework necessary for a lifetime of moving house was not as robust as it could have been.

I was born in Toronto, in the midst of a baby boom and a building boom. The city was reinventing itself for the modern age, and by extension so was its citizenry. Time to shake off that colonial past, develop some can-do spirit, give Hog Town a cosmopolitan makeover. The urgency for progress was dizzying, as if the city had just discovered a cache of mortar that had to be used up. Like all new things, everyone wanted it yesterday. You might be able to renovate a house virtually overnight, but not an entire city or its population. It would be many decades before a whiff of cosmopolitanism descended on Toronto the Good. In the meantime, the movers and shakers had set about redrawing the city, and they were assembling cranes and hoisting up the wrecking ball. Down came the old and dowdy; up went the tall and shiny. Houses, office buildings, hospitals, schools, shopping malls.

My generation was the lucky beneficiary of this modernization scheme. We entered brand-new schools where everything was pristine: there was not so much as a film of chalk dust in the classrooms or worn varnish on the gymnasium floors. I experienced this over and over, because by the time I was nine years old, I had already lived in three houses and attended five different schools. The pattern was firmly imprinted.

Psychologists today would have lots to say about the impact of a peripatetic life on a youngster. Perhaps back then there was a body of work that revealed disturbing statistics on the subject, some insight into the effects on so-called army brats—the children of servicemen and -women who were frequently uprooted from one military base to another with their parents. But for the most part no one considered the emotional, psychological, or social ramifications that numerous moves had on a child. My parents certainly did not. Neither of them was in the armed forces; they just moved a lot. Had there been any such research, they would not have paid it the slightest heed. Especially my mother. She was the reason we always moved.

I do not recall my young self being particularly flustered about moving from one house to another. I had tried to absorb it as an adventure, an opportunity to explore new places and meet a new tribe of youngsters who were ready to play with me. I tried to rationalize moving as a normal part of life: that all families moved into a house, lived there for a while, then packed up and moved to a different one. Like musical chairs, but with houses.

Except that my apparent amenability was a ruse, a necessary coping mechanism to please my parents so they would not worry about me. The reality for me was that moving was a black hole that sucked out familiar friends and hurtled me into an unknown universe to make new ones. Sure, being part of the great baby boom meant there was no shortage of young playmates, but for a shy, anxious child like me this was no consolation. I acquired—as if by osmosis—chameleon attributes: seeking the background, adopting a muted expression. I wore the mask of the polite and deferential; of the easygoing and compliant that, while not at all my natural character, would at least score friends. If I knew anything at that age, it was that no one likes a bossy-boots, and you are more likely to attract friends if you appear submissive.

It was the finality of moving that disturbed me, of being wrenched from the familiar and tossed into a quadrant far away with no hope of returning. Nowadays, when I track our various homes on a map of Toronto, I am surprised at how close they are in relation to one another. But distance is an abstract concept when you are nine years old and do not drive: tell a kid that you are moving four miles away and you might as well tell them you are moving to Saturn.

Moving is said to make a person more resilient, more able to adapt and integrate into different social situations. That was the reasoning my parents used. But it was not my experience: I grew more sensitive, more aware of how different our family was. An invisible line of demarcation between the normal and "us" was cleaved into my understanding. I felt like an outsider.

My mother was unimpressed with my sentimental attachment to friends. I confided in her my doubts about moving, my fears about missing my friends, but she scoffed, "Friends do not matter. You'll forget them the moment we're in our new home. New home, new friends."

No, I thought, that cannot be right: Friends are vital for people like me. They are facilitators and guides to the complexity of neighbourhoods, schoolyards, relationships, and life in general. My circle of friends was small, but they were good, loyal pals who were savvier than I.

My best friend was Cheryll. She lived one street over from me in the then new suburb of Don Mills. She and I had met in kindergarten, and we formed one of those adhesive friendships that, if you are lucky, will accompany you through life. Crucially, Cheryll had a grasp of the world that I lacked, and through her I learned how life operated outside the tightly controlled home of my parents. What I was to appreciate decades later was that childhood friends are the glue of one's past: who else remembers you as that tentative, awkward kid but a friend from primary school?

Still, I had to trust that what my mother said about friends was true, even if she refused to acknowledge that my personality made it difficult for me to make new friends. Then she said something so shocking that it lodged itself permanently in my consciousness: "People are important, but they will not get you ahead in life. Only property can do that. Remember that. Property first, people second."

Her words stunned me and confused my green world concerning the nature of relationships. How could she say such a thing? Hadn't we just learned in Sunday school that passage from John saying something about there being no greater demonstration of love than that of someone laying down his life for his friends? Not laying down his life for his property; for his friends.

I argued the point with my mother. This moving thing was grossly unfair. She stood her ground.

"Don't be so sensitive. You need to roll with the punches. You need to toughen up."

"But what about *your* friends?" I finally said with as much petulance as I could get away with without being spanked or sent to my room.

"Your father and I will make new ones, just like you will."

They did. Of course they did. They had a car and a telephone, and so their social circle expanded exponentially and effortlessly, whereas my social circle shrank because it was constantly being redrawn.

Exploratory forays into each new neighbourhood confirmed for me that my family was different, perhaps even weird in terms of their frequent moves. My opener when meeting potential playmates was "How long have you lived here?" It astonished me to meet people who had lived in the same house for more than four years. Or who had been born in their home; had only known the house they were living in. In turn, they reacted with suspicion when I rhymed off the places where I had lived, regaling them the way an intrepid explorer might regale fellow adventurers around a tavern table but who in the midst of the telling rapidly recognizes how foolhardy it must sound.

"Why do you have to move so much?" my playmates quizzed.

"I have no idea."

WHEN I THINK BACK to all the homes of my childhood, the one that resonates most strongly is Larkfield Drive. Perhaps the reason has to do with the fact that I was young; that it is the first home I remember, and that it was the only brand-new home we ever lived in. Larkfield Drive was in the new experimental development of Don Mills, and it was here that my world view was formed.

The area encompassing Don Mills was settled in 1817. Its name was conferred by Elizabeth Simcoe, wife of John Graves Simcoe, Upper Canada's first lieutenant-governor, who in 1793 wrote that the river that ran through this area east of the city of York (now Toronto) reminded her of the River Don in her home county of Yorkshire.

From the time Earth was formed up until the mid-1950s, Don Mills was largely untamed, an area of gentle hills, forests, rivers wending innocently through a landscape that gradually included farmland and pastures. A few miles away, Toronto was racing toward its hopeful status as Centre of the Universe: immigrants were arriving weekly to supply labour to a growing host of industries, businesses, and services. Expansion was furious. Bucolic Don Mills remained virtually untouched, until it bumped up against dump trucks and planning schematics, and then redevelopment pounced swiftly. In 1950, Don Mills was home to about two dozen farms; five years later, it was home to about fifteen thousand new homes—the first planned residential community in Canada, and a blueprint for future North American cities.

Don Mills was built around the Bauhaus principles of its founder Walter Gropius, a pioneer of modern architecture. The movement gained traction in post–Second World War North America, where it was lauded, or criticized, depending on your sensibilities, for its radical house designs: angular and sculptural in appearance; low to the ground, with split-level layouts. Oddly, while espousing leading-edge designs and worthy principles about green spaces, Bauhaus exerted draconian control and conformity, and it became one of those creative movements that sees itself as so ahead of the curve that it fails to recognize its own hypocrisy: to wit, streetscapes were subject to regulated design edicts, and homeowners were forbidden to change the colour of their homes, not even the front door.

My parents' home at 10 Larkfield Drive (since demolished and replaced by one of those monster homes that have bullied their way into older suburban enclaves) was a popular model in the development: a split-level, three-bedroom home with a broad, obtuse roofline. The front entrance was a recessed courtyard with irregular windows whose shapes mimicked the roofline. On the main level was a study/den, and behind it an open-plan dining/living room with a large glass wall and door that faced the backyard and patio. The kitchen, small but functional, had a side door that my brother and I were instructed to use whenever we came indoors from playing outside. The upstairs was compact: three bedrooms and a bathroom. Below the main floor were two lower levels: the first led to our family room, with its green-marbled linoleum floor; one more level down was the cellar, where the laundry was done and where my dad kept his few tools, though it could not be said that he was in any way handy.

Where our house differed from those of my friends was in its interior. My friends' homes had furniture with straight sides, glossy surfaces, sofas and chairs of easy comfort, the type of furniture that suited a Bauhaus home. Our furniture was unusually shaped, embellished with carvings, turned feet, winged armrests, filigreed handles. Mahogany chairs, tables, sideboards, and cabinets looked distinctly out of place in this modern surrounding, like a group of elderly gentlemen who have wandered into a rave. That my mother referred to some of the pieces by name, such as "the Adam" and "the Chippendale," added to the weirdness, and made my friends snicker.

"Why does she have names for her furniture?"

"I think they are like her pets," I gamely said.

Indeed, my mother stroked, buffed, nurtured, doted on her furniture, and ensured the pieces were in prizewinning condition. Young fingers were discouraged from touching them; the bite would have been severe. At the same time, that furniture, erect and imperious, appeared to hold us all to account, and the collection sat among us as if it were doing us a huge favour by deigning to live in suburbia.

Outside our Victorian/Bauhaus home, newness reigned—in the young fledgling trees planted throughout the subdivision that grew quickly and softened the harsh geometric shapes of the houses; in the smell of freshly rolled-out turf; in the slick, shiny blacktop driveways; and in the thousands of smartly dressed young families and their babies who moved into the area. It was like a specific demographic had been selected to colonize the area, and we were its pioneers.

The writer John Cheever, who hated the suburbs but ended up living in one, lamented in an article that appeared in *Esquire* in 1960: "My God, the suburbs! They encircled the city's boundaries like enemy territory, and we thought of them as a loss of privacy, a cesspool of conformity and a life of indescribable dreariness in some split-level village where the place name appeared in the *New York Times* only when some bored housewife blew off her head with a shotgun."

But Don Mills was not a cesspool of "indescribable dreariness": it was the place to live if you were young and ambitious, which my parents were. The average homeowner was between twenty and thirty years old, and included journalists, actors, artists, academics, advertising and marketing professionals, TV performers and writers.

An occasional visitor to our home was Robert Homme, who wrote and starred in the popular children's TV program *The Friendly Giant*. My brother and I were explicitly instructed by our parents to address him as "Mr. Homme" and not by his TV name of "Friendly." Mr. Homme happened to drop by one evening—obviously not wearing his alter ego's Robin Hood–type tunic and tights—to speak with my father. My brother and I were getting ready for bed, and Mr. Homme asked my parents for the honour of reading us a bedtime story. That is how he phrased it: "the honour." His humility touched me; if anything, it was an honour for us to be read to by the Friendly Giant. I have never forgotten his courteousness and gentleness, or his comforting, sonorous voice. Nor have I forgotten my awe: "Wow, Friendly is reading *us* a bedtime story!"

Larkfield Drive was as singsong sunny and carefree as its name implies. The sky was preternaturally cerulean; the air as clear and clean as a new pane of glass; the grass and shrubs in our large backyard as glossy as polished tsavorite. When my mind's eye roams the streetscape in front of our house, however, the grass is always, curiously, parched; as gold as a wheat field. I have wondered about this many times: why the backyards of my imagination are green and lush, while the front yards are dry and pale. Perhaps from the vantage point of a youngster the terrain beyond our property was a metaphorical wasteland: that life beyond our home had yet to bloom and colour for me, while the backyard where I played was as green as I was.

I barely remember the winters; what is fixed in my mind are the summers—long, hot, humid summers of perpetual sunshine alternating against a soundtrack of lawn mowers and the high-pitched drone of the cicadas.

Mr. Tamaki, our gardener, kept the property trimmed and our trees, shrubs, and flowers blooming in orderly profusion. My parents also employed a cleaning lady. Mrs. Kaiser was young, beautiful, and blond, and she went through our home cheerfully dusting, vacuuming, and washing. At the end of the day, she would slip into the bathroom to change her clothes, and emerge minutes later in a plain but figure-enhancing shift, makeup applied and hair done up in a slight beehive. She would wait patiently by the front door for the arrival of Mr. Kaiser, young, blond, and handsome at the wheel of a gleaming red convertible. Mrs. Kaiser would lift a patterned scarf over her neat coiffure and tie it under her pretty chin, don a pair of white-framed sunglasses, and when smiling Mr. Kaiser arrived, she would elegantly slide into the white-leather passenger seat and with a gloved hand would wave us goodbye. As we waved back, I often wondered why the cleaning lady was more glamorous and happier than the people for whom she worked. A few years later, after our black Monarch finally and blessedly bit the dust, my father bought an ice-blue Ford Galaxy 500 convertible. We could at least pretend to be the Kaisers, pretend that we were cool and carefree when we went out for long drives— at least until my mother insisted that we stop at every antique shop along the way.

I was permitted to have friends over to play, but not when Mrs. Kaiser was there, or when my mother had a telephone interview to conduct (she was a columnist for the local paper), or when my father was at home. We could play on the front or back lawn, but only if Mr. Tamaki was not there working and only if we were quiet. My father had a low tolerance of children; my mother subscribed to the Doris Lessing school of parenting: "There is nothing more boring for an intelligent woman than to spend endless amounts of time with small children." To my parents, play was a waste of time and children were a boisterous interruption to their quiet, smarter pursuits. Their eyeballs rolled whenever my brother and I pleaded with them to play in the sandbox with us, and if they relented, it came across as a huge sacrifice and never lasted more than three minutes. They did not want to play with us or converse with us; they conveyed to us that they had better things to do.

Eventually, my brother and I stopped asking. After all, we had an entire neighbourhood of playmates. Every home had at least one child. A notable exception was our next-door neighbours, a generous and childless couple, the MacDonnells, who kept a large freezer in their carport stocked with Popsicles and freezies, and who invited us kids to help ourselves. It was a child's paradise: all you had to do was walk out the front door and there would be a kid or three waiting to throw a ball or go for a bike ride or ask you to play house.

My parents' social circle was equally abundant. On the weekends, they had lively dinner parties, to which my brother and I were explicitly not invited. Bathed, readied for bed in our crisp pyjamas, we were allowed to greet the guests and to take their coats to my parents' bedroom, but once all the guests had arrived, we were shooed off to our rooms and ordered not to come out. I always disobeyed. I would sit on a step hidden from view of the main floor, and listen to adult gossip and laughter, stealing a peek at the women in their shimmering pearls, the flared skirts of their satiny dresses rhythmically swinging and swishing to the music on the hi-fi. I enjoyed the house when it was filled with adults, and I loved seeing my parents in high spirits, laughing with their friends. But when the guests had left and the evidence of the party was cleaned up, they retreated into their silent lives—my mother to her writing, my father behind a newspaper or book. Occasionally, my mother would break the silence and monotony by mentioning that she had seen a new house—it was always coded as "having possibilities." Something seemed to catch her fancy every week. Dad would lower his newspaper and listen to her avidly. He never discouraged her, nor did he ever encourage her, but he nonetheless would agree to go along "just to take a look" at her new discovery.

Move? Why was that necessary? And why was I not being consulted?

Being young sucked. I bristled against the powerlessness of childhood, and against not being allowed to express my emotions and feelings. Oh, the insignificance of being so young, and of having to weather the miserly affections of adults. I craved my parents' attention and love, but it was as if they were withholding it until my brother and I grew up and became interesting. Furthermore, I sensed that if I did not share their interests, there would be no hope of me having any kind of a relationship with them.

If my parents could not wait for my brother and I to grow out of childhood, I could not wait to be an adult and have my own home.

We all scrutinize our childhood and ruminate about those metamorphic, sometimes seismic moments like archeologists excavating some unexpected disruption in the advancement of humanity. No such rumination is ever undertaken without laying the blame at the feet of those who raised us, taught us, employed us, befriended us, dumped us, hurt us, or upheld us. They all contribute to the strata of our existence, making it as defined and impermeable as an exposed face of raw rock. We are set in the stone of our own making and histories.

In the years since the deaths of my parents (my father in 1999, my mother in 2013) I have come to understand that the madness concerning their serial house moves was not of a capricious variety but rather the kind driven by circumstances that must have affected them deeply. Both their upbringings were shaped by instability: my father's by grinding poverty and parental irresponsibility, my mother's by political tyranny and necessary immigration.

To my father first. He was the eldest of four children born to Lancashire mill workers who immigrated to Toronto in the early 1900s. They raised their family in a slum approached down a grimy lane in the city's Yorkville district. (My father lived to see his old soot-covered neighbourhood turned into Toronto's most expensive and desirable address.) At the age of five, my father was sent out to work to help support the family. He hawked newspapers every day at the busy corner of Yonge and Bloor Streets. On the Sabbath, he lit fires for Jewish families in his neighbourhood. It makes me extremely uncomfortable to think of sending a child of that age out to work, especially alone. Who knows what near misses of danger my father evaded, for he was a sweet-looking boy, blond of hair, blue of eye, and gentle of nature. The experience had a profound impact on him because it became his private crusade to escape the wretchedness of tenement life and to raise himself from penury.

The model that spurred this crusade was *his* father. Stanley was a dreamer, an unreliable provider, and a liar. His boast—and lie—that he once played for Bolton Wanderers football club was intended to mark him as being too special to toil in the workaday world of his new adopted homeland. Whatever money he made, he took to the pub, while his family shivered and went hungry at home.

My father had no intention of being the loafing, larking fool that was his father. He applied himself to his studies, and his diligence earned praise and prizes at school. Like many of his generation, he enlisted in the Second World War, and once it was over, he parked the trauma of that horrific tour of duty and took advantage of a government-sponsored university scholarship.

Stanley, meanwhile, shuffled reluctantly into steady work as a bus driver for the Toronto Transit Commission, with overtime to boot— or so he told my grandmother. He said he had been conscripted by the TTC to train new bus drivers in the growing city of London, about two hundred miles southwest of Toronto. Each Friday he would leave his family for London then return on Monday to Toronto in time for supper. It took Hurricane Hazel to end his deceit: He died in the midst of the raging storm in October 1954, of a heart attack. At his funeral, a TTC supervisor who approached my grief-stricken grandmother to pay his respects was surprised by her rebuke:

"Your company led my husband to an early grave, making him work seven days a week," she cried.

The TTC supervisor gently corrected her: "Stanley never accepted our offer of overtime. He said he needed to spend time with his family. In London."

"Nonsense," said my grandmother. "Our home is in Toronto, not London."

As fragments of lies were pieced together, the picture revealed a scandal: Stanley had been keeping a second family in another city.

The shock was devastating, not just for my grandmother but for my father and his siblings. My father, by then firmly employed in the nascent field of public relations, and with a family of his own, felt deep shame, and did all he could to distance himself from his father's fraud.

My mother's life could not have been more different. She was born in Hungary into a hard-working, upper middle-class family. Her father, the village miller as well as its mayor, was an industrious man, clever with his hands and with his mind and well liked by his community. He was the model of decency, an upstanding citizen at a time when Hungary was in shambles. At the end of the First World War, when Hungary traded its monarchy for a parliamentary system, a band of counter-revolutionaries going by the name of Lenin's Brothers began terrorizing an exhausted citizenry. They nationalized industries, businesses, transport, banking, and landholdings. They expropriated grain from farmers and executed those who resisted. This reign of terror lasted barely a year, but the damage cut as deep as the blade of anarchy can go. My mother witnessed overnight the confiscation of everything that her parents and their parents before them owned: land, farm machinery, tools, furniture, jewellery, heirlooms. Gone.

Many Hungarians fled their country, my grandfather among them. He boarded a ship to Canada, where he was dispatched to the gilded wheat fields of Saskatchewan. The farming family that took him in were blessedly kind to him. They taught him English, recognized his aptitude for engineering, and helped pay his way toward a formal certificate. After five years, he earned naturalization, and he brought over his young family. They settled in the manufacturing town of Oshawa, Ontario, where my grandfather secured a job at General Motors as a stationary engineer. In time, they bought a house, a bungalow, on King Street East. Its large backyard had an abundance of fruit trees, whose fruits my grandmother harvested and made into jams for the local Catholic Women's League. As their savings grew, my grandfather invested in his community. He bought rooming houses.

My mother, the middle child and only daughter, accompanied her father on his rounds to collect rent and undertake repairs. She saw how the acquisition of property reaped affluence and paved the way toward upward mobility. In her late teens, against her parents' protests, she moved to Toronto. She wanted nothing to do with Hungarian culture or with the marriage proposals from the sons of her parents' Hungarian friends. She got a job as a copy editor at The Canadian Press, which is where she met my father, who was a reporter at the time.

Theirs was an unorthodox marriage, one that was frowned upon by both their families: his English Anglican background paired with her Hungarian Roman Catholic one. Even in appearance they were starkly different: she with thick raven hair and dark chocolate eyes; he with blond wavy hair and eyes the colour of Lake Ontario. Despite their differences, they had a unified purpose: my father to rise above his poverty; my mother to rise above her ethnicity.

They were a sensible couple, though not always prudent: They once attended an auction with the intent of buying a bed and ended up falling in love with a painting. The painting depicts the dark interior of a simple Dutch or Flemish home. The canvas is illuminated by a pale band of sun splaying through a side window and landing on a mother cradling an infant as she delivers something into its mouth by a slim, long-handled spoon. A young girl, possibly the daughter, looks on in obedient silence. To one side of the scene dark flames flicker in the grate, almost like an afterthought. It is not an expert painting; body proportions are off, and the artist's hand was not skilled enough to render depth, giving the scene a somewhat flat, naive appearance, but its sentiment of hearth and home from a bygone era obviously resonated with my parents.

When I ponder my parents' backgrounds nowadays, I see that one of the compelling reasons any of us move is the hope that planting ourselves in a new place will magically replace something lost or absented in childhood. On the surface, in my parents' case, the reason for their moves is obvious—the escape from poverty and ethnicity—but was there also something subcutaneous? Some psychological compensation? Was my mother trying to restore for her parents what they lost in the Hungarian upheaval, to somehow atone for them being wrenched from their homeland and forced to immigrate? Was my father trying to prove through a rise up the social ladder that he was better than his duplicitous father? Did he feel he had to compensate for his father's failings with his own moral, upstanding image in order to curry acceptance?

In a symbolic way, Don Mills gave them that break, that fresh start. There had been two previous homes, both short-term ones, but Larkfield Drive marked a milestone in my parents' new life. A new house, in which you are its first owners, conveys special proprietorship: There are no past owners; there is no past history. You are solely responsible for the formation of its soul and personality. Though young and inexperienced, my parents had an intuitive understanding of that concept. They knew that a new home settling into its place in the earth requires vigilance to ensure that its many parts and facets function properly and safely, that its stability in both fabric and foundation depends on alert nurturing. They found this easy to apply to a house; not so much when it came to raising children.

My parents lived on Larkfield Drive for about seven years. Their next home was to define their lives, and to imprint and influence mine.

ORIOLE LODGE

3

The Cornerstones

The memory of my last day in Don Mills is so vivid it might have happened last month rather than more than half a century ago.

There was my young self on the final day of school, a sweltering late-June day, the air fragrant and clean, but so heavy with heat that it sent the apple blossoms in their drowsy demise fluttering like confetti to the ground. In my arms I clutched artwork of coloured construction paper, of drawings showing my first experience with Conté sticks, and paintings studiously rendered with fine brushes and watery paints that had been mixed with grown-up panache (or so I imagined) on a wooden palette hooked through my thumb. There were essays, too, and poems; and most important, my report card, which showed decent grades and the vital words "Jane has passed grade three and can proceed to grade four."

I was waiting outside Rippleton Road Public School for a neighbour to pick me up because that day our family was moving from Larkfield Drive to a house unknown to me. My parents had not felt it necessary to burden me with the details of or the reasons for the move, not even the location of our new home. I do not remember inquiring about where we were going to live. My parents looked after my needs and I trusted their direction. So much so that I only learned days earlier that we were moving.

A humid gust blew up, raining down another basketful of apple blossoms and at the same time threatening the papers in my arms to flee my already tight embrace. I hugged them closer to my body. Around me swirled a celebratory atmosphere as children sprung from the restraints of school greeted parents and relatives with happy squeals and were hustled into idling cars to be whisked off to their summer holidays.

I remained dutifully at the appointed spot, my mother's explicit instructions on Repeat in my head: "Mrs. Austin will pick up you and your brother in front of the school. Do not walk home." But from where I stood, I could not see my brother. A year younger than me, he had a mind of his own, so God only knows where he was.

In a flash the children, their parents, the cars, the celebratory hoopla, disappeared, plunging Rippleton Road into preternatural silence. Even the birds seemed to have flown off. It was just me and the cicadas. No Mrs. Austin. Something was wrong, some miscommunication, and I knew with the surety of those young years that it would be my fault. I twisted my white-leather perforated sandals from side to side on the sidewalk, making patterns in the film of dirt that had blown up from the playground. I waited. I let the breeze tease the skirt of my flowered dress, watching it swell like an umbrella being opened and then gently collapsed.

Still waiting. The drone of the cicadas grew louder.

Eventually, I turned away from the street and peered past the school to the vast, deserted grounds behind Rippleton Road Public School. Time to be decisive. An asphalt area sloped down to an expanse of sun-dried grass and a few young trees, and to the baseball diamond where we spent our recesses panning for fool's gold and which now stood like an oasis amid the veldt-like emptiness. At the far end of the schoolyard was a major road—Leslie Street. I had never had need or cause to walk to Leslie Street—to a nine-year-old it looked far enough away to be in another country—but having given up on Mrs. Austin, it seemed a logical destination, and I began to walk toward it.

When I finally reached a white ribbon of sidewalk that ran alongside Leslie Street, the intensity of the sun reflecting off it nearly blinded me. I held my hand up to shield my eyes, looking left, then right, trying to determine which direction might lead to our new home. I turned left.

People outside of Canada, so accustomed to hearing about blizzards and ten-foot-high banks of snow, can never quite believe it when you talk about the thick wall of humidity and the sheer, still scorching of a southern Ontario summer. It is an oppressive type of heat. That day the combination of burning sun and suffocating humidity walloped me like a punishment. And then there was the eerie silence. Aside from the odd car whooshing past there was not a soul about. It was as if the entire city had been placed under an evacuation order.

Beneath a punishing amber sun, I walked for fifteen minutes, thirty minutes, I am not sure how long, with no idea of where I was going. A car horn honked from the other side of the road. Stranger danger. I ignored it and kept walking. I heard car tires squealing as the car did a sharp U-turn and sidled up beside me. Warily, I turned my head toward it. It was my mother.

"Where on earth have you been?" she shouted across the front seat toward the open passenger window. "Why didn't you wait for Mrs. Austin?"

"I did wait. She never showed up. I stood waiting, even when no one was around."

"She was there. Your brother was there. He can follow instructions. What is wrong with you?"

"I *was* there! I stood where you told me to wait, and I did not move!" I slid sulkily into the passenger seat.

"You're impossible."

My irritated mother shifted the car into Drive. She continued her harangue, but there was a draft of relief in her voice, and I knew that she had been fraught with worry that something might have happened to me.

Her concern disappeared quickly as she brought me up to date: "We had a problem with the moving van—the driver refused to cross the old bridge, and so they had to bring in three smaller trucks and all our furniture had to be moved into them and then taken up to the house. Imagine! I was fit to be tied. And then one of the construction workers dropped a beam on the fridge, so we are going to need a new one."

None of what she said had much meaning for me. This "house" was a mythical place at that moment, though she spoke as if I should know it intimately.

"And in the midst of all that I had to drop *everything* because you went missing."

I turned toward the passenger window to ignore her. A small voice rose inside me: "This is how it will always be," it said. "You will never be able to rely on anyone but yourself."

The pile of schoolwork clung to the sweaty dampness of my dress as we drove on and on, past unfamiliar territory. Presently, we arrived in a barren landscape of newly paved streets that were alive with enormous dump trucks and gigantic diggers that thundered all over the place, kicking up clouds of dry dirt like monsters hunting for something to eat. Our car slowed down, and my mother broke the silence: "Here we are."

I got out of the car and looked up at the house. My mouth dropped open. It was the ugliest, darkest, most forbidding place I had ever seen. It looked like something from a horror movie. The bricks were dark, blackish red; not straight, linear bricks, either, but of various shapes and sizes, some blooming with black bulbous appendages, like hideous tumours. Worse, as I was soon to discover, the back of the house had a turret shaped like a witch's hat.

When I spun around, the house's setting arrived like a second shock. We were surrounded by a dust bowl of new-built homes lined up in tidy arrangement and in varying stages of construction. Our house sat on a slight rise, giving it prominence on the landscape and also emphasizing its incongruity. How could my mother refer to this as a "new house"; it was old, a ruin. We had moved from the modernist vibrancy of Don Mills into something out of *Little Dorrit*. Shame and embarrassment flushed my face.

"This is called the 'Henry Farm subdivision,'" my mother said as if instructing me in a new lesson. "Our new home was the original homestead when there was a farm here. It's called 'Oriole Lodge.'"

I did not care. I stomped sullenly behind her up the steps to the front door and wondered whether she truly comprehended the definition of "new." This house was anything but new. It was simply awful. Even the ancient-looking cedar trees we passed seemed to agree; their long, limp branches hung like arms in a state of resignation.

Where the hell were we? I paused on the steps to look back at the neighbourhood, trying to reconcile the two extremes: behind me was a scary old house of dark bricks and dark-green, peeling paint; in front of me, new roads meandered around the contours of the rolling landscape, with miles of cables, copper tubing and wire, and concrete pipelines banked up along the roadside. The heavy, sun-saturated air pulsated across an oasis of brand-new homes. Why could we not live in one of those instead of this monstrosity?

I looked up pleadingly at my mother, hoping this was a joke, or at the very least a stop on the way to our real new home.

"I hope they have the bathroom working," she muttered, ignoring my expression. She flung open the front door to the chaos and din of a building site, but before I walked in, she grabbed my shoulder and spun me around to face her hard eyes: "There are workmen here. Act polite."

Schoolwork still clutched to my breast, I waded through clouds of plaster dust, tiptoeing around strange tools and building debris, dodging a jungle of exposed wires that hung like venomous snakes from wall holes and ceilings or that slithered up from behind the baseboards.

When we arrived in the room that was set up as our kitchen, I headed over to a large table and finally emptied my exhausted arms. My mother immediately plucked my report card from the pile and with one sweep of her arm sent the rest—a year's worth of proud artwork, test results, poems, and essays—into a garbage can.

"But . . ." I wailed.

"We have no time for that. Look at this place. We have got to roll up our sleeves and get to work."

For the rest of the summer that is all we did—my father, mother, brother, and I. No day passed without a list of chores. One Saturday morning my mother led me through the dark-panelled library hung with glass-fronted cases that held my parents' beloved collection of books. At the opposite end of the room a pair of glazed pocket doors opened onto a small, round room of almost floor-to-ceiling windows. It was the middle section of the turret at the back of the house.

"This is called a 'conservatory,'" my mother explained. "It is used for growing plants."

We were not able to actually walk into the room because at least four feet of dirt impeded our access: it covered the entire floor and completely blocked the door to the outside.

Misreading my confusion, she said, "No, they do not grow them on the floor. Someone obviously did not look after this room. In Victorian times, a conservatory was used for cultivating plants, especially over winter. And it was where the lady of the house might recline and have her tea. Can you picture that?"

The room looked as far from being a place for a lady as you could get, but I knew my mother craved to be that lady.

She handed me a shovel. "Your job today is to dig this out. You are going to have to first shovel the area in front of the door so that you can open it and throw the dirt outside."

I spent the day digging and digging. It was a big job for a nine-year-old, but in our house we did not dare question our parents or their methods. Hard work was the ethos by which we lived. By late afternoon, my excavation work had uncovered a waist-high cement trough that encircled the entire room; a cast-iron radiator; a couple of plant stands—one of white wicker, the other of wrought iron. There were loads of discarded pots and fragments of pots along with trowels and other gardening implements. The big discovery was a floor of terracotta tiles, all intact. This delighted my parents, and they brought me a pail of warm water and a scrub brush to clean it. My work was rewarded with an ice cream cone.

On the days when I was free to play, my brother and I and the clutch of kids marooned with us in this subdivision in the middle of nowhere roamed the houses under construction. We peered into poured grey concrete foundations, tested the strength of the joists supporting the subfloors, bounded up staircases that led to roofless levels. We wandered through rooms of wood framing, probing the wiring and piping that would soon be covered with drywall. It was like viewing skeletons awaiting skin.

Back at our home we lived amid the renovations, working along-side a small crew of tradesmen who thought my parents insane for saving such a relic. The notion of renovation had yet to be embraced by the wider world, but my mother took to it naturally and instantly, as if she had been born with the knowledge and capability to under-take it. She had no prior experience or tradition with such things: her parents' simple bungalow was never altered, nor was it particularly decorated. She certainly did not have the plethora of house porn that exists today to inspire her or egg her on. Yet, she stick-handled the renovation and the subsequent decoration like a pro and was fearless among tradesmen.

By fall the house was complete—a remarkable achievement given its condition at purchase and its size. Originally, the house had seven or eight large bedrooms, but under my mother's redesign there were now four bedrooms, plus two playrooms—one for my brother, one for me. Two smaller bedrooms, thought to have been servants' quar-ters, had been made into a bathroom. My bedroom had views over fields of tall grass stretching like a Saskatchewan vista to High-way 401. Back then it was only a four-lane highway (as opposed to the sixteen lanes it is today), and my brother and I would sprint across it to explore the ravines and woods on the other side.

I got first dibs on the playroom and chose the smaller of the two: the light was better, and the floor was carpeted. Over the next few weeks I organized it. My own space. In one corner, I set up my Barbie dolls and created a home for them with pieces of small wicker furniture and the occasional small chair my mother found during her frequent haunts of the antique and junk shops scattered throughout downtown Toronto. Even Barbie, symbol of Swinging Sixties modernity, was not permitted to have new, plastic furnishings in our home. That Christmas, my grandfather made a canopy bed for my Barbie, and my grandmother made the bedding: bed curtains, lace coverlet, linen sheets, pillow, and pillowcase. I wept with disappointment that the bed was not the pink plastic Mattel version from the Barbie catalogue, but I grew to love it.

My Barbie nook organized, I got down to business and set about drawing a home for myself. I held an obsessive fascination for Ethel Kennedy and her eleven children, and I decided that I wanted a life like hers. I designed a horseshoe-shaped home with twelve bedrooms—one for each of the children (I was going to have ten, and I named them all), one for my husband and me, and one for guests. All I needed was a husband, but finding one was the least of my worries. I was not interested in boys, but I was obsessed with designing my home. A box of Smarties, the contents spilled on the floor and arranged in colour-coordinated pairs, became the inspiration for the outfits I sewed for my dolls, and the mood board for the decor of each room in my dream house.

In the Henry Farm house, I began erecting walls of my own and became out of necessity a solitaire. Without a nurturing mother, I pined for nurturing friends, but the disruption of the move, of having the previous structure of friendships and agreeable playmates torn from me so bluntly, had shaken my young foundations. I trained myself to be inconspicuous to avoid my mother's spasmodic attention.

"Go make friends," said my mother.

How does one "make" friends?

"You just walk up the street and introduce yourself to whoever you meet."

She made it sound so breezy, like drawing breath. But meeting new people—putting myself "out there," as she referred to it— terrified me. I was frightened of rejection. Friendships had occurred so organically before; now it was something I had to "do."

Our house did not help my search for new friends. Potential play- mates were too frightened to call on me and play inside. It looked like the home on *The Addams Family*. Not surprisingly, given its unusual appearance smack dab in the midst of a new housing development, the house—and our family—became a side show. People slowed down when they approached it; stared at it. If I was playing outside, they would stare at me, too, wondering what kind of child, what kind of people, lived in a house like that. Even when I was nowhere near the house, adults singled me out, whispering, "Her parents live in the old Henry Farm house," which elicited nods of understanding, though what they understood precisely I could not tell. All I knew is that our family was viewed as an oddity and an anachronism. The perception was not entirely incorrect: outside our home the world was in bellbottoms and miniskirts; inside our home we were strapped into metaphorical corsets.

My mother courted this distinction. She was in her element. She was already a minor celebrity as a columnist for the local newspa- per, and her "rescue" of a home slated for demolition, one that was discovered to be the homestead of a former premier of Ontario and his early-settler relatives, had bestowed new prestige on her. To her credit, it is entirely due to her efforts that Oriole Lodge is still stand- ing and that it was eventually designated a historic building by the Architectural Conservancy of Ontario.

In short order, my parents' lively Saturday-night parties resumed. My father crooned along with Frank Sinatra on the hi-fi and shook up the martinis; my mother passed platters of canapés and dips as she regaled her circle with anecdotes about our unusual house. She loved to talk about its history, and spiced up her stories with the mention of ghosts—a subject that had her audience transfixed, agape, and looking uneasily around the room. One such story was this:

Oriole Lodge was built by Irish settlers Henry and Jane Mulholland in 1806. Henry was bullish on Canada and what this vast frontier had to offer, and he made several trips back to Ireland to entice others to emigrate. On May 11, 1833, on his voyage back to Canada, *The Lady of the Lake*, the ship he was travelling on, struck an iceberg off the coast of Newfoundland and sank. Fifteen passengers and crew survived. Mulholland was not among the lucky ones. According to my mother, Mrs. Mulholland was on the veranda *of this very home* at the time of the disaster when she saw in the distance her husband on horseback riding up the driveway. She called to her children that their father was home, and they came running out of the house to join her. They waved to Henry, who waved back, and then he vanished into thin air. Word arrived soon after with the tragic news of his drowning. Whenever my mother told this story, I would notice the women quietly draw their evening wraps tighter around their shoulders and migrate back to their husbands.

The Mulhollands' grandson was George Stewart Henry, a farmer and a lawyer. In 1898, he brought the homestead back into the family's ownership, and lived in the house for the rest of his life, even while serving as Premier of Ontario from 1930 to 1934. A strong proponent of expanding the province's highway system, he served as Minister of Highways before his premiership. It is either ironic or fitting that the largest and busiest highway in North America runs right behind his old home.

In 1958, George Henry sold his estate—the house and 460 acres—for $2 million to a development company. He died ten days after the sale was completed. Two years later, building began on a suburban enclave that would be known as the Henry Farm.

George Henry's ghost and those of his relatives appear not to have moved out when my parents moved in. The house positively crackled with ghosts. Oftentimes, I had to pause when I heard a voice or a sound to discern whether it came from my parents or from a ghost.

These were no subtle manifestations. One evening, a din arose upstairs—a wild racket of yelling, knocking, and banging, like furniture being thrown around by someone who had gone berserk. Tucked into bed, I heard it distinctly. My mother, who was downstairs in the kitchen, heard it, too, and called to my father, "John, what on earth are you doing? You'll wake the children!" My father, who was upstairs, called down to her, "I hear it, too, but it's not me." My brother and I sprang from our beds and stood with our father at the top of the stairs, looking down at my mother at the bottom of the stairs, all of us listening to this cacophony and screaming coming from the ether. And then it stopped abruptly. We stood for a moment looking at one another, and then without a word we trundled back to what we had been doing: my mother to cleaning up in the kitchen; my father to reading in their bedroom; my brother and I to our beds. That is how we dealt with ghosts: no discussion, no questioning; we accepted them and went on with our lives.

Darker manifestations than ghosts had begun to pervade our lives.

My mother had grown increasingly tyrannical and restless, as if possessed by an inner disturbance. Inside the house she was a bundle of barely suppressed fury, dark-brown eyes darting from one anxiety or desire to another, frequently exploding with a volcanic temper. She became a compulsive buyer of antiques and curios, often of a religious nature. She came home one day with a pair of large brass candlesticks and a monstrance that she claimed to have saved from a church that was being demolished. No one I knew had altar candlesticks and a monstrance in their home. She fretted and fussed with the decor and the arrangement of furniture, and while she had beautiful taste in all that she did, it seemed to be compensating for a deeper anxiety.

One source of discontent was me. She was hypercritical of my appearance, once slumping on the edge of my bed and wailing, "Why did God give me such an ugly daughter?" We never had real conversations: everything was a scolding, and any passions I expressed were deemed an affront to her curated realm of Minton china, majolica pottery, and lace placemats. She was driven by a furious, seemingly insatiable aspiration, hurrying to make something more of her life, to create the perfect home, the perfect life. All that stood in her way were two stubborn children and a psychologically needy husband. The irony is that home imprisoned her as soundly and completely as any addiction can. Perhaps there were money problems to which I was not privy, though my parents were in no way extravagant and nothing was ever bought on credit: "the never-never," my father called it. Only the ring of the doorbell would return my mother to a model of gracious ease and sparkling wit.

Perhaps the reason behind this moody agitation lay in what happened several weeks later.

One cold January evening just before supper, the phone rang. I answered it. It was my father. In a dead voice he said, "Tell your mother that I am at the subway and I am going to throw myself in front of the next train."

I had been given no instructions on how to respond to such a declaration so I called to my mother, "It's Dad."

She seized the phone from me, and I slipped out of sight to give her privacy while I listened around the corner.

"Don't be ridiculous," she hissed into the phone. "You get on the next train now and get right home. I have had just about enough of your theatrics." She slammed down the receiver.

Her callousness alarmed me.

"Is he going to kill himself? Should we go get him?"

"Nonsense," she snapped. "He'll be home." Then, as if noticing me for the first time: "Have you done your homework?"

An hour later my father walked through the door. My mother did not run to him with relief and a kiss, or welcome him home, or say anything to him other than a terse "Your supper's getting cold." He sat at the dinner table like a beaten prisoner, eyes too heavy with unspoken grief to lift from his plate. I sat next to him, sensing his anguish and feeling angry that I lacked the words and the deft emotional skills to offer comfort. I had absolutely no language for this. In moulding me into a paragon of Victorian manners—the anachronistic adage "Children should be seen and not heard" was the war cry in our household—my parents had trained me to be dumb and numb: I was as mute as a piece of furniture.

That evening, as I lay in bed, I could hear my parents' hushed voices as they argued behind their bedroom door, though I could not make out the content of their conversation. Even the house ghosts seemed to be hovering and listening.

Two nights later, the morning of my fifteenth birthday, my father threw himself down the stairs. He survived the attempt to end his life. Once again, I did not know how to respond. We never spoke about emotional things in our family; in our home we let the walls absorb the silent pain, and the foundation support and steady us. I never found this approach satisfactory, but it was the way my parents wanted things, and there was no option but to fall in line.

Was this some sort of mid-life crisis? My parents were by then in their forties, after all. Was it an early warning of the depression that would one day grip me? We comprehend, too late, the shadows that reside in our parents: they die before we can revisit the past with them and allow our bitterness at their perceived failings to be transformed into empathy.

After my dad's suicide attempt, my parents went away to Bermuda for a change of scenery. I was sent to live for a few weeks at the home of friends of my parents. They happened to have a handsome son who was a year older than I was, so the arrangement suited me perfectly fine.

My parents had two weeks in sunny Bermuda, but I had it better: I got two weeks in a home without drama. These particular friends of my parents were academics, and their son was similarly clever. What their home lacked in fascinating decor it more than made up in stimulating conversation. It was a bookish home, calm and convent-like in atmosphere, but at supper, the dinner table became a forum of roving ideas, news of the day, and opinions expressed without censorship. I was asked my thoughts on current events, but being unused to this freedom, I worried that any contribution would be shot down as "nonsense." Far from it. My hosts were lovely, and they coaxed this restraint out of me, so that I warmed to it, unshyly voicing my views or asking questions of things I did not understand. When my parents returned from Bermuda, tanned and relaxed, I tried to replicate this dynamic discussion at our own dinner table. I cannot say they were thrilled.

AFTER FOUR YEARS in the Henry Farm house we moved in 1969 to Mason Boulevard, at the edge of what was then known as the Toronto city limits. The house was much smaller than Oriole Lodge, but crucially, it meant that my father's commute to work would be shorter, and that it would ease his mind. Unfortunately, it had the opposite effect. He felt acutely the loss of prestige that came with owning a distinctive home, and felt this new one, though perfectly nice and with a beautiful ravine backyard, was inferior. He grew more tightly wound and looked as if he might spring apart again at any moment.

He did so on the morning of my sixteenth birthday, once again throwing himself down the stairs. As with his previous attempt, he was unharmed physically, but from the whispered arguments between my parents and calls to a doctor there was no doubt that he was unravelling. I did not know whether I could survive another birthday with a suicidal parent. To this day, long after my parents have died, I continue to approach the morning of my birthdays with immense trepidation.

My desire for more loving, mentally stable, less house-obsessed parents grew, and as it did, I became despondent. In hindsight it might have been simply a case of being sixteen, but at the time I felt as confined as a prisoner under a life sentence with my mother as warden. Now that I was in my mid-teens, she had embarked on a plan to mould me into a woman with a country-club lifestyle. She wanted an attractive, aspirational, well-dressed, polite young daughter who would date attractive, aspirational, well-dressed, polite young men. After years of telling me how unattractive I was, I do not know how she figured this would succeed.

One day, I had a big argument with her. It was a school holiday, and I had gone with a friend to see a movie. My mother was incensed that I had not thought of devoting my day off to household chores but had, instead, indulged in selfishness.

"If you have time to go to a movie, then you have time to do the laundry," she roared. That night, she flounced out of the house to the movies with my father.

I was tired of not being able to do the right thing, or at least of living with people who felt I was doing the wrong thing. I believed myself to be a good daughter, who was helpful, dutiful, respectful. I had nothing that could be remotely called a social life, but when

I did go out at night, I was always home before curfew. It felt like I was breaking apart: I did not fit in outside the home, and I did not fit in inside it. I longed to run away but had no idea how to make that happen. The only option was to end my life.

While my parents were at the movies, I raided their medicine cabinet, then sat at the breakfast table and downed the lot—Aspirin and sleeping pills, I imagine, though it never occurred to me to consult the labels on the bottles—until I began gagging. Our dog, a gentle border collie named MacGregor, watched me with big, sad eyes. I was unexpectedly overcome with guilt about leaving our beloved dog behind—though to be fair, he received far more love and attention from my mother.

I decided at that moment to telephone the hospital and tell them what I had done. Within minutes an ambulance was screaming up our street. "What would the neighbours say," I imagined my mother's reaction to be. I was mortified. As soon as I opened the front door, one of the paramedics grabbed me and shoved me into the downstairs loo, where he stuck something down my throat to make me vomit. They were not the least bit sympathetic to my situation.

"Where are your parents?" one of them yelled.

At the movies, I said meekly. I told them which cinema.

They flung me onto a stretcher, strapped me to it, and rolled me into the ambulance. Lights, siren, and we were off. It was terrifying.

At the hospital, I was put into a cubicle and forced to drink something that induced more vomiting. No one spoke to me or consoled me.

Not long after, the curtain around the cubicle was flung open. My parents walked in.

"Have you any idea how embarrassing it was to be paged over the address system in that cinema?" my mother said theatrically. "What must the neighbours be thinking?"

"The movie was just getting good," teased my father. "I'll never find out how it ended."

We drove home in silence, and I was sent straight to bed. The incident was never spoken of again. The next day, our family doctor made a home visit. He checked my pulse and my heartbeat, and prescribed Valium. I sincerely wished he had prescribed it to my parents. My remaining high school years were spent in a quasi-doped state, my teachers wrongly assuming that my sudden lethargy was due either to boredom or to a scandalously wild social life that included illegal drugs. But then, no one asked what was going on at home.

A YEAR BEFORE I WAS to graduate from high school my mother decided that we were all going to move to the country. "Fresh air! Exercise! A simpler life!" she enthused.

I could not believe she was deciding to do this at such a critical point in my education, and that she expected me to finish my final year at a completely different school.

My mother cared not a whit. Life was all about changing and adapting, and she wanted another house to fix up. It would do us all a world of good, she said. To her, houses were the most important thing in life. I can tell you, it did nothing for my confidence to be playing second fiddle to a pile of stone and brick.

As my mother flounced around, looking at possible homes to buy and strategizing our next move, my brother and I held our breath. This would mean not only a change of schools but a change in the way we were taught. By moving to a rural school in my last year of high school, well, I might as well have thrown my entire education out the window. The school would be no more than a schoolhouse, and I might be one of two, possibly three, other grade thirteens.

"Fiddle-dee-dee," said my mother. "Think how unusual you will be! Think of the adventure!"

She did not seem concerned at all that my father would now be commuting to work much farther than he had ever commuted. A commuter bus and train service had been proposed for the area, she insisted, failing to add that it was at least ten years away from becoming reality.

None of us had the courage to talk her out of this. Instead, we dealt with it by ignoring her.

Off she went to find her dream stone farmhouse, and soon enough she found it: an Ontario Gothic wreck set against a ripple of scrubby hills. It was in Campbellville, about forty miles west of Toronto, which in the early 1970s was akin to *Deliverance* territory. In a move of singular audacity, my mother bought the house without my father's knowledge. When he found out, he was incandescent; not outwardly so, more in the way many British people are incandescent: with a composed, even cheery exterior while mentally calculating murder. From the set of his jaw and the change of blue in his eyes— from sky blue to the colour of a blade—I knew he had been pushed far enough.

Before major renovations began in earnest on this new acquisition, my mother threw a large and drunken surprise party at the farmhouse for my father's fiftieth birthday. Everyone was instructed to wear casual clothes and to bring a garden chair. This was quite a departure for my mother: she never allowed us to wear jeans; hated the thought of anyone dressing down. We actually had to go out and buy jeans for the first time.

It turned out to be a splendid party, the only time my parents really let their hair down in front of me and allowed me to do the same. Maybe my mom was right: maybe this house would be a good thing for us after all. At the party, one of the gifts my father received—intended as a joke—proved prophetic: a For Sale sign. It was as if he had been handed the greatest power in the universe. He was about to be given the opportunity to exercise it.

A week after the party, my mother drove out to the farmhouse to meet a builder. While there, she slipped on the icy driveway and broke her leg. She was taken to hospital, where her leg was mended and put in a cast, and then she was decanted to a convalescent home for a couple of months. She was rendered completely immobilized. Seizing his chance and showing rare defiance, my father drove out to the farmhouse with his new For Sale sign and posted it on the fence. It was a speedy sale. My mother was beyond furious.

It was a win-win for the rest of us: my father did not have to worry about a lengthy commute to work, and my brother and I had a few months of stability without the threat of being moved to another school. By then, I would be out of high school and off to university, with any luck far from Toronto and from my mother's constant pre-occupation with houses, moving, and renovating me.

When my mother finally did return home and was firmly back on her pins, she redoubled her efforts to find a home in the country. Just before I left for university, she purchased another stone farmhouse, this one outside the town of Milton, a step up from *Deliverance* territory. We drove out as a family to see it. When we arrived, we stood at the top of the driveway, dumbstruck.

"Isn't it beautiful?" my mother sighed dreamily.

We stared ahead at what could only charitably be called a "disaster." The house was basically a burned-out shell; a dilapidated barn nearby looked as though it would not survive someone exhaling within ten feet of it.

My brother and I, who were barely on speaking terms with one another at the best of times, looked at each other with an expression that we both read as *Okay, this does it. She is definitely crazy.*

Once again, we were conscripted into renovation work, but not for long: My brother, always a wild child, had had enough and took off on a road trip that lasted more than a decade. I left a month later for university.

By the time I returned home at Christmas the burned-out wreck was unrecognizable. Once again, my mother had sprinkled her interior design fairy dust over another ruin and had transformed it into something stunning. One fire-scarred room was turned into a wood-panelled family room with a huge open fireplace flanked by built-in bookcases. The large country kitchen was bright and welcoming, with modern appliances and conveniences blending in with her beloved pine Canadiana furniture, among them a large harvest table. Every room had been artfully decorated with the antiques my mother had collected since the 1950s. Outside, there was an in-ground pool and a large latticed gazebo. To one side of the property was a pond, stocked with fish and encircled by more than one hundred poplar saplings that my brother and I had been tasked to plant one weekend. On the other side of the property, the old barn had succumbed to fire. My mother had ordered construction of a new, albeit smaller, barn, which was now home to a dozen sheep and two cows that she named Juicy and Delicious.

I escaped all the house shifting and shaping when I went away to school, but I did not exactly avoid the moves: In the three years I spent at university, I lived in four different off-campus student homes. But then, was that not par for the course for everyone? What I knew for certain was that I was done with old houses, with renovations, with constant moving and upheaval. It was ridiculous and unnecessary; it wreaked havoc and instability. Done with that. I was not going to be the home I was raised in. Once I finished university, I was determined that life on my terms would be settled and stable.

MASON BLVD.

4

The Hunt

The Husband has come around to understanding the need for us to move house, though it has been a tough sell. He is comfortable in Brixham but agrees that the seagulls and the location of our home are drawbacks. For nearly two years, he has been driving back and forth every other weekend to Essex—a six-hour drive each way—to look after his elderly parents, and a move that would shrink that distance is looking pretty enticing.

Convincing him to move was the relatively easy part; convincing the British house-buying public to buy our home was another story.

At first, the signs for a quick sale were promising: The town was on the upswing, we were told. The newspapers' Homes sections reported that floods of people were itching to move to the seaside, and that one of the sought-after destinations was *our town*! But none of this bore fruit, and in fact maybe none of it was true; perhaps it was all part of the shills and tricks the news media use these days to sell newspapers and aspiration. For nearly a year our home languished on the market.

One reason was Brexit. The referendum had been held in June 2016, and the shocking result sent the country into a collective paralysis, if not financially, then psychologically. No one knew what to do next or what to expect. There was no plan. Those who put their trust in the politicians' bombast and lies, and those who voted to leave purely out of spite, slunk back to their respective corners to see what would shake out.

The political stasis sent the housing market, especially in the rural areas and particularly in the apparently much-vaunted seaside, into a seizure. For sellers like us it was depressing and nerve-racking. After five months, I could no longer suppress my feelings behind a brave face. When The Husband went out for a run or for a coffee, I would sit at home on the sofa and weep, asking God, asking St. Joseph (patron saint of house hunters), asking anyone, why we had not sold. I felt utterly trapped in this home. It reached the point where I begged The House itself to intervene and be kind to prospective buyers: "Remember, it's not you—it's us. You are a beautiful home, but we need something not quite as special as you."

And then someone came along, nonplussed by the busy road, the steep steps to the garden, and the seagulls. Someone bought The House. *Halle-effing-lujah.*

Still, just because we have sold does not mean we have sold. This is England, after all. When someone offers on your home and you accept their offer, this does not indicate a done deal. It is a complicated, frustrating system. Here is how it works:

When you find a house on which you want to put an offer, you contact the listing agent for that house. England does not have anything as efficient or collegial as North America's Multiple Listing Service. If there are ten properties you wish to view, and each has a different agent/agency, then you must deal directly with ten different agents. The estate agent contacts the vendor, makes the offer verbally, and it is either accepted, rejected, or countered. When the price is agreed, no money is exchanged—not a penny. Whereas under the North American system an immediate deposit or down payment formalizes the intent and agreement to purchase, under the English system both parties remain uncommitted. It is akin to accepting a proposal of marriage while both parties continue dating or sleeping with other people. At any point in the process either party can call off the deal without penalty. Madness.

Second, once your offer is accepted, you order a survey or home inspection. An inspector, without you present, goes through the house you have offered on and makes an assessment. A few days later a thick, spiral-bound book drops into your mail box. Its contents attempt to explain the guts of your intended home, highlighting areas—roof, electrical system, wall structure, foundation, the eaves and drainpipes—that need attention. However, despite the impressive hundred or so pages you receive, and the £600 you have paid to have it done, it is not exhaustive. The surveyor might cast a flashlight in the direction of the attic but often does not actually go into it to check its condition; he or she will regard the roof from the road, not from the roof; a prognosis of wiring and plumbing is based on what is visible. In other words, it is a purely superficial reading of the house.

If the survey reveals subsidence or other structural issues, or if the improvements you plan to undertake on the property will be more expensive than you expected, you can renegotiate the purchase price. If the seller is set on his asking price, then you can bow out of the deal, and your house hunt begins anew. This process is repeated until you get a survey that does not scare you off.

You then enlist a lawyer, who conducts a series of searches on the property to ensure there are no liens and to determine whether your intended property is in a flood zone, or if a tin or coal mine lies beneath it, or whether it is subject to a chancel repair tax, or whether it is part of a duchy or has restrictive covenants attached to it. Your home may well sit on land owned by a duke, a prince, or a queen.

Once the deal is in the hands of the lawyers, you play a waiting game. Eight to ten weeks is the norm before contracts are exchanged. However—and it is a big *however*—this stage of the house-buying process is still a free-for-all. If another buyer comes along and offers the vendor more money than you have offered, the vendor can accept their offer. You have then been, as the Brits say, "gazumped." Likewise, buyers can turn around and offer less money to the vendor than they had originally offered. This happens in cases when the market slows or nosedives. But it can also happen when unforeseen expenses appear on your survey (subsidence, roof leaks, failing windows). This is called "gazundering." A third pitfall, known as "gazanging"—you know you are in Britain when you come up against terminology like this—occurs when, having agreed to a sale, the vendor gets cold feet and decides to remain in the property, leaving the buyer hanging. Or when the vendor complains that he or she cannot find a suitable home to move to. If a home is advertised as having "no chain," it means the vendors have not entered into a contract to purchase at their end. This is the sort of situation you want, because if there is a chain, then it has a domino effect when someone three places along the chain changes his or her mind and opts out of the agreement to purchase, and suddenly everyone else's deal is threatened with collapse. This is where the insanity of the system reveals itself.

In the North American system (and I believe this is the same with the Scottish system) you sign the agreement of sale and submit with it your down payment/deposit. It is done the day your offer is accepted, at which point both parties agree to a closing date, which is when the deeds change hands and the banks transfer the remaining funds to the vendor. It is usual for closing to take place anywhere from five weeks to six months from the date of signing. This means both parties can then book movers; arrange for school transfers, change-of-address notifications, utility cancellations, and hookups at the new address. Under the English system, you are unable to book your mover or undertake change-of-address business until contracts are exchanged, when the sale agreement is then legally binding, which is normally one or two weeks *before completion*, the day you move out or move in. This creates an atmosphere of such mind-boggling anxiety that who but a clueless Canadian would put up with it?

Such a system is perfect for commitment-phobes and ditherers, which the British are, by and large. Only when your purchase finally goes through do you begin to appreciate why the British move so infrequently, and why they are a nation of such heavy drinkers.

It is our last day in Brixham. We are definitely moving, and we know that because the proceeds from the sale of our house are now in our bank account. The movers have come and gone. The bits and pieces we dare not trust to movers are stuffed into our small, rusting, pale-green car. The House has been cleaned and scrubbed; each room has received parting prayers of thanks to the spirits. All that remains is for us to bid the town a fond farewell and move on.

The problem is, we do not have a place to actually move to. We have viewed around sixty properties—a conservative estimate—and have not been successful at securing one because we have either been pipped at the post on houses we wanted or have been unable to find something we could both agree on. As a result, we have taken a rental house while our search continues for a permanent home.

For no particular reason we have narrowed our house hunt to Bristol. Bristol is where John Cabot set sail for the New World; where the engineering genius of Isambard Kingdom Brunel built the SS *Great Britain* and the Clifton Suspension Bridge; where Charles Wesley wrote hymns and co-founded Methodism; where Daniel Dafoe's imagination was stirred to create Robinson Crusoe; where Bob Hope, Cary Grant, J. K. Rowling, and Damien Hirst were born; and where the likes of Samuel Taylor Coleridge, Robert Southey, and William Wordsworth settled for a time. Bristol is the home of adventurers and nonconformists. I like to think of myself as adventurous and nonconformist, but then, I am someone who fell for the cliché of living by the seaside, so maybe not.

We have no connection with Bristol whatsoever, no personal history, no community safety net; we have no family or friends living in or near Bristol; but we have plumped for Bristol because it has history, culture, walking trails, fast trains to London, a diverse population, and an edgy attitude. In other words, it is ideal for us. We hope.

What I discovered about The Husband and myself while we lived in Brixham is that we are by nature introverts. Small towns are not always best for such people. A low profile is hard to keep in a small town unless you are the surly, curmudgeonly sort. The Husband is friendly, but he is also shy and not a joiner; I am more gregarious: easily talked into going for a walk, a tea, a movie, or having a chat at the drop of a hat. As a writer, however, I also require huge chunks of solitude. It is awkward trying to explain to people that you are in the middle of writing a book or an article, and that you cannot come out to play for another several weeks or months. They never understand, and they think your excuse is lame and that you are just fobbing them off. I work better without social commitments to maintain or disappoint. Ah, but then come the periods of non-writing. This is when my hard-earned isolation is sharply felt, and a desperate craving for company and conversation inserts itself into my personality. Which in turn leads me desperately wheedling my way back into social groups or dropping hints to overseas friends that I am free to Skype and FaceTime. The social life of a writer is one of polar extremes.

But here we are, The Husband and I, taking our final promenade down the length of Brixham's breakwater toward the lighthouse. With each step I cement three and a half years of memories in this town with nary a smidgen of sentimentality. It is ironic that I have waited to leave this place as eagerly as I waited to move here.

It is early afternoon, and out on the breakwater the late-January wind is calm, and the sun is showing the town and coastline to its best effect. It feels like a smug benediction. We are leaving behind good people and easy routines. The Husband has reservations about leaving. He is happy here; and I have thrown his world into flux. My attempt to reassure him sounds hollow even to me: "It is beautiful, but I just cannot remain here," I say to him with as much conviction as I said three years earlier "We have to live here."

The Husband's needs for our new home are few: a south-facing garden, and proximity to an amiable café that opens early in the day.

My requirements are less prosaic:

- lots of natural light
- high ceilings
- two bathrooms
- three bedrooms
- a level backyard that is visible and accessible from the kitchen
- off-street parking
- a walkable neighbourhood close to amenities
- not on a main or busy road
- no seagulls

And that only covers the house. I want to be in a community, near a church and a library, within walking distance of the city centre, places of interest, and unusual shops. I know what I want and I also do not know what I want. But this list will be the framework to keep me on track, to ensure I do not mess up, because, God knows, I cannot afford to do this again.

What I really want is a house where I can open all the windows and doors and let light and life blow in. I want to hear and smell the everyday—a neighbour's back door opening; a murmured conversation from some indeterminate backyard; the rustle of tree leaves and the aroma of flowers; the sound of a shrub being clipped, a baby crying and being soothed by a parent; the sweet trill of birdsong. There was none of that in our Brixham house. Quite the opposite. There was always the sense of sealing ourselves from the world. Leaving the house required an intake of breath and a steeling of character because our front door opened directly onto the street and thus lacked one of those small walkways that gently ease you into the outer world. Re-entering the house after some errand or excursion was like returning to prison. The only escape was out the back, through the kitchen door, and up the vertiginous stone steps to where the seagulls, perched like guards along a watchtower, waited to assault us. We were rarely able to open our windows, and even then, the view beyond them was just the bricks on the houses opposite us or the stone wall behind us. We had to crane our necks to glimpse a sliver of sky. I need more of the world than that on a daily basis: I need to see green and blue together. I need to witness the moods of the sky, the movement of clouds, the sway of bushes and trees.

In North America, my list would be a no-brainer. Millions of homes in our price range fit that brief. Not so in England. The word here is *compromise*—a word I have had the good fortune never to invoke. In England, housing stock is older and infinitely more varied. It sits on land that has in all likelihood been used in the past for purposes other than housing: industrial, agricultural, ecclesiastical, aristocratic, or royal; land that has been worked or lived on for the greater part of two millenniums. As a result, the terrain twists and turns and dips: it adheres not to a legislated or decreed building or land-use code but to historic undulations, former riverbeds, slag heaps, ancient burial mounds, chancel land. Nothing is standard about English homes, or about British homes in general; if anything, irregularity is the standard.

Halfway down the breakwater, our mobile rings: It is an estate agent in Bristol. A house she has dangled in front of us for the past month is finally on the market. She can show it to us today at four o'clock. We check our watches. It is two o'clock. We are two hours from Bristol in good traffic, and good traffic is a moving target in this country.

We turn our back on the lighthouse and speed-walk back down the breakwater, hoping we do not run into anyone we know who might delay our sudden departure. We break into a jog, then a run. The Husband and I bark through our checklist:

"The house is clean?"

"Yes, and every room is cleared."

"Do we need to set the alarm?"

"Nope. Told the agent we wouldn't. New owners arrive tomorrow."

We close in on our car parked on the quay.

"You start the car. I will run the house keys to the estate agent," I pant. "Meet you at the corner, by the ice cream shop."

Minutes later I rejoin him at the appointed place and jump into the passenger seat. Just then a seagull lands in front of our car and struts indolently across the road, taking its damn time.

"Hit it," I sneer to The Husband.

But of course we will not: there are lots of people around, and we do not want to risk a mob riot.

I open the car door to shoo it away, and it finally takes the hint.

We are off. Our small car kicks up road gravel as we speed out of town like fleeing criminals, and the ensuing dust cloud excuses us from having to look back.

The seagulls weren't done with us. As I punch into our mobile the directions to the Bristol address, a big blob of seagull shit splatters across the windscreen.

"Bastards," we mutter in unison.

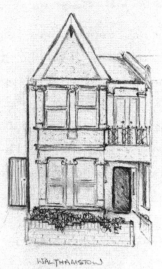

WALTHAMSTOW

5

The Find

We arrive at the Bristol house exactly at four o'clock. Miracle time given the notoriously unpredictable traffic conditions on the A380. Make that reason sixteen for our move: you need a private plane if you hope to avoid the congested roads of South Devon.

Greeting us at the property is our agent. She knows we have seen some sixty houses. Her wry smile suggests she is about to open the oyster containing the pearl of our dreams. This has to be pretty special if she can pull off that degree of confidence.

It is a Victorian terrace: it is the style we want, which we have seen more times than we care to count. Forty out of the sixty? Possibly. We could walk into a Victorian terrace now and navigate the layout blindfolded.

The Husband gives the exterior a once-over, pursing his lips as he takes in the surface conditions. I see that the house is standing upright and has all its windows, which at this point is all that matters to me. It is a two-storey double-bay-front style, and the house is clad in what the agent calls "brick" but looks like rough-hewn stone held together with thick mortar. There is a bit of Doric embellishment—gouged in places—around the windows and the door frame, neither of which has seen a lick of paint in three decades—minimum.

The agent unlocks the door. It swings partially open, banging against a ledge above the door where the gas meter lives. We squeeze in. There is a second door, partially glazed, called a "porch door." It opens and bangs against another obstruction, this one a wooden shaft painted bright red that houses the wires for the electrical panel. At least, I think it is the electrical panel; it looks ancient. The hall is long, narrow, and dark, with a flight of stairs facing us. Immediately, I notice that the usual architectural feature of a plaster arch with classical details has been ripped out somewhere in its history. Perhaps there is a way for it to be rebuilt and reinstated.

The first room we arrive at is the sitting room. In days gone by, the Victorians entertained guests here, and unashamedly showed off their prized possessions. It was the lushest, most decorated and architecturally embellished room, the vernacular versions boasting newly efficient cast-iron fireplaces and grates with mirrored over-mantels of wood, stone, or marble, and glazed-tile side panels; high ceilings with deep cove moulding and an ornate ceiling rose; deep skirting boards and window trim. Today, in this particular room, there is no evidence of any of that, only the ghostly outline of a departed ceiling rose. The chimney breast remains, but a board covers up the fireplace cavity, and who knows what horror lurks behind it. The original plaster cove moulding, though battered, is at least intact.

There are two small sofas and a coffee table between them. A change of layout could allow the room to potentially seat six to eight people.

The next room, normally called "the dining room" or "second reception room," is being used as a bedroom. It is not a bad size. The chimney breast has been removed, which makes the room more spacious. A small window faces the side return leading to the rear yard; French doors would be great there.

We return to the dark, narrow hallway. My heart is sinking while my head struggles to see past the gloom to the house of my imagination. I want to be wowed by a house, but we cannot afford wow—we have to buy shit and somehow turn it into wow. My mind cycles back to the estate agent's shill that stirred our initial interest in this property: it is on one of the best streets in this part of Bristol, it has a long backyard, the place needs work, the owner has gone into care; it is a sad situation.

Well, she got "sad" right. The place has suffered abuse. It looks unloved, and it is not loving me back. I detect a stroppy, grumpy vibe, and picture an overweight, gammon-faced older guy in a sweat-and-dirt-stained undervest.

As we progress, the house gradually, grudgingly, recovers itself: it gives off a sense of apology for its sorry state, while at the same time grousing about having to kowtow to Ms. La-di-dah and her magazine expectations.

For my part, I feel disappointed—indignant, even. All vestiges of the sort of Victorian charm you come to expect from a house of this vintage—hallway arch, ceiling roses, stained-glass transoms, fireplaces and mantels, cove moulding, sash windows—have been ripped out. The term "architectural cleansing" comes to mind. The walls are yellowed from nicotine, the woodwork battered. The floorboards are black with age and ground dirt; I have seen better in barns. And yet I cannot help but feel immensely sorry for this place. It needs a bath, some better clothes, and love. It deserves tenderness, and a chance to be rehabilitated. Dangerous sentiment, that: it is a short leap from pity to the house-buying equivalent of a mercy fuck.

I can tell right away that I do not love this place, though I am desperately trying to reverse that impression. It is like finally encountering someone you had been dying to meet, only to find yourself struggling to come up with a conversation opener to erase the awkwardness.

The anxious eyes of our estate agent are on me. She has half a dozen people chomping at the bit to see this place.

I spout short, positive platitudes in an attempt to buy time: "Love the high ceilings . . . Those floorboards will look great once they are sanded . . . The natural light is amazing." I need to keep her onboard and as engaged as much as she needs to keep me motivated and engaged.

I risk a look at The Husband. Elevens at the bridge of his nose. Not a good sign. He had brightened up about seeing this house when he learned that it was on a street that bears the name of his favourite football team. But now it is a different story. He refuses eye contact.

While he does not love the house, neither of us dares give any signals that might be construed as negative. We are exhausted from house hunting, and from the feeling that we are adrift; that our current address is Limbo, and that all our worldly goods are out of sight, as if they reside in the iCloud.

The Husband is not a big-picture thinker. He has no vision when it comes to property. He sees wiring, meters, and guttering that need to be overhauled, whereas I see walls that need to come down and a finished product. I wonder if our furniture will fit.

"Isn't this just what you were looking for?" says the agent.

I stand at the bottom of the staircase and jiggle the newel post to test the stability of the banister.

"Oh yes!" I reply, stalling.

This house will require a lot of work and money, and the space feels cramped. There is not one room that requires only a lick of paint. On the upside, light streams in on both levels, and it is four in the afternoon in late January—at this time in our Brixham home we would have been checking the clock to see whether it was time for bed.

While we like this area of Bristol, this particular patch is not entirely known to us. The area several blocks north is slightly trendier and more upmarket; this part is on the sketchy side. And yet it is close to the Bristol and Bath Railway Path—we can walk into the city centre in twenty-five minutes; the train station is a five-minute walk; ditto for the shops and restaurants on St. Mark's Road.

As I turn to head upstairs, I notice The Husband has returned to the front door, muttering about "signs of forced entry." He checks the visible things: signs of damp, the state of the brickwork, roof, eaves, ceiling, the boiler. He gravitates to the windows: there are strange locking mechanisms on these, almost homemade. He gives it all a growl.

While he checks the visible, I want to check the invisible, which is difficult to do with an estate agent at my heels. She scrutinizes my face, my gestures, my movements, like a forensic detective while I look up the stairs and listen for ghosts.

Does a house have memory? Most certainly. It is visible, and it is audible. It can be seen and read on its walls, in the ridges and gouges of its door frames and banister; it can be felt underfoot in its floorboards; it can be heard in the way the wind treats it—does it whistle through like a thief, or knock respectfully from the outside? A house's memory can also be gauged by its odour: I turn my head away from the agent and sniff the air. It smells stale, like an unhappy marriage.

I climb the bare wooden steps slowly, listening, smelling. At the top, I run a hand along the rough door frame of a bedroom. I inspect the doors: they are original but are thick with white paint, and some have been patched with wood filler, while others have panels that have been replaced, as if someone had kicked them in. I pause again and listen for something that is not there but is there.

I move into the master bedroom. Good space, bay window, and there is a cast-iron fireplace. The mantel is not original; it is home-made. The fireplaces and chimney breasts in the two other bedrooms have been removed. There are no cupboards or closets in any of the rooms—typical of older English homes.

I pace slowly through the rooms, allowing my imagination to take flight and to see past the miserable state to what the house could be. My mind tumbles back to previous homes I have bought where my initial impression had been instant and positive. Perhaps I am being more cautious now, and that is a good thing. I cannot afford to make another error in house buying. The asking price on this one is £305,000. We are fortunate to have the resources of most middle-class folks, but we did not anticipate blowing it all on a house. The reality is that this is the mid-range price for a house in Britain. It will be the most expensive house either of us has bought. And then there is the £70,000—the remainder of an inheritance I received—that will be used for the renovation. I tally that up in Canadian dollars, which is stupid because this is England, not Canada, but still, yikes, roughly $650,000. We would be better off buying a ruin in France, Spain, or Italy and fixing that up. But I have already had that conversation with The Husband, and he shut me down quickly. You cannot remove an Englishman from England. It is somewhere in the Geneva Convention.

Back downstairs, I head toward the kitchen at the end of the hall. Someone has tried to cheer up this room by painting the walls in a French blue to contrast with the white wooden cabinets, one of which is hanging off its hinges. The kitchen table is covered in a blue-and-white polka dot vinyl cloth, with a pot of cheerful primrose—red, yellow, and white—placed atop. On the window ledge above the table is a tea set in a pretty pattern. I pick up the little milk jug and turn it over. *Fait en Normandie*. It is adorable. I return to what is not adorable. The stove: Does it work? It looks unsafe. The fridge is small and cheap but looks like it works. I open a half-glazed door to a back area and find a grotty utility room with a washer and dryer, both of which look fairly new. I open the door next to it: it is the bathroom. The white fixtures look new. I step back into the kitchen and visualize a new interior: knocking out the kitchen, utility room, and bathroom, and turning the space into a large kitchen diner. The back wall could be opened up and fitted with graphite aluminum bifold patio doors. Love those.

A side door leads to the backyard. I venture outdoors. The yard is level, but like the house it is forlorn, a veritable dumping ground of waste. The area of garden closest to the house is a tangle of brambles and tall, pale grass. The back section is shingle heaped with a pile of old wood, bricks, concrete, and garbage. The entire plot is devoid of greenery; not so much as a shrub. The space is fenced but only loosely; a section on the right has collapsed completely. A pair of rusted iron fence panels and a gate lean against what is left of the wooden fence, and there is an old chimney pot with a crown-shaped top that reminds me of Tenniel's drawings for *Through the Looking Glass*. I take a closer look through the rubbish pile to see what else might be salvaged.

It is not a large garden, but it is manageable, and it is south facing, which would satisfy The Husband. I cast my eye over the neighbouring yards, all of which sprout mature bushes and small trees. Well, there is hope, at least.

Back inside, I tally up the positives: The pine floorboards, though beyond dirty, are original, and two of the fireplaces and chimney breasts have already been removed in rooms where I would have wanted them removed. The three bedrooms are of a good size, though one will have to be sacrificed for an upstairs bathroom. There is good natural light throughout.

The market is hot and getting hotter, and I am worried about sustaining The Husband's attention in this process so we do not price ourselves out of another market. We have spent a year looking at houses. One of our options has been to chuck everything into storage and travel. Is that what we should do? I pace through the house a second time, then a third. The agent checks her phone. I so want to have a base, a home. I want to unpack, settle, then travel.

We have both hit house-hunting fatigue. If I have to look at another house, cozy up to another estate agent, do another comparison list, feel another crush of disappointment that our budget has limitations, I am going to lose interest in the entire business, and that is saying something.

I am already feeling the sheer marital exhaustion of it all. This was so much easier when I did it on my own as a single parent. As a couple, we are getting bitchy and resentful toward one another. Even with The Husband taking a back seat to all this, I still feel under pressure. I resent his lack of interest in anything to do with renovating or his lack of ideas and decisions about one house versus the other. He resents my gadfly nature, my enthusiasm, my prodding of him for answers and decisions.

"This is perfect," I hear myself say to the agent. "We need to have a chat about it, but I am sure we'll be putting in an offer."

The agent's eyes shine with surprise and satisfaction. "The house is going on the market tomorrow, and there is an open day this weekend. Offers will be presented to the vendor early next week."

Our interest duly registered, we go off to find the hotel we are booked into for the night, and to get something to eat.

Over supper, The Husband nurses a beer. He does not appear happy.

"We're buying a house on a street that looks just like Walthamstow," he hisses. "We could have just stayed there."

He will not let go of his beloved Walthamstow, his former stomping grounds for twenty-five years. A depressing coincidence cuffs me: whereas Walthamstow was once the poorest, most deprived borough in London, now we are considering buying a house in Easton, possibly the poorest, most deprived borough in Bristol, and one of the most deprived areas in the entire southwest of England.

"We could never have afforded an entire house in Walthamstow," I remind him for the thousandth time.

It does not appease him. I need to get him to focus on the now. And I need to rein in my expectations. I draw out a sheet of paper from my bag and sketch the floor plan of the house we have just seen to show him how it could be the right house for us. True, neither of us loves the house, but maybe loving a house is overrated.

Of the nine items on my list of must-haves, this house scores a seven. It loses out on off-street parking (no room) and three bedrooms (pending the smallest one's conversion to a bathroom), but we win on natural light, high ceilings, two bathrooms (post-reno), a level backyard accessible from the kitchen (it will also be "visible from the kitchen" post-reno), the house is not on a main road, there are no screeching hordes of seagulls, and the house is in a walkable area close to amenities.

"And the bonus?" I say with forced enthusiasm. "It's just a ten-minute walk to Ikea."

A look of forced surrender fills his eyes: "Oh goody."

I am feeling guilty and reckless. This is not how I wanted our lives to turn out. I need him to be decisive, to challenge me, because if it were up to me alone, I would not buy this house. This house is a compromise, and I cannot remember if or when I have ever had to compromise. Compromise is not necessary when you are both in sync.

I have already disappointed The Husband by uprooting him twice in three years; now I fear I am about to disappoint myself.

6

The Unacknowledged Catalyst

"There is something to be said about Little Britain," I say dreamily to The Husband.

Little Britain was a television comedy series in the UK that made its debut in 2003, but the term has since become shorthand for a type of parochial mindset associated (often incorrectly) with those who live on suburban housing estates. And here we are, smack dab in one.

We are in the backyard of our rented temporary accommodation on the outskirts of Bristol. A hot spring sun has surprised everyone this Saturday, and the drone of lawn mowers and weed whackers pervades the neighbourhood as everyone jumps into action to take advantage of it. The Husband has already mowed ours. We sit in patio chairs facing a small enclosed vista of green trimmed lawn; sturdy, unbroken fences; and a bed of early flowers that stand erect and poised to unfurl petals of perfection. Serenity and contentment bloom in this neat-as-a-pin patch of England.

The Husband, eyes closed, face raised to the sun, acknowledges my comment with a grunt that translates into "I have heard you, but I do not wish to engage in a conversation about the subject because it is about houses and your comment carries a suspicious whiff that seems destined for a larger discussion that is intended to confuse me. Kindly keep your thoughts to yourself."

It is two months since we moved into this nondescript circa 1980s housing estate. All our belongings are in cardboard boxes and plastic tubs, numbered and catalogued on a homemade, handwritten manifest. They are crammed into the garage and into one of the three bedrooms. To emphasize our transient state, I have refused to unpack anything beyond the bare essentials.

For a place that sits between two of England's most historic and architecturally rich cities—Bath and Bristol—you would be hard-pressed to find a more unimaginative housing development. The house we are renting is bland to the extreme: Externally, it is a dull canvas of tawny brick and white PVC windows; not so much as a finial of embellishment. Internally, it has a living room and a kitchen/diner opening to a fenced and shrub-filled yard; upstairs, there are three bedrooms, and a bathroom with a toilet that has to be repeatedly flushed and a shower that has all the pressure of a royal handshake.

But the longer we are here, the more I begin to wonder whether Little Britain offers the perfect solution to our house hunt. This specific house we are renting is not for sale, but it would be easy enough to find one around here. I turn my thoughts to how I might dress this one up to suit us. First to go would be the net curtains; they seem to be a thing here. The house would need cosmetic changes for sure. It does not have an iota of charm or character, but you can buy that now. What it does have is everything else: the light and the room we need, built-in closets, and that rarest of finds in British homes—off-street parking *and* a garage. The house sits on a quiet court and would be a perfect lock-up-and-leave. The neighbours are friendly and considerate. It is a walkable area, with winding pathways and manicured parkettes between each of the courts, which saves you from walking on the busier main roads. A retail park is a five-minute walk away, with a few shops, a handful of big-box stores, and (to The Husband's joy) a Costa and a Caffè Nero. Ten minutes in the opposite direction is a friendly news agent, an extremely efficient NHS—National Health Service—centre, and a multiplex cinema. Easy, practical living. If we bought here, there might be money left over to travel, maybe enough to buy a holiday home in Spain.

But Practical Living and I have only a passing acquaintance. I will ditch Practical Living the moment its polar opposite, Character, waltzes into my range of vision. And yet, ask me to change and you might as well rip out my heart. I cannot pull myself away from the desire to buy a wreck, to take something forlorn and perform a Lazarus on it. There must be some undiagnosed or unknown psychological disorder that draws me toward such places even as a part of me resists it, even when such a risk could rupture my marriage. You see, I court stability, I dream of stability, I can afford stability, and yet I cannot give myself entirely to it.

What makes me gravitate to such properties, to the type of house that others see so clearly as a money pit, hard work, and aggravation? It surely is not financial prudence: my penchant for overimproving a house ends up costing me more in the long run. And yes, it is in my bones and blood: you do not spend two-thirds of a lifetime with maniacal renovators without any of that rubbing off. I acknowledge that. But there has to be another reason for the renovation itch. Am I doing this to impress someone? My husband? My late parents? Myself? Admittedly, an element of pride and confidence is at work here. And control? Possibly. I also want another kick at the renovation can. I want a big project; I want to be a martyr to the cause of rescuing an English home, regardless of how modest it is. I want to prove to myself and to everyone that I have the vision, the design chops, and the fortitude to pull it off. But even that reason does not strike me as entirely authentic.

The sun caresses my face and relaxes my brain; my body melts comfortably into the lawn chair. I decide not to think about houses and renovations for now but to consider, instead, this addiction of mine, to see if I can deduce what it all means. Why *do* I do this? Why this fixation, this near mania, with homes and redoing things? During much of my working life I was an editor, where my job was to disassemble a story and reassemble it to a clearer, polished, more correct version. Sounds like a gateway to renovation to me. Maybe a few decades of that habit permeated other areas of my life.

By buying and renovating a home, it is as if this disassembly personifies a constant, almost pathological, craving to strip back the veneer, to uncover—or is it *recover*—something that is missing, or a flaw that needs fixing, or . . . uh-oh. I roll my eyes. Of course. There is that, too. Like the surprise appearance of flower shoots that have heroically pushed through dark, viscous soil after a long winter, I see exactly what I am pushing through and what I am aiming to restore. It has nothing to do with a house.

An all-too familiar memory overtakes me like a sudden rash, and predictably—because this memory has tormented me for thirty-five years—the image materializes of the fat pig forcing his way through the door of my hotel room, pushing me onto the bed, and raping me.

I have written elsewhere about my rape and I am not going to revisit the details here, only to say that the awful events of April 1983 have never left me, that the blessed relief and epiphany I received decades later in a North Yorkshire convent abides within me still, but that the memory of what happened that terrifying night, like a scar, never fades. More than a violation of the body, rape is a violation of the soul, and damage that deep, that intimate, is near impossible to heal. The best you can do is erect a barrier and warning signs around the memory as if it were a toxic waste site, and let it be.

I remember, while I was being raped, frantically separating my soul from my body, believing I could save the most treasured part of me from being sullied by this animal rutting on top of me. But when it was over, my soul re-entered a damaged body and mind, like a homeowner returning to a house that has suffered fire damage or a violent robbery. From then on my life was cleaved into two distinct periods: BR and AR—Before Rape and After Rape.

In the past I flirted with the idea that my restlessness, my need to move, might be symptomatic of the rape, but to have acknowledged it fully would have opened a can of worms that I was unable to cope with back then. It would have been an admission that the experience had power over me. Instead, I kept an eye on the trauma in my rear-view mirror, always conscious of staying ahead of it, not letting it overtake me, though from time to time it did.

Here, now, focusing on it, considering it at my leisure, I see that relief from the rape memory, like the other memories consigned to The Basket of Painful Psychological Imprints, demands to be scratched from time to time. Whenever I wedge the flat end of a crowbar beneath the corner of a cupboard and pry it off the wall, or when I whale a sledgehammer into a wall or tear up tiles and carpeting, I am not only renovating—I am engaging in revenge therapy. The dust, the mayhem, all of it obscures and confuses the pain. We are taught to fear chaos, but for me it is a kind of fuel. I hunger for it, and nothing can sate my appetite except the upheaval of moving into a new house, a new shell, until I tire of that particular meal and seek something else to taste.

Maybe there is no house that can satisfy me; maybe the rape was so destructive to my sense of self that I have become like the walking wounded: unable to rest, unable to settle. I should come with a warning label: "Has been raped. Coping mechanism in this particular human specimen is an insatiable desire to move, renovate, and decorate homes."

I wonder whether a similar psychosis drove my parents. They never would have articulated it as such, much less discussed it. Perhaps they did not equate moving with what haunted them unconsciously. For my mother, moving and decorating gave her power—however illusionary—over her immigrant status and all that her family had lost in Hungary. For my father, each move distanced him further from his father's deceit and his family's poverty. We are all running from something, whether the beast pursuing us has actual legs or stalks us in our peripheral vision.

I look over at The Husband. His face is still lifted to the sunshine, and it holds a relaxed smile that I have not seen for many weeks. No, I cannot confide any of this to him. If he knew the subtext of this move, it would trouble him deeply, and I cannot bear to burden him with that.

WE ARE A MONTH AWAY from collecting the keys to our new home, a month away from taking, by law and honour, ownership of a house neither of us loves. Like the housing cads that we are, we insist on playing the field right up to the day of the wedding in case something better wafts into view. We are not entirely convinced that the house we have engaged to buy is for us, or that we want to undertake a full-scale renovation. Privately, I am game, knowing full well that the responsibility—and the blame—for this folly will rest entirely on my shoulders.

The Husband is not at home in the habitat of disorder and plaster dust; of project budgets and room schematics; of men in saggy, cement-encrusted jeans weighted down with tool belts that expose bum cracks. But he is not exactly talking me out of it, either. He is prepared to let me have my fun, which also means he is prepared to sit back and watch me screw up the whole thing.

Our pressing need at the moment is to find a builder. And we also need to get out there and do some comparison shopping of fixtures and fittings. But he cannot be bothered, and he gets angry when I suggest it, which he tends to do when he is pried from his comfort. And yes, he could leave it to me to get on with things, but I do not drive in the UK (I am terrified of the narrow streets and right-handed driving) and am therefore unable to dash from place to place checking out products and services the way I used to do in Canada.

But forge ahead I must. I tell him this: that I am just going to do my thing without his input or buy-in.

He shrugs. "This is your house." That angers me more.

"It is *our* house. If you are not interested in how your house is going to look, then fine. But we need to be decisive. And if you do not want to be decisive, that is fine, too. But for you not to respond to my suggestions or ideas, or if you are intent on delaying your opinion for whatever reason, well, I am not having any of it. We cannot afford that sort of shilly-shally."

Deep down I understand the subtext of his lack of engagement: This is *my* house in the sense that this is *my* move. He is not pleased about being displaced, about being wrenched against his will from what was to him entirely amenable. Perhaps I would behave the same way if things were reversed. While he is signing off on his involvement in the house, he is not doing so purely out of stubbornness. Like me, he is disappointed that our money does not stretch to buying something better. You work all your life, you save, you are prudent and not given to extravagance, and at the end of it all your money can only buy average.

Not that he would blurt it out like that. He is a quiet, meditative man of small and simple needs. A good and decent man. His stability and common sense were what attracted me to him, and I came to value those traits even more because they are so lacking in my makeup. I fell in love with how uncomplicated and calm he was. But now, like a room that needs to be repurposed, I require more of him, and perhaps more is something he just cannot give. He was never uprooted the way I was; his parents moved house fewer than a handful of times, and one of those moves was only three doors down from the previous house. What I am putting The Husband through is not just new territory—it is a shakeup of life as he has known it. This is about as frightening as if he were asked to stride naked onto the stage of Wembley Arena and sing "Livin' La Vida Loca." Seagulls, steep steps to the garden, a dark house; he could cope with those. Being without a home, and venturing into the deep, dark, money-sucking hole called "renovation," he cannot.

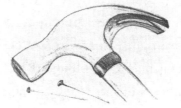

7

The Property Delusion

The Husband leaves our rented house to walk to the nearby retail park for his early-morning java fix at its two chain cafés: Costa and Caffè Nero. He says he prefers Costa because occasionally the manager gives him a free coffee.

"That's because you look sad and bereft," I tell him. "And you dress like a street person. He's doing it out of pity, not kindness."

"At least it isn't costing us money."

A jab at my renovation spending.

From behind white net curtains I observe the back of his lanky frame, clad in worn jeans and a khaki jacket that I keep threatening to throw out. Sunlight glances off his hair—mostly ginger when we first met twelve years ago, now silvery grey: I wonder whether the colour change is my fault. As he rounds the corner I think: He could do with a bit of renovating himself. I swat the words away immediately—they could have come directly from my mother's mouth—but it's too late, and with one of those lightning-quick, unedited moments of self-reflection, I realize that I have, in fact, been guilty of trying to renovate all three of my husbands, though to be fair it was only when it came to their clothes, which is like wanting to give them a fresh coat of paint. Is that so bad?

With The Husband out of sight, I plop on the sofa and switch on the TV. Time for some research.

I absolutely love property shows, and Britain's television airwaves are blessed with many. The Husband gets uneasy when I watch home-buying or home-renovation shows, especially when I watch with tablet or laptop in hand, swiping through properties for sale in the same search areas where the prospective TV buyers are hunting. He just knows I am going to look at him with those shall-we-move-there eyes. It works both ways: when we watched an episode of *Location, Location, Location* where the potential homebuyers were sizing up homes in his old stomping ground of Walthamstow, an area of London that has experienced skyrocketing house prices, I could feel the heat of his regret.

Lately, I have taken a shine to *Homes Under the Hammer*, which features homes purchased at auction and follows their subsequent renovation. I enjoy comparing the before and after, and seeing how the owners reconfigure the layout and generally improve the property's potential. There is nothing easier and cheaper than engaging in the fantasies of others. I also enjoy observing changes in the buyers themselves. A renovation alters you, not always in a good way but definitely in a reflective way.

On occasion I tune into *Property Brothers* for the comfort of its presenters' Canadian accents, but increasingly, their so-called radical

transformations leave me cold. An aesthetic of soulless, dull conformity. The denim jeans of the house porn world. A stylist puts a kid's
drawing or a family photo into a white or black Ikea frame, and that
is as close to "individual stamp" as you are likely to see.

Years ago, a decorating magazine asked to follow a kitchen renovation I was doing, but as soon as they realized they were dealing
with someone with ideas of her own, they backed out. I had told
them I would be using white or black appliances; they told me to
use stainless-steel appliances, which were new to the market at the
time. The home-decorating media are slaves to the glossy weaponry
of their advertisers, though at the time I was naive to this fact. Do
not get me wrong: I liked the shiny stainless-steel appliances, but
they were expensive, and I also felt they would look out of place
in the French-country design I envisioned for my kitchen. I stuck
to my guns: white or black appliances. The magazine folks stuck
to their guns: stainless steel. It was spiralizers at dawn. We parted
company.

My fascination for houses predates the internet and the vast world
of TV and print offerings. As a teenager, I was more likely to pick
up *Country Life* than *Glamour* or *Seventeen*. I devoured *Country Life*,
and spent happy hours fantasizing about buying such homes. And
they were so cheap. In the 1970s in England, you could buy a ten-
bedroom Tudor pile with a ballroom, tennis court, in a woodland
setting for £10,000. "Only ten thousand pounds!" I said to my father,
stabbing the magazine listing with my finger. "For a historic mansion!
With a tennis court! Let's buy it." He was already being hounded
about houses closer to home by my mother; he did not need me to
add foreign hysteria into the mix. Gamely, he said, "You buy it." With
$200 in my savings account, how could I? But it did not stop me
from dreaming. It made me even more determined to one day live in
England—the land of cheap and fabulous housing.

In the past few years, property portals have become a rich source of escapism for house-mongers. Pinterest can be an addictive source of decorating inspiration, but more times than not it throws up images of shiny renovations, of artistically staged and immaculately furnished interiors cleansed of personality. Dream homes to some, but to me they are lobotomized dens of minimalism. Where is the spirit? The fun? Who are these sad sacks, these folks bereft of character or too insecure to show it? They have fretted over the perfect shade of white; they have scoured magazines, catalogues, and shops for just the right accessories, as if curating a museum exhibit. Or they have enlisted an interior designer who has reduced the whole business to a "look" or a "vibe" that is "on trend." How I loathe that term "on trend." Life has been sucked out of these interiors; the throw cushions have been Botox-ed; the wall hangings are all splashes of colour and no story. I am more impressed with a home that displays quirky things from your travels; or a knick-knack that one of your kids gave you for Mother's Day; or shelves heaving with real books, not those arranged in colour-coded blocks. If all you can show me is a curated stack of glossy coffee table books sitting on a glass credenza, then I cannot see us having a long conversation. I have no truck with white walls, but I mourn the loss of individuality dictated by the home-decorating tribe, who on the one hand urge you to put your stamp on your interiors and on the other hand want your stamp to look like the one they are pushing at that moment.

The best ideas are those encountered randomly, serendipitously: a clever arrangement found in a friend's home; in a shop window; in a historic home, a museum, the lobby of a hotel; something glimpsed through a gate, fence, or open door while travelling in a far-off country or just wandering around your neighbourhood; something in a book; or gleaned from nature. They percolate and brew, these ideas, their taste improving or going slightly off as you stir in new ingredients culled from new discoveries. This is why I am not a fan of mood boards: they are too dogmatic, too incapable of the yield-and-flex necessary for the kind of quirky style I favour.

And yes, TV—not solely property programs but regular fare—and movies can be good sources, too. The problem is that my eyes drift easily to the background, checking out the goods in a character's home. It is not uncommon for me to whisper to The Husband, "Don't you love the shape of that chair" or "Check out the vase on the third shelf" while one of the characters is being murdered.

When I watch a movie, I scrutinize the background: I have come away from a movie lukewarm about the story but in love with the decor. The layout and design of the kitchen, the tiles used in the bathroom, the placement of the furniture, the arrangement of photos and art. It is often the small details in a character's home that tell me more about them than does the dialogue. That sage paint colour on the walls of Mr. and Mrs. Wilson's dining room in *Dennis the Menace*? Loved the calming effect. The perfect-for-conversation kitchen in *It's Complicated*? Wonderful. Or the one in *Something's Gotta Give*, with the amazing soapstone countertop on the kitchen island? Want it. In fact, I will take the entire house. Ditto for Meg Ryan's brownstone in *You've Got Mail*. Admittedly, most of these interiors are created on a Hollywood sound stage where perfection and illusion are the stock in trade, but they feed the idea factory in my head nonetheless. The day cannot be far off when we will watch a movie with special glasses that pop up product details about an item used in a particular scene.

When did we all become so home and product obsessed? When did these take centre stage in our lives?

Never before has both the concept and the ownership of home been so important. Home is everywhere: in advertising, in magazine copy, in TV programming, in the financial sector, in news reporting, in retailing. It is not so much about owning—though possession is a definite factor—as it is about manipulating aspiration, emotion, and security. The tincture of a memory becomes a permanent marker that makes you want to trigger that experience every day. Conversely, a certain trigger can banish or at least minimize negative memories. We do not simply live in homes—we fetishize the privilege into an experience.

Home was once the place to hang your hat and rest your head, until it was transformed into the ultimate acquisition. You did not just want a home—you wanted a lifestyle.

Around the late-1970s, my generation succumbed to the *Dynasty* effect. *Dynasty* was a TV soap opera about a wealthy Colorado family. That is all I know of *Dynasty*. It competed with another soap opera at the time, *Dallas*, about a wealthy Texas family. You were either a fan of *Dynasty* or a fan of *Dallas*. I was for *Dallas*. That said, I credit the uptick in the demand for upscale interiors to *Dynasty* because it had glitzier sets and espoused a more luxurious aesthetic. Suddenly, young homebuyers refused to consider any home that did not have a master ensuite bathroom. They wanted a *Dynasty* home on a Ford-assembly-line salary. The rest of us inched our way into home renovation via starter homes and starter marriages. We began in the basement, where we transformed concrete walls and floors with wood framing and drywall into TV rooms with VCRs, banks of speakers, and libraries for our vinyl records. We moved on to the backyard, adding decks and fencing. Next up, kitchens and bathrooms. I remember a former neighbour showing me her kitchen renovation, all cantilevered glass ceilings and granite worktops, and telling me it cost $50,000. That was 1982, and it seemed an obscene amount of money. A lot of us were dreamers; few of us could afford to turn the dreams into reality.

Where the serious armchair renovator hung out was in front of *This Old House*, a television series that began in 1979 and is still on the air. The show took old, dilapidated American homes and pains-takingly renovated them. The series became the springboard for a more thoughtful approach to home ownership and home improve-ment. People loved the idea of buying an old home, a piece of history, and fixing it up. Norm Abram, the great master carpenter, presented home construction as a meditative art with his Zen-like calm and pithy mantra "Measure twice, cut once." He had a workshop with every tool known to the human race, but he was not boastful about it; he treated the tools as if they were as necessary as a knife and fork. A new generation was taught to revere the handmade, the hand crafted. Unflappable Norm was paired with Bob Vila, a tightly coiled motormouth who looked to be on the verge of throwing a punch. Each week, the tension was less about whether the foundations of the house being renovated would survive underpinning and more about whether Bob and Norm would come to blows. When Bob left the show and was replaced by the infinitely more chilled Steve Thomas, you could feel the collective shoulders of continental North America relax.

Perhaps by coincidence, or perhaps inspired by the popularity of *This Old House*, two men who had been fired from their jobs at a hardware store in Texas decided to open their own. A year later, Home Depot was born. By 1984, it had grown to nineteen stores, with sales approaching $300 million and a slot on Nasdaq. Five years later, it was the largest store in the United States. It offered work-shops for the do-it-yourselfer, stocked tools (you, too, could have a workshop like Norm's!), construction materials, fittings, and fixtures. It also sponsored the steadily growing number of home-related pro-grams and media. You were not a boomer if your Saturday morning did not start at Home Depot.

Today, hundreds of home-related television shows flicker across North American and British screens. In addition—sometimes supplementing the TV shows—there is a plethora of decorating magazines, and countless how-to tutorials online or offered at your local hardware store. In Canada alone, more than eight hundred thousand jobs are connected to the home-renovation industry.

I cannot recall whether my interest in home improvement came out of interest or necessity. I suspect it was necessity. Single or married, my funds were always limited. I could never afford the "done" home. If my parents instilled anything in me, it was that renovating was an act of generosity for both the house and the wider community. When you improve an old house, you improve the housing stock for future generations. It did not matter if you did not know how to do it yourself; what was important was that you had the vision to do it. My parents did their share of removing rubble and undertaking minor demolition work, but they never attempted skilled work beyond painting, wallpapering, and a bit of furniture refinishing—they had no aptitude for it—and wisely left it to the professionals.

I followed suit. I have learned minor skills from watching various trades and from online demonstrations, but for the most part I hire professionals.

But these property shows on TV—I love them. They are addictive. They are the gateway drug to a full-on renovation. Spending time on the sofa in the thrall of these shows is never wasted time; it is intelligence gathering. The fact that there are entire channels devoted to home buying and decorating is a fantasy come true. They take the edge off reality. Political scandals, the world on the precipice of war with the despot du jour, wild fluctuations on the stock market, terrorist attacks, and home invasions? *Pfff!* Many of us medicate with property programs. Life drills down to saner, safer territory when you are faced with choosing between granite and Corian, rather than between bombing or not bombing Russia.

But like so many illusionary things that promise to improve your life, there is the element of a con to it all. I call it "Grand Designs syndrome."

Grand Designs is a British home-design/reality TV program in which people embark on some enormous project to build the home of their dreams. Want to take a crumbling monastery in Tuscany and turn it into a B&B? Or turn a garage in central London into a family home? Or build a house into a Spanish cliff? Or rebuild a shabby French manor house? *Grand Designs* is your destination.

The projects are fantastic, inspired designs, the ultimate labour of love, but they come with no shortage of drama. *Grand Designs* does not flinch from showing homeowners on the verge of breakdown, collapsing under the stress of it all. These are warrior renovators. There have been times when I find it hard to watch—the homeowner cries when the bank calls in its loan, or the family has to live sequestered in a cramped, cold caravan while their money flows like a fast-moving river into their dream-house pit. There have been cases where one of the homeowners dies in mid-reno. It is enough to make all but the stoutest viewer vow, then and there, never to try this at home. Then it is over. The ending is (usually) happy, the dream is fulfilled, and your relief is that you have been able to experience it all without the burden of ownership.

The con, which I have fallen for at times, is this: These TV programs make the work sound like a doddle. You can take this wall down for £500 or remake this kitchen for less than £3,000, they tell viewers and naive participants. Sure, it might cost £500 to take down that wall, but they do not tell you is that it will cost an additional £1,500 to hire the labour to do the job. And yes, that kitchen might cost you £3,000 if you live in Wolverhampton or $5,000 if you live in Winnipeg, but if you live in London or New York, that same kitchen will likely cost you £25,000 or $40,000. Many of these property makeovers are done in more affordable areas of the country and in less desirable towns and cities where labour is significantly cheaper.

I do wonder about some of the participants on property shows. I like to read them, to see what they are really searching for, in case I recognize myself in them. They do not just want a three-bed semi; they want a home that will make them feel as rich as the Beckhams; they want a home that will erase disappointments, whitewash an unhappy past; a home that will validate them to their circle, allow them to give the middle finger to their boss. They want a cocoon that makes them feel like movie stars the moment they walk through the door after spending the day as nameless grunts on a production line or on a hospital-ward floor.

People scoff at these shows; they say a life cannot be transformed by a home. I disagree. I do believe that your life can be improved, if not transformed, by where you lay your head. I have experienced it myself. Where I draw the line is when people believe that such improvement can be achieved by material consumption. So often these TV homebuyers walk into a home and cannot see past the stylist's work: they look at the dishes on a glass table, the innocuous art on the walls, the creamy linens and throw cushions on the beds, the grey-painted walls, the plantation shutters on the windows. It is apparent that they do not want a new house—they want a new life-style. But then, can you blame them when the design gurus harangue us that our homes are inadequate; or shame us about not maximizing space, or not being creative enough, or not keeping up with trends?

We are led to believe that home, and by extension our design choices, are the reason for our dissatisfaction with life. They are the flaws in our drive for perfection, and if we can just banish them or change them, then we will banish our demons. No one seems to worry about the gigantic bill at the end of it, of the spectre of bailiffs repossessing your gorgeous home.

A smug superiority comes over me when I watch those shows. I tell myself that I am different from those naive sops: I am more sensible and practical; I have control over my purse strings. I am good. I have convinced myself of all that and more.

My attention returns to the program on the TV screen in front of me. I am transfixed by the wreck some brave soul has bought, and am itching to see how it turns out. Will they keep that Edwardian mantel? Will they knock through the wall separating the dining room and kitchen? Will they refinish the floors, or will they opt for the quick fix of carpeting? Suddenly, I am part of the creative world: the armchair designer.

A movement flickers at the corner of my eye. Uh-oh. The Husband is back. Here he comes, walking up the path. His key will be in the front door any second. I grab the channel changer and switch to *Frasier*.

8

The Keys

The morning we pick up the keys to our new house, a news item over the car radio announces, "After months of feverish house prices and rabid buyers, the property market has cooled, buyers and sellers are suddenly cautious, and prices are drifting back down to saner levels."

Turning the key in the car ignition, The Husband gives me one of those frosty I-told-you-so smiles and says with mock cheerfulness, "Nice to know we bought at the height of the market."

We arrive at the house for the first time as its reluctant owners. No historical documentation remains of our house or of its previous owners and occupations beyond a covenant between one Aaron Heywood and one Thomas Doble requiring the first eleven odd-numbered houses on our street (which includes ours) to pay a perpetual yearly rent charge of £3 5s as of November 6, 1895. Nothing exists to show whether this was ever enforced, and so the covenant has been declared void.

We still do not love the house, and from the state of things it does not look as if it loves us, either. There is a sulky tension on both our parts: we are the resigned owners of a house that has been disturbed after months of blissful solitude.

I force myself into a state of positivity, both for the house's sake and for The Husband's. It is vital that he feel we made the right decision, or rather that *I* made the right decision, since this venture is my responsibility, as I am frequently reminded. Even so, his body language shows disappointment. He is questioning our decision to buy it. He is questioning his decision to trust me on this. Truth be told, so am I. But this is the best we have found in our price range, and we have put a ring on it. This is home.

We wander through the house searching for a modicum of comfort in this rattling, old skeleton. A bottle of prosecco, a housewarming gift from the person acting on behalf of the previous owner, sits on top of the fridge. A kind touch. We have brought a carton of tea bags, two mugs, two spoons, and a bright-red kettle, in a half-assed attempt to fashion a kitchen. But mostly we sit or stand or stomp from room to room, mugs in hand, taking it all in, wondering where to start. Bizarrely, given the state and condition of things, we decide to attack our new home with an arsenal of cleaning products and sponges. A smiling Henry vacuum cleaner, left behind, peeks helpfully from beneath the stairs.

The old trope of a renovation is this: "Locate the stud, then hire him." We need to find a builder. Fast. I have made calls to several builders I found online. The ones I have actual conversations with are not available until September at the earliest, or more likely the following year. The rest do not return calls. If we have had trouble securing a home, then it looks as if securing a builder will be twice the nightmare.

Eventually, two builders do show up to quote for the job; both are nice, youngish, and appear to have the chops for the job—we saw samples of their work—but one focuses solely on loft conversions (we are undecided about whether to plump for one), and the other is unable to begin for several months.

The one who quotes for the loft proves especially helpful.

"You've got your work cut out," he declares, his eyes roaming the main floor of our house.

I ask if he can recommend any trades. He pulls out his phone and says, "What do you need?" and proceeds to give us the names and phone numbers of an electrician and a plumber.

Can he recommend a builder?

"I know a guy." He pauses, as if he has had a change of heart, but then he carries on and mentions someone named Francis. "He has been off work for a while—mental breakdown or something like that—but he's ready to get back into it."

We take down the details. As someone who knows a thing or two about mental breakdowns, I am sympathetic, and happy to help anyone get back into it, as long as he does not flake out on me.

I call Francis. He agrees to meet us at the house the following week.

On the appointed day, I answer Francis's knock on the door. We greet one another with the eager-to-please smiles of the desperate-to-please. Late thirties, with dark hair, handsome features, and a cheerful personality. He looks like a builder: confident in bearing, muscular in body. He has boundless enthusiasm. He strides into the house and goes through it with the enthusiasm of a youngster who has been given a new toy.

"Wow. Look at the potential!" He turns to us. "This is perfect. It's a blank slate."

The Husband's face brightens.

I step forward.

"Basically, this is what we need: Create a bathroom upstairs in the smallest bedroom—that is the priority. In the kitchen, we want the interior walls taken down—get rid of the utility room and the bathroom—to make one large space. And we want the back wall to have bifold doors, so we can improve the light and access the backyard."

"That will look amazing. And since there's nothing above this back part of the kitchen, which I gather will be your dining area, right?"

We nod.

"Then how about we take the ceiling right up to the rafters and install three Velux skylights. It'll be wow."

Yes, I want wow.

"There is a side return," I say tentatively. "We wondered about extending the kitchen."

Francis looks out the kitchen window at the side return. He thinks for a moment. "Doable—but expensive. You're looking at an additional thirty-five grand."

I try not to blink.

"But frankly, it's not a huge amount of space. You wouldn't be adding much more room to the kitchen. It would be an unnecessary expense. And with what you've got in mind already, you'll have lots of space."

Well, he seems honest and sounds like he is not a budget breaker. I like that.

"What other projects are you working on?" I ask politely. "Anything we can see?"

He rhymes off a few projects; offers to show us one the next day that is not too far away. We agree on a time to look at it.

Francis seems to know what he is doing. I voice my biggest concern: "Will you work exclusively on our home until it is done?" I do not want to be two-timed.

"Absolutely. I was actually going to use the next few months to work on my own place, but I'm happy to take on your project."

"How long do you think it will take to do all this?"

He shrugs. "Six to eight weeks?"

A FEW WEEKS LATER, HAVING VISITED one of Francis's projects and being reassured by the quality of his work, we agree on a start date of June 12. Rule one in the renovator's handbook is not to trust a builder who says he can start pretty much right away: if he's any good, he will have been booked up months in advance. But I am impatient, bordering on rash. I convince myself that I am generally a good judge of character, and that I have a good bullshit detector. But what do I know? Have I asked Francis if he is accredited? Of course not. Have I seen his work? Yes. Have I spoken to the clients of that work? No.

We pay him the first instalment to renovate the kitchen and the bathroom. It is a fair whack of money, but the work will be extensive, and we want it done right. His quote was in line with what we were quoted by the other builder and it is for the work only: it does not include fixtures, fittings, and cabinets, which we agree to purchase separately. He suggests we use the kitchen cabinet company he uses, since they are reasonable and reliable.

We have a builder now. One huge hurdle crossed.

Francis's start date gives us a month to do what work we can manage on our own. We can tidy up the backyard and take the refuse to the dump. We can rip out some of the ramshackle cupboards inside the house, strip the wallpaper, and pull up the carpet in the master bedroom.

I have a bit more bounce now; so does The Husband.

"Let's look at this project as an opportunity to strengthen our marriage," I say during a tea break in the backyard.

The Husband says nothing. I will take that as an okay.

THERE ARE ENDLESS STORIES about couples who embark on a big renovation and then split up. I am determined that ours will not be one of them. However, it is true that a renovation sharpens your relationship. You size up each other's mettle, assess one another's abilities—or lack thereof. Whenever I clock The Husband's concern, I have to remind myself that he has never done a big renovation, whereas I have lived through nearly three-dozen moves and more than a dozen renovations.

After seven years of marriage, it often feels as if The Husband and I are still getting to know one another. We arrived late in life in one another's orbit, fully formed with entrenched traits, preferences, cultural reference points, routines. I had been married twice before and had three children. The Husband had never been married; had never had children. We first laid eyes on one another in a café along a dry and dusty path on Spain's Camino de Santiago de Compostela. Our reasons for walking an ancient five-hundred-mile pilgrimage route were as starkly different as our personalities: He was getting over the death of a fiancée seven years earlier; I had turned fifty and was looking for adventure and figuring out the next stage of my life. He was looking back; I was looking forward.

We were each accustomed to our single status and had settled into our respective silent lives and routines. Our individual histories, neuroses, stories, and patterns did not invade our courtship because we were never in one another's company long enough for them to reveal their colours and shades. We were like parallel lines that never quite intersected, or needed to, merrily and steadily moving along. How can one ever see fully, completely, the person to whom one is attracted, especially when one's eyes are blinded by the unarticulated expectations and fantasies unwittingly foisted on the object of one's affection?

When The Husband and I began to talk about marriage, I had asked him playfully whether he would like to live in Canada. His response surprised me: "Absolutely not." It hurt a bit. He went on to explain quite defiantly that he did not want to adapt; did not know what he would do in a strange country. He would be apart from his family and friends, he said, away from his routine and everything he knew. The idea was completely foolish. Completely out of the question. I do not think it occurred to him that his concerns were exactly my concerns about moving to England. Then again, I have always been a pleaser.

Moving meant leaving my children behind, but they were by then adults with lives of their own and jobs in different parts of the country. If I remained in Canada, I would be a plane ride away from at least two of them anyway. Moving also meant leaving behind my mother. I felt guilty about it, but she dismissed as nonsense my concerns; said she was happy that I had met someone (and someone she finally approved of) who would take care of me. She was an indomitable, fiercely independent woman who did not want to be coddled in her old age yet resented not being so.

Misgivings aside, I have not regretted the move. When I am asked how I came to live in the UK, I have said teasingly that I drew the short straw, but the truth is I was happy to move. Strangely, I always felt more of an infinity with England than with Canada; somehow knew that I would one day live here. When I was sixteen, and on my first visit to England, I recall how, upon landing on English soil, it felt like a private homecoming. The words, in fact, had risen unbidden inside me: "You are home." And along with them was an inexpressible yearning to put down roots here. I have always agreed with the sentiment that the place where we are born and the place where we belong are not always one and the same.

And so The Husband and I married, and I flew away from the life I had in Canada, and endeavoured to settle in and embrace English life.

People meet and come together in random ways. You question whether it is serendipity or whether God is just messing with you. I have often been inclined to think it is the latter. How can two people so different in temperament, passions, and interests be happy together? And when were our specific roles determined? Why have I been cast as the ringleader, the organizer, and he as the long-suffering, silent partner? Sometimes we barely speak the same language, frequently responding to the other's statements with "What?" as we struggle to discern the other's accent, cultural tics, and terminology.

When did this man who I had been drawn to so instantly, who appeared when I was not looking for anyone, whose patient, effortless, easygoing nature and love of travel seduced me, abruptly change into cement shoes and refuse to be stirred by this adventure of renovating our own home? I want him to engage in the experience of renovating. I want him to share a bit of my passion. I want him to bond with this space and with me. I want this house to bridge the chasm between us.

This morning, we perch on beige-canvas folding chairs in our new backyard and face the back of the house, with its dreary, beige, pebble-dash facade (which I see painted a crisp white or a pale grey). The backside of a Victorian terrace is not an attractive sight. The sun is bright, and the day is warming up, but all the same our hands are cupped around mugs of instant coffee, willing some spiritual warmth to melt our worries. Steam rises like inspiration, and I move my face closer to the cup to receive its heat and aroma. I broach the bonding aspect again.

"What we need is something that will make us bond," I say. "An experience. Something that we can be proud to look upon and say, "We did it." We have done the Camino. We have done Machu Picchu. What we need is a house to renovate. Something where we can get stuck in. Work with our hands. A creative project."

The Husband looks at me as if I have been living all this time with another man. In addition to not being comfortable with change or moving house, he has zero ability or interest in anything to do with do-it-yourself. DIY is for another breed of male, whom he respects but with whom he has no fraternity. He will not so much as hang a painting. I wonder whether someone was overly critical of his efforts to make or repair something when he was a youngster, and that the sting forever put him off attempting it again. That said, he does enjoy shovelling snow and chopping firewood. Should have moved to Canada. His preferred domain is a café, preferably small, independently owned and not patronized by people with crying infants in tow, where he can read the newspaper and drink his two cappuccinos. He never wanted to renovate anything; he wanted to travel. This neat, precise man is at home with solitary pursuits: he runs, he hikes, he does not like being disturbed. You will not find him arguing about the day's news events or political shenanigans. He wears a pained expression when his football team wins, as if fist-pumping the air in victory would be an indecorous gesture, hurtful to the losing opposition. He is so restrained in speech and temperament that I do not honestly know if he has passions. His dress sense, like his manners, is on the formal side. He is not a Renaissance man, but he is most definitely a Victorian man.

"This Victorian house is so you," I say to flatter. "It resembles your character and personality perfectly. Even your build—tall, erect."

He looks deeply offended.

"What?" I say. "It was a compliment!"

He stands up abruptly and walks away.

I shake my head and drain my mug. Where to start? I decide to go to the library and see what I can find out about Victorian terrace homes.

9

The Victorian Terrace: Icon of an Empire

In the early hours of September 2, 1666, fire broke out in the bakery of Thomas Farynor on Pudding Lane in London. Who knew that his Restoration fire would spark the rise of the Victorian terrace?

The weather had been unseasonably dry and hot that summer. Like most London homes of the time, those on Pudding Lane were of wood-and-pitch construction. It did not take long for an innocent spark, driven by parched air and wind blowing north from the Thames, to burst into a wildfire. As the flames leapfrogged from Farynor's bake oven to a haystack to a dung heap to a thatch roof, the fire gathered force and roared a course of magnificent destruction. In four days, nearly all of London was destroyed: thirteen thousand homes consumed; more than seventy thousand people left homeless—which accounted for about 90 percent of the population.

Remarkably, only six deaths were reported, though it has since been determined that because deaths of the poor and middle class were not recorded, hundreds of people actually perished in the fire.

What happened next is a lesson in chaos theory.

London began rebuilding immediately, without plan or prudence. While builders tried to seek out property owners and rustle up workmen, Charles II encouraged the homeless to leave the City and settle elsewhere, in effect escorting from the premises much of London's surviving workforce.

Meanwhile, speculators and earnest builders clamoured for the king's attention to their grand schemes and visions for rebuilding the City. One of them was Nicholas "If Christ had not died for thee thou hadst been damned" Barbon. His unusual middle name was consistent with the trend for religious slogan names among English Puritans in the seventeenth century.

Astute and ruthless, Barbon was a bit of a gadfly. He trained in the Netherlands as a physician, then as an economist. When the Great Fire flared up, it stoked his ambitions to get into the building trade, where he saw a profitable opportunity to trade his speculum for speculation. It should come as no surprise to learn that he pioneered the invention of fire insurance.

Barbon, the Renaissance man with a Machiavellian heart, was quick with the shovel. While London lay open like a charred carcass, its boundaries, roads, and any semblance of order obliterated along with the housing stock, Barbon began digging west of the City, where there was open land. He progressed eastward, linking Westminster and the City in districts later known as the Strand and Bloomsbury. He must have been a supremely arrogant man, for he ignored every building restriction and legal objection and plowed his way through them. He treated the land as if it were his own. He razed buildings without permission and in their place erected residential and commercial buildings from which he reaped immense financial wealth.

It was Barbon who came up with the idea of treating a continuous row of houses as if it were the facade of a Georgian palace, with the entrance of the central abode marked by pillars and a sprawling pediment. Thus did he become known as the father of the terrace home. Examples of his work are still around today, in London's Grosvenor Square and in Bath's Queen's Square. A generation later, Thomas Cubitt took the idea and built on it.

In 1685, Barbon published the treatise *An Apology for the Builder, or A Discourse Shewing the Cause and Effects of the Increase of Building.* In it he philosophizes that of the three things that man is governed by necessity to provide for himself—food, clothing, and a home—it is the need for home, for shelter, that propels man to build, and this, argues Barbon, is the foundation of all:

> *It is the interest of the Government to incourage the Builders; not only because they presume and increase the subjects but they provide an imploy for them, by which they are fed, and get their livelihood.*
>
> *There are three great ways that the People in all Governments are imployed in: In providing Food, Clothes, and Houses. Now those ways are most serviceable to the Government, that imploy most of the People; Those that are imployed in feeding of them, are the fewest in number: for ten men may provide food enough for a thousand: but to cloth, and build Houses for them, requireth many hands: And there is that peculiar advantage that ought to be ascribed to the Builder, that he provideth the place of birth for all the other Arts, as well as for man. The Cloth cannot be made without houses to work it in. Now besides the vast*

numbers of People that are imployed in digging and mak-
ing the Materials, the Bricks, Stone, Iron, Lead, &c. all
those Trades that belong to the furnishing of an house, have
their sole dependencies on the Builders, as the Upholsterers,
Chair-makers, &c.

Conferring the role of Grand Provider on builders was done for
Barbon's singular gain, but his treatise does make one consider
the importance of builders. Without them, where would we live?
Where would we work, pray, or be healed of disease and illness?
How would we travel, shop, eat out, if not for facilities that shelter
us from the elements and cater to our comfort? I would rank builders far ahead of chefs any day. Anyone can cook; not everyone can
build.

Today, builders are frequently chastised (sometimes justifiably so)
for their cowboy behaviour: their shoddy workmanship; their outrageous costs; their speculation; how they bank land and manipulate
the housing crisis; how their plans rarely integrate with nature. But
one of the most widespread complaints against modern builders is
their penchant for cookie-cutter homes. And yet, what could possibly
be more cookie cutter than the Victorian terrace?

THE VICTORIAN TERRACE did not rise fully formed overnight;
its apogee came at the latter part of the nineteenth century. Up
until then, the style mavens of the day crossed swords over which
was better: Gothic revival or Classical revival. The Gothicists
believed that Classical architecture was rigid, that it put form
ahead of function; the Classicists regarded Gothic architecture
as an unholy and unsightly pastiche. The Victorians, for the most
part, cast their lot with the colourful and fanciful interpretation

of the Gothicists, and ransacked the architecture handbook: The foliated pillars that framed their doors were a nod to the Classical era; their fan-shaped transoms hailed from the Palladium period; timbered gables evoked the Tudor era; stone quoins referenced the Queen Anne period; the balance and proportion of their buildings were courtesy of the Regency; while the symmetry was thanks to the Georgian style. The Victorians never did anything by halves, and this being the era of upward mobility, they were not about to be shy about it, either.

Concurrently, Britain was moving from an agrarian economy to an industrial one. Mass production was in full swing. Canals and railways allowed heavy materials to be transported economically all over the country—cast iron from Scotland, terracotta from the Midlands and the southwest, slate from Wales and Cumbria—so that house building no longer depended on available local materials. As well, advances in technology gradually brought electricity, central heating, and indoor plumbing into house design, so that it became commonplace rather than the exception.

The Industrial Revolution triggered a demand for housing like nothing the UK had ever experienced. People flooded into towns and cities from the countryside in response to the cry for labour, and when they arrived, they needed places to live. The speculative builder answered the need with the tried-and-true template for cheap urban housing on narrow plots of land: the terrace. The housing boom of the 1850s produced millions of terraced homes.

Of course, in class-stratified Britain there were Victorian terraces and then there were Victorian terraces, but there are common elements to the style apparent today in middle-class versions: enclosed front gardens with iron railings and gates; rear gardens delineated by low brick walls; uniform facades forming a ribbon of unbroken continuity.

Roofs were generally steeply pitched and clad in black-slate or red-clay tiles, with hips and gables embellished with elaborate wooden barge boards and ornate ridge tiles and finials. Multi-storey bays were usually given their own steep roofs, joined to the front pitch of the main roof.

Some styles had crenellated roofs that mimicked a castle parapet above the projecting bays; while the front courtyards, with their low stone walls squaring off the boundary line, evoked a protective moat or the enclosure system. If an Englishman's home is his castle, the Victorian terrace fulfilled that brief across the classes.

Under the Victorians, chimneys bloomed from being a utilitarian standard into a tall and decorated feature, with projecting courses of brickwork, stone carving, and other ornamentation. Even the lowly chimney pot got a makeover. Many were shaped like crowns, making them look like giant chess pieces or imparting a regal nod.

Large front bay windows, often of two or three storeys of ornately decorated surrounds, became a dominant feature after 1850. Inside the home, these big bays coupled with high ceilings brought in lots of light (until the Victorians hung their enormous, heavy curtains). The sash design of the windows allowed for generous ventilation, playing to the trend toward healthy living. There was a discreet bonus to the bay windows: a more generous view of their street-scape allowed homeowners to keep tabs on the comings and goings of their neighbours.

By the latter part of the 1800s, the Victorian terrace had grown out of the hard, ugly soil of the Industrial Revolution and flowered into a pretty architectural specimen that could be—and was—planted everywhere.

It was not just attractive—it was handsome and heroic looking, a distinguished (if not slightly pretentious) specimen. Today, it is as beloved and cherished an icon as the cream tea, and just as pervasive.

It is not a stretch to consider that Britain's continued infatuation with the Victorian era, when the United Kingdom was at the height of its international prowess, accounts for its enduring popularity. It is a sort of psychological trigger for the country's identity, even today. Imposing in height, trim in girth, the facade conveys power, probity, and precision. It brings Norman control and Greek beauty tidily together in one design.

When I look up our street, lined on both sides with two-storey bayed Victorian terraces, I wonder whether more than simple residential accommodation was a factor in the design. The uniformity of the facade speaks to democracy and egalitarianism in one long, uninterrupted sweep, but it also looks militaristic. The lower bay windows are thrust out like proud chests; the upper bays are capped with a peaked helmet that stands in sharp relief from the vertiginous roof rising behind it. Solid, erect, orderly, Victorian terraces stand shoulder to shoulder like suffragettes or soldiers. Nothing says "No one fucks with us" more than a parade of double-bayed Victorian terraces.

Internally, the layout has the flexibility to suit a multitude of ages and generations: two reception rooms plus a kitchen on the ground floor; two, three, or four bedrooms on the upper floor. As sanitation improved and bathrooms were brought indoors, the easiest place to put the bathroom was at the back of the kitchen. It is a surprise how many British homes today retain their ground-floor bathrooms. In others, the smallest bedroom has been sacrificed in order to relocate the main bathroom upstairs, allowing then for a natural extension of the kitchen. It is a floor plan that works for a professional couple, for a family of four, for retirees, for singletons. It can be dressed up or down, stretched to the loft for conversion into master bedroom suites or added storage, or into the rear yard to create large kitchen-diners.

As I wander through these homes, it is hard to avoid the hard edge of masculinity in the design. I find myself from time to time imagining how a woman might improve on the model, how she would unpick the maleness of this house design and imbue it with more common sense and practicality.

The most obvious design flaw of the Victorian terrace is its narrowness: the average terrace is fifteen feet wide. That makes the average front hall only thirty-three inches wide. Getting a modern sofa through that space is like pushing a twelve-pound baby through the birth canal. Surgery is almost inevitable.

As I embraced the idea of owning a Victorian terrace, it was gratifying to learn that there are practical reasons to love it, too. A terrace has lower fuel costs than its detached counterparts. It is also less expensive to maintain: English Heritage found that repairing a standard Victorian terrace house over thirty years was 60 percent cheaper than building and maintaining a new home.

There was a lot of architectural meat in a Victorian terrace, even in a middle-class one. Sadly, a lot of that meat has been chewed and spat out. Nowadays, you are lucky to find a home that can claim a few of its original features. Some people have ripped out their bay window and opted for a flat, double-glazed window. Or jettisoned the stained-glass transoms, the fireplaces and handsome over-mantels, the pine doors, the plaster arches, the built-in pine cabinets. Sometimes it was done in the name of modernization; sometimes it was done for money. As unemployment tore through successive postwar periods, the gentle beauty of the English Victorian home fell into decline. Anything that could be removed was traded for food or money, or chopped up and used for firewood.

What we have since discovered about the Victorians is that for all their pretensions to morality, contentment, and middle-class family values, for all their display of affluence, they were masters of deceit and illusion. If Victorian society had been a city, it would have been called Hollywood.

Adultery was rife, particularly in London, where the ratio of mostly married men to prostitutes was 25:1. No surprise, then, that syphilis became the plague of the era. The Victorian home, therefore, became a carefully staged construct of domestic bliss and God-fearing probity.

Nowadays, probity is for prudes; but surprisingly, the Victorian terrace as a type of housing stock continues to be sought after for its charm and practicality. With some adjustments it can be the ideal home for modern living. I was banking on it being the ideal home for us.

10

The Preparation

The Husband and I, not knowing where to start with this mammoth renovation, decide to tackle the wood-chip wallpaper. It covers the living room, the upper and lower halls, and the stairwell—walls and ceilings. It is a bitch to remove. When it does come off, it does so in small, flaky segments. Occasionally, we hit gold, where the adhesive's grip has worn away over time and allows for the wallpaper to be satisfyingly pulled away in long sheets. We end up in unspoken competition to see which one of us can find those patches of keyless wallpaper.

Removing wallpaper is tedious work, but it does ripen conditions for daydreaming and reminiscing. I am the type of person who actually looks forward to mundane domestic tasks for that very reason, that performing them will let my mind wander to the places it needs to go at that particular time. Now, scraping the surface, shimmying the blade of my scraper under the edge of the paper, prying it off the wall, I begin to feel like I am scraping the surface of my life. Each scrape removes another level and another, sliding deeper into the past until a pocket of air is reached that allows memory to gush in. Before I know it, I am back in Don Mills, answering the door of our Larkfield Drive house to greet my best friend, Cheryll. Do children still call on one another to come out and play? Or is it done by text, or scheduled in advance as managed playdates by nervous parents? I feel fortunate to have lived in a time when children could come and go from home and no one would worry.

Cheryll lived on the street behind ours. Sometimes she would walk into a neighbour's backyard, hop the fence to get to our yard, and knock on our back door. You could do that in those days—use other people's backyards as shortcuts around the neighbourhood without being screamed at about trespassing on private property. We were taught to respect the boundaries of others and to keep to the fence line. Other times, Cheryll and I would take the long way to our respective homes.

Cheryll was one of those extraordinary childhood friends, slightly wiser, slightly more daring, the one with the more interesting toys. She had a mass of long, bouncy, gingery-blond hair that framed a galaxy of amber freckles on white skin. She had a maturity beyond her years that my parents appreciated. She spoke to them on a chattier, more relaxed level than I could ever manage with adults, let alone my parents. She was full of news from around the neighbourhood about who was moving away, who was moving in, who was sick, who was off on a trip. My mother, as a local-newspaper columnist, was particularly appreciative of Cheryll's intel.

Along with her facility in social situations, Cheryll possessed a big imagination. Her head was a vivid, exciting playground. When we played house, it was never anything as predictable as mimicking the home life of our surroundings; no, our pretend house was in Japan, or Holland, or in ancient Egypt, and Cheryll ensured that we dressed the part. She had a dress-up trunk to die for. I have no idea where she got her ideas or all the outfits—probably from a travelling grandparent—but the stuff was always thrilling and surprising.

She was an easy friend; a forgiving one, too. Ours was a fluid, relaxed friendship. One day we would play with dolls, the next it was house or drawing, the day after we might raid our brothers' toy boxes and spend an hour or two playing with trucks and cars. I can still hear the tinkle of conspiratorial laughter as she directed our play. She did not allow herself to show hurt feelings. If anyone called out childish taunts against her, she would shake her head of thick curls, wrinkle her nose, and laugh as if to say, "Aren't they weird?" and continue on her merry way. This was the fundamental difference between Cheryll and me: she laughed off stuff like that; I would have taken to my room for two days. As my mother frequently pointed out, Cheryll was the type who could roll with the punches.

I slow down my wallpaper stripping and listen to the past. Nostalgia is a welcome blood clot to the present. Soon, Cheryll's big laugh comes bounding out from some far quadrant of my brain. This is not the first time I have thought of her in the last few weeks. Strange that she keeps popping into my head. Whatever happened to her? Where is she now? What is her life like? Why did we lose touch? I am overcome with a sudden determination to find her, to be reassured that her life turned out okay. Yet, how ridiculous. I have a hundred things to deal with right now. Focus, I tell myself. Get this renovation done, then you can look for Cheryll. But that has been so much my pattern, of fixing myself to a single direction, and delaying another avenue of interest until I have more time, more money, more nerve. I resolve to start looking for Cheryll.

I continue scraping the wall in tiny, incremental movements, as my mind methodically works through the steps I would need to take to locate Cheryll. I have no idea where on the planet she lives. Is she still in Canada? That alone is a big search area. I do not recall her married name; maybe she is still under her maiden name.

My arm feels weak. I take a break, step back from the wall, and look at the work ahead of us: this is going to take ages. I move in and resume scraping. Bits of wood chip flutter to the ground, forming a small pile at my feet. Possibly, just possibly, if I find Cheryll, I can resurrect our friendship, and I can begin to restore—renovate, yes!—a bit of my past. The thought rumbles like a long train coming into the station, and there is an unexpected moment of clarity. I had never considered the possibility that all this moving and renovating might be about me trying to rebuild and renovate myself. The rape attack is a definite spur, but so, too, is my disjointed upbringing and chasing after perfection. Maybe this is not about a house; maybe it is about me. As that possibility enters my head, my scraper eases under a corner of the wood chip and a huge sheet lifts away miraculously and easily from the wall.

At the sound of it, The Husband pokes his head around the corner. He eyes me jealously. "Well done," he says. "I'm putting the kettle on. Want a tea, a coffee?"

I do not, but I agree anyway. It feels as if I am on the verge of a big self-discovery, and at this point I would rather continue to work away at the wood-chip wallpaper and play a bit longer in memory land. It is not so much escaping into the past as it is about processing the past. Sometimes the present becomes clear only when the experience of the past is allowed to settle and mature. It takes time to process a lifetime. Scraping wallpaper: this is manual labour with benefits.

The Husband and I go out to the backyard and sit on a pile of bricks. The sun and the vivid blue of the sky make a mockery of our surroundings. The yard is still a mess of rubble, weeds, scattered bricks, and rotted lengths of lumber crawling with wood lice. I cannot even visualize how it might look all fixed up. I glance at the collapsed section of fence on one side: the entire run will have to be replaced. Another expense.

"Having fun?" I ask him brightly. If I allow my mood or my enthusiasm to waver, if I look as if I am distracted, The Husband might think I am rethinking this whole project.

He rolls his eyes. "'Fun' perhaps for you."

"It's an adventure, or rather, we should look at it as an adventure. Remember, this is our bonding exercise. Strengthening our relationship."

I do not blame The Husband when he snorts derisively. My mother used variations of that line on my brother and me: "Renovating is fun." "It is an adventure." "You should be grateful to do such work." And, "This is what families do—a family that works together stays together."

Actually, no family I had met then or since did the scale of renovation that our family did. Come to think of it, I am surprised our family survived intact.

Mug drained, I walk back into the house, pick up my scraper, and start chipping away at the wood chip and the past.

AT DAY'S END, WE RETURN to the relative sanity and cleanliness of our Little Britain home. I rustle up a quick supper—frozen vegetarian pies tonight; thank you, Linda McCartney—and then head upstairs to the room that serves as my office.

I scrounge through piles of boxes, haul out smaller boxes and manila folders crammed with crimp-edged snapshots from the late fifties and the sixties. Must organize these, I remind myself for the umpteenth time.

How is it possible for so much memory to exist in a single, small celluloid print? I dump the contents of one envelope and rummage through random pictures from a host of decades. I am sure I have a picture of Cheryll and me. There it is. One of my parents must have taken this photograph, because the picture places us in my backyard, against the dense bottle-green spruce hedges my parents favoured. In the photograph, Cheryll and I are standing either side of a white-stone bird bath, holding hands. We had raided Cheryll's dress-up trunk that day, and she decided to dress me in a Dutch costume complete with wooden clogs. She dressed up in a quasi–Native American tunic and sash. Funny, my memory of that day had us reversed: the Dutch costume suited her flouncy strawberry curls, while the Native American one better suited my tanned olive skin and long, straight, dark-brown hair. I am struck now by her generosity; I had not recognized it at the time. Most friends would have taken the more attractive outfit for themselves, but not Cheryll.

Our friendship fizzled once my family moved. I am surprised my parents did not do more to nurture my existing friendships. As I said, they liked Cheryll a lot. She was the standard to which I was unfavourably compared: "You are so glum and shy. Why can't you be more upbeat like Cheryll?" Or, "Why don't you dress like Cheryll? She always looks so smart."

I last saw Cheryll at a shopping mall on the outskirts of Toronto. Was it thirty or so years ago? I first heard the sound of her voice—familiar, animated, slightly hoarse—and my head swivelled toward it like a divining rod. There she was, talking to someone. She could talk to anyone. I stood off to one side so as not to interrupt her conversation. But at that moment it was as if she had sensed a change in the air: she turned her head, saw me. Her mouth made a big O, and she squealed. She hustled toward me, grabbed my arm, and dragged me back to introduce me to the person with whom she was speaking: "This is Jane! She was my best friend from school! We were in kindergarten together!" Cheryll always spoke in exclamation marks.

I was on a lunch break from work; so was she. She worked in a women's clothing store in the mall, she said, and was expecting her first child. I gave her my phone number, with the promise of a longer chat when we both had more time. It was a hurried conversation, and by the time we went our separate ways, I had no real sense of what her life was like.

A month or so later, I returned to the mall and went to the store where she worked. I learned she had gone on maternity leave.

Truth be told, I had not tried terribly hard to find Cheryll. It was the mid-1980s: my first marriage was on a nosedive, and I did not feel sociable, or up to talking about my failure as a wife. With divorce looming and two little boys to care for, my mind was heavy with how I was going to support them, and how I was going to survive the ignominy of being a single parent. My reluctance to seek out Cheryll and re-establish our friendship was also due to a deeper sense of personal disgrace: My rape had happened a few years earlier and was still a shameful secret. I wanted to erase it from my memory, and to do that I needed a clean slate—a new set of friends, a new job, a new life, a new place to start over. It would not do to have an old friend like Cheryll learn the truth of what had happened to me. These days I think I could tell her, and I do not think she would judge me.

Was this something I should do now: find Cheryll? Perhaps it was better to sit with the idea. Reconnecting with old friends can sometimes leave you wishing you had not made the effort.

I once drove 125 miles to visit an old school chum with whom I had reconnected online. When I arrived, I did not recognize her; was, frankly, shocked by her appearance. She was grey and bitter, dressed in a patterned housedress, the kind that women in the 1940s might have worn while doing housework. During our entire visit I could not see anything of the mischievous and happy friend to whom I had once been so close. I kept my car keys in my hand, stealing glances at my watch and wondering how soon I could leave without appearing impolite.

Life had not been kind to her, and it appeared she was intent on returning the favour. Her home was unkempt. Unwashed dishes sat piled in the sink and spilled over onto the countertops. Ashtrays teemed with spent cigarettes and ash, which the summer breeze blew onto her worn furniture. Dust coated everything, and in the unforgiving rays of the afternoon sun you could see more of it hovering, waiting to land. She had a collection of owls in every conceivable medium, and their saucer-like eyes looked eerily like the black stare my friend wore behind her large, round glasses.

I had tried to cheer her up with lively conversation, but she would not have it. She told me she had cancer while she puffed furtively on a cigarette. I asked how her treatment was going, but she shifted the conversation back to me and asked sternly why I had looked her up.

"Because we were friends, and I wanted to see how you were."

She countered abrasively that what I really wanted was to compare how much better than hers my life had turned out. It was a lie, and it stung. She was evasive and prickly on every subject; loaded for bear, as they say. Nothing I could do or say generated any warm feeling. Much later, after I returned home, I discovered that she had embezzled from her place of work and was under house arrest at the time of my visit.

Surely Cheryll would be different. I think of her bubbly, sunny disposition; her bouncy walk. Surely time and life had not sucked the effervescence out of her, too.

My mind wanders from Cheryll to the other little playmates I had back then. What of Sharon Scott, who lived across the road on

Malabar Court? Or George Lawrence, who tied his shoelaces to the piano leg in kindergarten and for whom I gave up my recess to help unknot them? What of Bill and Laurie Austin? Kate Rainsberry? The names percolate like a dormant gene zapped to life, but instead of happy reverie, ruefulness swoops in. I am back to blaming my parents. How could they not see that their compulsive moves, their fixation with homes and social aspiration, denied me the foundational pieces for my own development, such as a solid circle of playmates? How much better all our lives could have been, how much more emotionally stable we could have been, had my parents understood that children need to feel fixed and rooted to a place. But they put no currency in that. It was always about them, always about their bloody houses.

STANLEY AVENUE

11

The Layers Revealed

We are still on the wood-chip wallpaper. We have discovered more of it, on the hall ceiling of all places, and scraping it from an awkward angle ramps up our annoyance levels. The Husband offers to take the bullet on this one. He is taller, so he can reach it easier. Plus, he is a gentleman. Still, there is no mistaking a touch of self-flagellation in his offer, that scraping wood chip off the ceiling will be penance for buying this dump in the first place.

As for me, I am warming to the house. I do not totally love it—maybe I will not ever totally love it—but I have a morbid fascination of seeing where this renovation takes the house, where it takes me, and us as a couple.

Removing the wood-chip wallpaper does not faze me. There is a hypnotic quality to the work that gets into my pores and cells. With scraper in hand, I dig gently but firmly at a corner and use the smallest of actions to wedge under an edge until there is enough of the paper to allow it to be torn from the wall. As I home in on one stubborn section, my focus becomes concentrated, like narrowing one's gaze on a pinhead. Scrape, scrape. The rhythmic action, the intense shortened field of vision deliver me into a contemplative trance. Soon, the scraping is nothing but white noise, and my mind is tumbling down the rabbit hole, straining for the sounds of my past.

With one exception, all my previous homes permitted me to have my way with them, to do what alterations needed to be done so that I could settle into them. This Bristol house is different. Each morning when The Husband and I leave Little Britain and drive toward it, I do not approach the prospect with the excitement of previous renovations but with a cautiousness, a preparation of mind. Like going to church. It is a common house, nothing special. Its location, its architecture are, as they say in this country, bog standard. But for some reason this ordinary house seems determined to draw me into a level of self-reflection that I was not expecting, nor had wanted. It has taken me in hand and led me to a scraper and a bucket of warm water, apparently believing that this is all I need to direct my mind to the past, consider the present, and to glean from this exercise patterns, symmetry, and insight. My guide is not the grumbling old man I sensed on our first visit to this house; I think he was just the caretaker, a squatter. I think he got fed up and left. This other manifestation is benign and definitely more task oriented in terms of getting me to meditate on why home—and by extension, moving—has been so dominant a force in my life. This house is a spirit teacher.

HOW DO HOMES LAST SO LONG? Bricks are essentially sand, clay, and water; stone is nothing but sediments of sand, minerals, and water.

Furthermore, when we look upon a home, why do we categorize it as an old home or a modern home? Are not all homes ancient? Are they not all built from sand sifted up from some long-vanished lake or ocean, and of stone hacked from the vast strata of bedrock that comprises the earth? Whether the sand or stone comes from the crags of Scotland, the Apennines of Italy, the Picos in Spain, the Canadian Shield in North America, or the Andes in Peru, our homes are birthed from a geological lineage millions of years old. Even the sharp-squared brick of a newly built home is fired from the earth's prehistoric quarry of sand, soil, and lime. All our homes and buildings are literally as old as the hills.

How is the rubric of stacking stone or brick determined to ensure the durability and stability of a home? And what is it in that conglomeration of hard materials that go into building a home—of brick, concrete, stucco, stone, wood, plaster, glass, steel, aluminum, PVC pipes, and copper wiring—that makes the whole ultimately soft to us, one that so readily absorbs our emotions and memories and fears?

When a marriage breaks down, does the marital home suffer, too? It is one thing for houses to resist centuries of battering by Mother Nature, but what of the blunt forces of human nature? How do houses withstand the reverberation of anger, or of inconsolable grief, within their walls? How do they withhold secrets and pain without cracking, or absorb extreme joy without their windows shattering in their frames?

What is it about the homes of other people that makes us swoon with desire? That makes you want to pull up a chair, stare, and luxuriate in the surroundings and imagine that the home belongs to you? With some homes you are happy to leave, and the sooner the better. Some do not try hard enough to evoke comfort. Then there are the ones that try too hard, exuding the perfumed and surgically enhanced glamour of a superannuated movie star.

A third type of home enchants at an almost cellular level. You want to take in every inch of it—the arrangement of knick-knacks on bookshelves; the sight of a row of herbs on a windowsill; the interplay of light and shadow; the choice of colours and furnishings; a passageway leading into the garden. I confess to being mesmerized this way when visiting or seeing images of Spanish, Italian, and Moroccan homes. Is there an alchemical formula at work in the homes to which we are attracted? Is it 20 percent nostalgia, 30 percent colour, 10 percent furnishings, 15 percent botanicals and plants, 25 percent lighting (natural and electrical)? Surely the formula is different for everyone. In the same way that a meal tastes better when someone else cooks it—their specific ingredients? the convivial nature of the conversation? the surroundings?—some houses look, feel, and smell better than our own. Is it a case of the other person's grass being always greener? Perhaps it says something about our lack of confidence in putting together a home, or about our general state of discontentedness.

I THINK I HAVE FINALLY HIT peak move, peak renovation. This particular renovation feels more like a clear-out of the cerebral attic. I cannot say I am loving it, nor am I loving this trip down multiple memory lanes. The past can be a painful companion. Then again, the chance to piece together fragments and to make peace with others does bring solace, if only to understand the why behind all these moves.

There are moments when I can barely face this reality of how many times I have moved in my life, and I find myself, as now, staring into space and counting them off on my fingers to maintain a mental log of the upheaval. Here it goes:

As a newborn, I was brought home from the hospital to a wartime bungalow on Craigmore Crescent in Willowdale; then we moved to the split-level Bauhaus design on Larkfield Drive in Don Mills. Next it was to the old Henry Farm house, which was surrounded by modern new homes but lacked a completed junior school; in the six years we lived in that house I ended up attending six different schools. After that we moved to Mason Boulevard—another two schools. Blissfully, I remained at Lawrence Park Collegiate for the rest of high school. Ah, stability. After graduation I was off to Carleton University in Ottawa, and spent three years there in four different off-campus houses. Each summer, I moved back home to Toronto: it was always eight months at school in Ottawa and four months in Toronto, then packing up and moving back to Ottawa for eight months, then back to Toronto. Six moves right there. When I returned home at the end of university, my parents were by then living in a farmhouse in Milton. The commute from Milton to my summer job in downtown Toronto was onerous (it was long before the days of GO Transit), so I got an apartment on Maitland Street in downtown Toronto. Three months later, I was offered a job in Woodstock, Ontario, and so I packed up and moved into a flat on Huron Street. A year later, I was back in Toronto with a new job and a new apartment on Isabella Street. Marriage followed three years later, and with it a move to another apartment, this one on Balmoral Avenue. We bought a house a year later and moved to Romark Mews in Mississauga; two years later we moved to Gloucester Avenue in Oakville. We had a child, and eighteen months later another child, so we moved to a larger house on Kingsmead Crescent in another part of Oakville. Then my marriage broke down, and I moved out and into an apartment a few blocks away. Four months later, I moved back to the marital home. The marriage ended, and I packed up and moved to Woodbine Crescent in Hamilton. Three years later, I married my second husband, and we bought a house on Hyde Park Avenue. When that marriage failed, I moved to Stanley Avenue. Three years and three different jobs later, I moved to Pelee Island for five months, sold my house in Hamilton, and then moved into my mother's home on Lawson Street in Oakville. When I found a home of my own on Elmer Avenue in Toronto, I moved with the kids there. But that did not last long, because I got laid off from my job. Eight months later, we moved back to Hamilton and onto Herkimer Street. I lived on Herkimer for seven years—a record!—and then downsized to a condo on James Street South. Then it was marriage number three, and I moved to England—first to Howard Road in Walthamstow, London, then King Street in Brixham, then into our rental in Longwell Green, and finally into our home in Bristol.

Well, look at that. Couldn't even contain them on a single page. So how many moves is that? Thirty-two homes and eight schools, not counting university. It is no surprise that sometimes I wake in the middle of the night, cocooned in darkness, with a surge of panic racing through me: Where am I again? The confusion clears once I realize that I am home.

All this moving and renovating once made me worry that I was becoming my mother. Not anymore. Bolted horse. Barn door. I have made peace with the fact that much of my mother's restlessness resides in me, and no matter how much I rail about never wanting to become that person who moves constantly, that is who I am. I also recognize that rape trauma is a factor in my inner agitation. I recognize now, in a way I was unable to do before, how and where my compulsion to move kicked into high gear after my rape. The rape occurred when my then husband and I had just moved into a new home. Within the year, I was dropping hints that it was time to move again. When I became single again, I thought moving house was a way to push away the stigma of divorce, but the reality was that moving house created a level of agitation that would psychologically garble the rape memory enough to send it spiralling into a corner of my brain, never to show its shameful face again.

Years later, I continue to play out the residue of the trauma, one house at a time. Those two components—the rape, and my mother's influence and behaviour—are behind my desire to move: one is the fuel, the other is the driver, though their roles interchange from time to time, and I am never quite sure which is the driver and which is the fuel.

This new knowledge is a consolation. Better to know why you do what you do than simply that you do it. Recognition confers the frame of reference from which you can harness self-control. In the same way that reformed alcoholics continue to refer to themselves as alcoholics and pray for sobriety, I will continue to call myself a property nomad, and pray for stability.

12

The Loos and Don'ts

Want to know how it feels to be an immigrant? Renovate a house in a different country. Or just hire an electrician. Electricians have a way of making you feel like you have dropped through the space-time continuum of common sense.

In the six years that I have lived in Britain I have managed to delude myself into thinking that my foreignness is a non-issue, that I have seamlessly adapted to British life because, well, why would I have not? Canada and Britain are part of the Commonwealth; everything we were taught at school was built upon the foundation of British history, literature, and culture. Britain was our motherland. Canada had yet to fully develop a sense of nationhood, and so Britain stood as our constitutional cipher, the standard to which we aspired. It is fair to say that a certain generation of Canadians felt pretty much British, assured of a common tradition of values, as well as of language. Of course, there were differences: Britain had charming accents, the Queen, and adorable thatch-roof homes; Canada had mountains, central heating, and we drove on the right side of the road. Like many of my generation, I had Great Britain, its people, and its mighty heritage on a pedestal.

It is not until you actually buy a home in Britain that you understand the stark and deeper differences between these two countries.

Take fixtures and appliances, for instance. In Britain, where the houses are small and narrow, there is no such thing as an integrated stackable washer/dryer. They are MIA. (There is an all-in-one washer/dryer, but they are impractical if you have multiple washing loads to go through, and they are fairly ineffective on the drying front.) In North America, where floor space is usually not a factor, you can buy an integrated stackable washer/dryer. Or rather, you used to be able to buy them: it appears they are made by only one manufacturer nowadays. But why? These are models of economy and space saving, which every home could use.

Then there are the kitchen appliances. In the UK, stoves are huge, with lots of separate ovens, half of which you do not use; whereas refrigerators, which you use constantly, are slim and lack depth, and have drawer-like freezer compartments that are about the size of a package of printer paper. They certainly cannot accommodate a casserole dish.

Shall we move on to the heating system? In the older stock of British homes (which is the majority of housing stock) there are no basements, and therefore no furnaces and hence no duct-directed heating. You must get accustomed to boilers and radiators. I hate them. They are clumsy and obtrusive, but there is no way to avoid them unless you want to shell out squillions to have your basement dug out for ductwork. British engineering created robust ductwork in

Victorian factories and offices but, strangely, the idea never migrated to the Victorian home.

Heating the Victorian terrace means embracing radiators and boilers, which constitute a home's central heating system. North American homes are (usually) heated by forced-air gas furnaces that push warm air through a duct system and up through floor vents. In the UK, homes are heated when a boiler (usually gas-fired) heats water and moves it around the house to heat the radiators. In a country where square footage is at a premium and room sizes are teensy, radiators suck up a good three feet of wall space, whereas floor vents take up not more than a foot, and even then, you can place furniture over it and still get hot air. Due to space constraints in British living rooms it is not unusual to find that the sofa has been pushed up against the radiator. Presumably, no one worries about the possibility of their sofa catching fire, nor are they concerned that their sofa is covering the sole source of heat in the room.

I asked about the possibility of installing a duct system in our home but was politely told "This is how we do things over here" and handed a catalogue from which to choose a radiator. Sigh.

If mechanicals are one thing to get used to, there is also the matter of British construction terminology and argot to decode: *Job done* does not mean the job is completed; it means *Okay* or *I've got it sorted*. *First fix* and *second fix* do not refer to heroin-injection schedules but are akin to the North American version of *roughing in* and *finish*. There are others: *glazing* (windows); *skirting boards* (baseboards); *architrave* (door frame or trim); *worktops* (countertops); *gutters* (eavestroughs). Then there are the categories of trades that come with their own nomenclature: *sparky* (electrician); *chippy* (carpenter); *brickie* (bricklayer); *fitter* (kitchen installer); *decorator* (painter, so not someone you would go to for interior-decorating advice). Haven't yet come across a nickname for the plumber. And then there is the pithy, oft-said phrase whenever I ask about doing something a certain way: "It's not done in this country." It is meant to silence me and put me in my little expat place.

So, to the electrician, or sparky, who uses that exact phrase on me when I ask why I cannot have an electrical socket in the bathroom.

Mark is the guy on this job. He is tall, lean, with close-cropped dark hair, and we like him the moment he bounces into our house to quote for the job. He thinks aloud as he surveys the site, asking questions, considering different options, but not exactly wanting a response or input.

He stares down at the floor in our hall for a few minutes, and then drops to his knees and startles us by ripping up a couple of the floorboards. I feel surprisingly protective of the house, as if some guy were sneaking a peak under its skirt.

It is the first time I have seen what lurks beneath the floorboards in an English home. It is not pretty. Under the boards on the ground floor there is no subfloor, just dirt, bare brick, and post and beam foundations, along with entrails of wiring and piping, bits of builders' debris, and garbage thrown in for good measure. There is no poured-concrete foundation; and certainly no room for a cellar, let alone a full basement. The space is not remotely finished—it looks like it could have been dug yesterday. I cannot say I feel entirely comfortable knowing that not much more than a foot and a half of brick footings and some timber planks are all that hold up our home.

Mark stretches on all fours across the opening, peers into the void, then springs back up. He stamps the floorboard back into place and stands with his hands on his hips, staring at his feet.

"Right. Upstairs." And off he bounds up the steps, two at a time. We rush after him.

In the master bedroom, he rips up another floorboard. This time we all fall on our knees to observe the guts. It is similar to downstairs minus the brick foundation and dirt. Instead, there are thick tim-ber joists separated by lath and tarpaper-lined troughs filled with all manner of junk: the necessary wiring and plumbing pipes threaded alongside or through the joists; the dust, and evidence of previous work—discarded nails, screws, bolts, wire cuttings, snap-off blades, a Subway wrapper, paper coffee cups.

"What a mess," I say by way of apology to Mark.

"It's normal," he says, and shrugs. "Everyone [he means all the trades] tosses in their crap."

I am horrified. I do not like the idea of sleeping an inch away from a trough filled with garbage along with a heap of dust and dirt. I do not want the clutter from someone else's past under my floorboards. Is this what it is like throughout the house? In everyone's house?

"Is there a contraption that can clear out all this debris, like a big industrial vacuum cleaner?"

He looks at me as if I have just said something that is either ridic-ulous or brilliant.

"Nothing I've heard of. Besides, it's no big deal. I've seen worse. You won't even notice it."

But it is a big deal to me. I have allergies, and I am a clean freak. Has James Dyson not thought of this? A device that can suck out the loose matter beneath my floorboards would be a godsend. Just because you cannot see something does not mean it is not there.

Mark hammers the boards back down.

"Right, then. If I'm honest, this house is gonna need a full rewire."

We nod. We expected as much. And if there is anything you do not scrimp on during a reno, it is the wiring.

Like I said, we like Mark. He has the energy of Tigger, and the deduction skills of Sherlock. But he is a code stickler, which is a good thing in the long run yet a pain when he refuses to consider my request for an electrical outlet in the bathroom.

Here's the thing: the British are paranoid about electricity and bathrooms.

You cannot have a socket in the bathroom to run your hair dryer or styling tongs, though it is perfectly fine to have a socket to run your shaver. (Why has no one invented a hair dryer or curling iron or hair straightener that runs on the same current as a shaver?) You cannot even have a light switch *inside* the bathroom. Yet, it is apparently fine to have your light switch inside the kitchen, and to have electrical outlets all over the kitchen countertops close to water—sinks, dishwashers, washing machines, kettles. I can run my hair dryer in the kitchen next to the kitchen sink, but it is against code to run it in a bathroom next to the bathroom sink. Why?

"Please?" I plead with Mark. "I'm North American. We dry our hair in the bathroom."

He will not discuss it.

Months later, when our main floor WC is fitted in space under the stairs, I assume the light switch will be placed outside the door, as it has been in the upstairs bathroom. But it is not. It is installed inside the WC door. And the reason you can do that is the light switch in this case is on a chain that is attached to a string. Thus, you can have a string to turn on a bathroom light inside a bathroom, but not a switch protected by a wall plate. I cannot see the reason for this.

Mark and I move on to the matter of laundry facilities. Most British homes have their washer and dryer in the kitchen (if there is no separate utility room), either as stand-alone units at the back of the room or integrated into the cabinetry. Recently, the host of a television property program railed against the British habit of locating laundry facilities in the kitchen. It is not an ideal placement for the laundry, but anyone who has schlepped laundry from the top floor to the basement of a North American house and back up again would welcome washing facilities in the kitchen. Apparently, this same TV presenter is not bothered by the main bathroom of a house being located right off the kitchen, which I consider a greater "ick" factor.

Many of the Victorian terrace homes we viewed had bathrooms adjoining the kitchen. In an earlier decade people scurried from the upstairs bedroom down the stairs, through the back of the house to the outdoor privy. (Or used the pot under the bed.) It is a bit of a surprise to learn that the outdoor privy in Britain is still in use. In 2010, about forty thousand homes still had an outdoor loo. Mains drains did not come to parts of Britain until the 1950s, and some areas were without mains drains until the 1990s.

Over time, extensions were built onto the backs of homes to incorporate the privy as a way to bring it "indoors." As these extensions were updated, better insulated, and equipped with modern fittings and fixtures, the privy was entirely integrated into the home. But it was still on the main floor, off the kitchen.

Moving the bathroom upstairs was something The Husband and I agreed on from the get-go. We are on the same page with that one, even if it means sacrificing a bedroom.

The other very British feature in a house is doors. The British are door crazy. They have doors that open to more doors. No sooner are you in the front door of a home than you are greeted less than three feet away by a second door. The Victorians were (as are the British in general) sticklers for privacy. Their interior doors open in a counterintuitive direction, so that as the door swings open, you do not see the room immediately, which allows the occupant in the room to recover from doing whatever someone in the living room would be doing that you were not supposed to see. Farther along the hall there is a door to the second reception room. And then another door to the kitchen, and more doors, depending on the layout, to the utility room and bathroom. Upstairs, there are the standard door requirements—doors on bedrooms and bathrooms, though again, in the case of the bedroom doors, they open so as not to disturb the occupant.

Doors were useful in Victorian times to shut off the cold from various rooms, to allow heat from fireplaces and radiators to remain in certain rooms and not be wasted in the lesser-used rooms. With the introduction in the 1970s of central heating this multitude of doors rather impeded the flow of heat in the Victorian home, but by then the British were wedded to their doors. In newly built homes, you will still find a ridiculous number of interior doors despite the fact that the British gush about the open-plan living of North American, European, and Asian homes. I guess you have to be British to understand the attachment to doors.

My idea was to remove all the doors except those to the bedrooms and bathrooms. The Husband will have none of it. He likes his doors.

To brighten the long, dark front hall and create a sense of space, I suggest we remove most of the wall between the hall and the second reception room. He does not like this idea, either. I also suggest we convert the window in that room to French doors opening to the side area of our garden. He is okay with that—it adds another door, after all.

I DASH OUT THE FRONT DOOR to buy a dustpan at the corner shop. As I go through our gate, I almost collide with a woman in a niqab.

"Oh, sorry! Good morning," a bright voice sings out from behind the black. "Gorgeous day, isn't it?"

"Yes, i-it is," I stammer. I am not used to conversing with fully veiled people, though I have learned to pretend that it does not bother me. I like observing the range of people's facial expressions when I speak with them. It is how I recognize people and relate to them. I gain as much by seeing their eyes, the set of their mouth, the condition of their hair, the tilt of their chin, as I do from hearing their words. I gain no such clues about this woman except from her voice, which has a no-nonsense Brit clip and, to my ears, indicates a practical yet chatty type of person.

Here is another stark difference between British residential areas and their North American counterparts: cultural diversity. Residential areas in North America are for the most part homogenous in terms of cultural, social, and racial makeup, where differences are more muted. Not so in Britain. Our street, as with most residential streets, is made up equally of blacks, whites, and all shades in between; of well-to-dos and not-so-well-to-dos; of professionals and students; of retirees and young families; of immigrants and natives; of Christians, Muslims, Jews, and Sikhs; of people with brown hair, grey hair, and green hair. There is no sense, really, of anyone's social situation on this street. The hip dudes are on bikes; their Muslim brothers are in BMWs with tinted windows. It is a truly and visibly diverse neighbourhood, not an assimilated one.

Once we move in, I look forward to exploring it and getting to know our neighbours, like the gal behind the niqab.

Ah, moving in. Will that be in August? It is only May right now, and August seems a long way off, from a May point of view.

13

The Neighbourhood

"There's a Christmas tree in our front garden," mumbles The Husband, not looking up from his work. He is in the master bedroom, on hands and knees, pulling staples and small nails from the floorboards in preparation for sanding the floors.

"Yeah, I saw them. Cute, eh? Wonder how high they will grow."

I am looking distractedly out the window at the street. A group of Muslim men and boys in their white thobes and taqiyahs are parading silently on their way to Friday prayers at the mosque around the corner. It is the middle of Ramadan.

Right this second, a cultural—or is it a linguistic?—difference is playing out in our soon-to-be bedroom, because when I turn to The Husband, he is looking at me with incomprehension. We have reached one of those "We both speak English, but I do not understand you" impasses.

Whoever assumes that English and Canadian are the same language has never been in an English/Canadian marriage. It is not just the accent, but the cadence, the place of emphasis on a word, the shorthand speak that his culture understands but that mine does not. Couples in same-culture relationships develop a linguistic shorthand that both understand. If I said to The Husband "Goin' for a Tim's," he would not know what the hell I was talking about. (And because Tim Horton's outlets do not—praise the Lord—exist in the UK, he need not worry that I will ever say that to him.) I once asked if we were "taking a subway," and he could not understand why I wanted a fast-food sandwich on the Tube. We almost came to blows one time when I referred to his "housecoat" and he insisted he did not have one.

"Yes, you do."

"No, I do not."

"It is hanging on the back of the bedroom door."

And still he could not understand what I meant, until he finally said, "That is not a *housecoat*. It is a *dressing gown*. *Housecoat*. What an absurd term."

"Who but people born in the 1920s uses the term *dressing gown* anymore?"

When we realize that we are speaking about two different things, we revert to those oft-used responses "What?" or "Sorry?" or "Pardon?"

"What?" he asks now.

"Christmas tree?" I query.

"Grow?" he asks. "Looks pretty dead to me."

"The three miniature evergreens? In our front garden? Is that what you mean?" They are hidden among a dense tangle of foliage. I am surprised he even noticed them. I make a mental note to transplant them before building debris gets dumped on them.

"Not those. I mean a real tree."

"But they *are* real."

"Not those. *The Christmas tree.*"

"What?"

Again I look down from the window into our front courtyard. There, leaning against our low wall, is a desiccated, rust-coloured fir tree with strands of silver tinsel struggling to liberate themselves from the ignominy. Arranged around the base of the tree, like presents, are several bags of garbage. At least, I hope it is only garbage.

"The bloody nerve!" I explode.

The Husband keeps his head down and returns to the forensic work of plucking staples from the floorboards.

"Where did that come from?"

The next day a few more bags and boxes have accumulated around the new dead tree.

"Really?" I look at The Husband accusingly, swiftly holding him accountable for the behaviour of every Englishman. "Is this a thing in your country? Dumping crap in other people's front yards? Is there no respect for private property, no sense of trespassing? We all just heave our trash wherever we want?"

His lips form a tight line. He tends to go silent whenever my rants veer close to the failings of his country. I often wonder if he is thinking: If you don't like it, go back to Canada.

I stomp downstairs, where Francis, who has started work on our house, is tearing out the kitchen. He started three days ago and is making good progress. The kitchen has been gutted, and the interior walls are almost down. Tomorrow, he will cut out the back wall for the patio doors. His guy will be measuring today.

I tell him about the garbage collecting in our front yard; about how this flagrant, cowardly behaviour annoys me.

He laughs. "I've ordered a skip. It's coming in a day or so. You can just toss the stuff in there."

But he has either missed my point, chosen to sidestep it, or is not fussed about it. I storm out the front door and, hands on hips, look down at the desiccated little tree like a dog that has done its business there, and then glare across the road and up the street, hoping my mean-lady looks will put the fear of God into the culprit.

Predictably, it does not. Each day a little something more is added to the offering. Like the chumps we are, we load the pile into our car and take it to the local dump. At this rate, we will need a skip just for the extraneous crap from our neighbours.

The skip arrives. It is precariously lowered onto the street in front of our house. The following day it is evident that our skip has become the community dumpster. It contains items that have in no way come from our house.

"When did you order a cross-trainer?" The Husband asks, inspecting a box in the skip.

"This would never happen in Canada," I snarl.

He mutters something and goes off in search of floor staples to pluck.

On a street of Victorian terraces there is little to differentiate the individual houses, little insight into the nature of the inhabitants save for the colour of their front doors and the state of their front court-yards. The courtyard, with its lower perimeter stone or brick wall and wrought-iron gate, is sacrosanct to its owner. It is a buffer from the outside world, a declaration invoking a strict private-property pol-icy but in that distinctly British way of "Look, admire, but do not dare touch, trespass, or disturb" as firmly as if razor wire were erected around it.

There is an inbred suspicion in the British psyche that is absolutely personified in the Victorian terrace. The British are as fanatical about walls, fences, barriers as they are about interior doors. This is a people who are rule setters and policy-and-procedure makers first, and your mate at the pub second. Perhaps this is due to the population density. Space is so squeezed in this country that people are forced to live, work, and travel cheek by jowl; personal space has to be established and respected. It takes a newcomer some time to get accustomed to it.

The lack of roominess in terrace homes, the lack of basements, and the land-locked, externally inaccessible nature of terrace homes means that the front courtyards often become holding pens for cast-off furniture, building materials, old toys, and assorted garbage. When you are having work done on your home, the front courtyard comes in handy as a place for all manner of supplies, waste, and cast-offs. Unfortunately, some households let this disarray linger long after the renovation is complete.

This is where the Victorians and we of the modern era part company. The Victorians were all about pretense and house pride. They never displayed their garbage. They kept a tidy patch. Nowadays, there is no shame to having a messy front garden. Some wear it like a badge of honour, an elevated virtue, as if to say, "I am so busy that I have no time or energy to think about it. And come to think of it, neither should you. Mind your own bloody business!"

If an inventory were taken of British homes based solely on the state of the front courtyard and facade, it would reveal that the majority are on the scruffy side. The British do not tend assiduously to the external appearance of their homes the way North Americans do. Perhaps because there is not much property frontage to tart up, or that proximity to the sidewalk (low courtyard walls and gate notwithstanding) makes any embellishment that is not planted or tied down fair game for light-fingered passersby. I have met people who have had plants stolen from their courtyard, including some that were dug up. Visible displays of decoration or landscaping are frowned upon. No one wants to appear showy. No one wants to tempt thieves and other pariahs. On a street of Victorian or Georgian terraces the unspoken maxim is "Plainer is safer."

Inside, it is often a completely different story. Many are the times that have I approached a tatty-looking front door, bins teeming with bottles and jars, small front gardens appearing weedy and forlorn, pebble dash stained and in need of a paint job, masonry gouged, and yet the interior of the house in question is decorated to a bright, shiny standard, with clean and polished floors, and intriguing art on the walls. This startling change of character extends right into the back garden, where little oases of lushness and enchantment, of charm and delight, can be found. It is completely at odds with the signals the front facade gives off, proving that you cannot judge a British house by its curb appeal.

There are a few offenders on every street, and ours is no exception. Several front gardens show neglect—overrun with weeds, cluttered with old doors, fragments of windows, bottles, bits of wood, plastic flower pots whose contents have shrivelled into unidentifiable remains. One or two have mounds of garbage bags and assorted crap piled up against front bay windows. My heart pities the poor house that must endure this mortification. You would not see rubbish like this in North America unless the home was that of a reclusive psychotic murderer. Then again, most North Americans have garages, so perhaps they are better able to hide their mess.

At the opposite end of this lack of house pride are the homes whose courtyards bloom with shrubs and flowering trees, whose window boxes brim with colour. What a balm they are. A few enterprising souls have built from old wood pallets little shelters for bikes and bins and topped them with green roofs that sprout moss and sedum to attract the birds and bees. They are lovely.

In the middle—and with no amount of pride do I acknowledge current fraternity with this group—are those courtyards that are tidy but bereft of personality, a place for recycling boxes and large, ugly, black garbage bins. Once the renovation is done, I hope to make our courtyard more attractive.

A few lucky homes, perhaps eight on our street, retain the original iron railings that once encircled every courtyard on the street. Only about a dozen have their original stained-glass transoms, or the cheerful checkerboard encaustic-tile walkways leading to the front door.

I have tried not to be unduly petulant about the loss of our home's original architectural features such as the stained-glass transom and courtyard railings. Our Easton neighbourhood has a history of poverty—at one time it was the most deprived in all of England—and I daresay that if I had a choice between feeding my children or enjoying the colourful prism cast by a piece of stained glass, I, too, would have flogged mine for food.

The matter of missing iron railings is particularly distressing. Up and down the streets of our neighbourhood is the rusty, amputated evidence that something beautiful and strong once graced those low courtyard walls. While pondering the architectural cost against the scant pounds and shillings their owners might have reaped from selling them off, I discovered a sadder story that explained it all: the elegant iron fences that embellished the courtyards of Victorian terraces were ripped out not through any personal desire or need on the part of the homeowners but by an act of Parliament.

In 1941, during the Second World War, when iron was needed for munitions, Prime Minister Winston Churchill passed a law compulsorily requisitioning all iron fences and railings erected post-1850. Exceptions were made for those of historic merit or interest. Naturally, the poorer residential areas of Britain were hit first. Council workers poured into streets with sledgehammers and cutters and carted off everything that could be melted into firearms. It became one of the most successful unifying causes of the British war effort, so much so that more iron was collected than was needed. The tragedy is that the government, not wanting to hamper morale, continued with the pillage regardless, and quietly dumped thousands of excess fence railings into landfill sites, council sidings, rivers, and oceans.

I TAKE A BREAK FROM wood-chip scraping, and wander through the rooms in our Victorian terrace, imagining the history it has witnessed. It is not an old house, only about 125 years old—a new build by British standards. But human history has shaped this place. War bombs and great poverty have shaken its walls. Grief and love have intermingled in its mortar.

Parts of this Easton neighbourhood have a weary, beaten-down look. There are pockets of squalor, but there are also pockets of quiet elegance. When you venture into places like this to buy a home, it is tricky to determine which direction the wind will blow stronger— toward squalor or toward elegance. Easy to dismiss a place based on first impressions.

Long before there were houses here, deer, rabbits, foxes made their home on this land—foxes still; I have seen them. Men—kings, even—on horseback thundered through these parts in centuries past, hunting deer, boar, wolf.

Easton (from the Saxon *Est Tun*, or East Farm) was a hamlet about a mile from Bristol, in the Royal Forest of Kingswood, which served as the hunting grounds for the king and assorted nobility. The

Empress Matilda, mother of Henry II, settled midway between Bristol (then *Brycg Stowe*—"Place by the Bridge") and Easton after she lost her battle for the English throne to her cousin Stephen of Blois. She built an enormous castle and garrison—its keep was reputedly the size of the keep at the Tower of London—to the east of Bristol, effectively cutting off Easton's trade with the city of Bristol. Easton was forced to reimagine itself and develop its own livelihood, so its inhabitants made implements and weapons as well as food for the castle and garrison. Noticing that the royal herd was mysteriously thinning, the nobility regarded those who lived in Easton with suspicion, and the phrase "without the gate" was used to refer to those who lived outside the garrison gate—the Eastonians—and gradually came to imply anyone of ill repute.

Despite being "without the gate," Easton attracted the aristocracy. At the beginning of the thirteenth century a who's who of royalty had manor houses here: Edwards I, II, III, IV, V; Richards II, III; Henrys IV, V, VI, VII, VIII; Queen Anne; and the Duke of Clarence among them. It was an area of meadows and pastures, of arable farmland and two rivers: the Frome to the north and the Avon to the south. It also had riches underground: coal began to be mined around this time.

Easton's pastoral beauty lasted until 1858, when the Industrial Revolution came knocking. The urgent need for human hands brought thousands in from the countryside to Bristol. In 1800, Bristol's population was seventy thousand; by 1850, it had doubled; and fifty years after that the figure had doubled again to three hundred thousand, so great was the need for labour in shipyards, banks, coal mines, cotton mills, distilleries, pulp and paper mills, potteries, and sugar refineries. Easton itself had three mines operating in 1883 as the Easton Coal Company: the main shaft was eleven feet in diameter, a thousand feet deep, and it was fitted with two cages. Thirty miles of tram roads were dug underground, where more than fifty horses toiled in the grimy depths.

Above ground, houses went up in Easton at an astounding rate, especially between 1880 and 1890, when our house was built. The former royal hamlet was now a booming residential suburb. As Easton's physical landscape changed, so, too, did its social makeup. In the eighteenth century, the city rolls listed Easton residents as farmers, lead merchants, gentlemen; barely a hundred years later, the occupational roll listed dairy men, fruit and vegetable merchants, malters, ironmongers, and miners. Bucolic fields of old were now criss-crossed with steel rails rumbling with trains carrying coal from the pits.

Areas that are forced to serve the urgent needs of man are doomed the moment those needs succumb to economic and political vagaries. In 1911, Easton's miners walked off the job, seeking an extra three pence per day. People suffered terribly during the three-month strike: children went to school barefoot; feeding centres were set up. If you owned a bicycle and worked as an errand boy, you were considered well off. When the strike ended and the Easton pit was closed, a series of disasters—the First World War, then the Depression—besieged the area: and crime gained a foothold.

The final nail in the coffin for Easton was the Second World War. All those Victorian terraces that sprang up in the late 1800s became a useful marker for German bombers: pilots only had to spot the coal slags and the long streets of row upon row of terrace houses to know they were closing in on Bristol's shipyards and factories. On their way to bomb the city, German planes dropped a few on Easton. One, in April 1941, shattered two streets so badly that a huge hole in the ground revealed the coal seams of the colliery below.

Easton devolved into an eyesore, a cautionary tale of urban blight. In the 1950s and 1960s, plans for a "new Easton" were trotted out by successive governments, but none of the attempts stuck. Stillborn and infant mortality increased. Unemployment ran at 20 percent; immigration rose to 35 percent; poverty doubled; crime and violence soared. Drug dealers and hookers were about the only people in Easton who earned money. A survey measuring poverty and deprivation based on seven criteria was conducted throughout Bristol. Of the ninety-nine zones surveyed, Easton was one of six zones that ticked all seven criteria. As recently as the 1980s, half the houses in Easton were deemed unfit for habitation.

And then a welcome reversal breezed in. Urban theorists such as Jane Jacobs and Richard Florida have long cited artistic and entrepreneurial energies as the drivers of regeneration and positive gentrification. Some areas are resistant to public policy and government measures but manage to find their footing through grassroots initiatives. So it was with Easton, where renewal happened organically. In the mid- to late-1990s, when a fine Victorian house in the area would set you back just £18,500, creatives and young families braved Easton's sketchy reputation. Banksy was among them: his graffiti art lives on several buildings.

Today, Easton is a mosh pit of cultures and identities: churches, mosques and gurdwaras coexist with man buns, dreadlocks, pink hair, and artistic collectives producing menstrual art. You are not likely to encounter anyone wearing a tie here. It also has graffiti, lots of it: mostly the good kind. Cafés, bakeries, hot-desking space, and trendy eateries attract the young, the educated, the flexible, the tolerant. A walk from our house to St. Mark's Road passes sari shops, halal butchers, Indian grocery shops, a bakery, an artisan pizzeria, and a smattering of restaurants—Moroccan, Bangladeshi, and Indian. An Italian restaurant is opening up soon in space formerly occupied by a vegetarian restaurant. Italian. In this area that will count as exotic.

Equally important to any area, maybe even more so, are the family-run corner stores, the community centres and church-run programs offering book clubs, yoga and Pilates classes, food banks, and mental health groups that are vital to successful and long-lasting regeneration that help retain that village feeling.

It is obviously paying off: The most recent census (done in 2011) shows that Easton has a higher proportion of young children and people in the twenty-five-to-forty-four age bracket than the England and Wales average. It bodes well for us newcomers that our attraction to this area others might view with trepidation is finding its way back to respectability.

HERKIMER STREET

14

The Hamilton Homes

It is mid-May, and a respite from reno hell arrives in the form of quick trip to Canada to visit my kids, friends, and the dentist. People consider it eccentric of me to cross the Atlantic for a dental appointment. Believe me, eccentricity has nothing to do with it; it is self-preservation.

Before he retired, my fiery, Irish dentist imparted some firm advice. I was pinned in his examination chair, and when his assistant mentioned that I was moving to England, Dr. McKenna stopped prodding around in my mouth, and fixed me with a stern look: "Never trust a British dentist." I smiled, nodded as best I could with an aspirator in my mouth, but he leaned in closer and said it again. "Seriously, do not trust a British dentist. You're taking your life in your hands when you do that." His warning has been borne out by

British friends and acquaintances, who have regaled me with their dental horror stories. Obligingly, I now schedule my biannual visits to Canada around appointments with Dr. McKenna's successor and a team of gentle hygienists.

Of course, there is a side benefit to this: the dental office is located near all my former homes in Hamilton.

Although I was born and raised in Toronto, circumstance moved me to Hamilton, where I lived for nearly twenty-five years, though not, as you now know, in the same house. I had earmarked myself for a settled life after university, but the reality was that within a decade of graduation, I had married, had two children, and moved house eleven times.

My husband at the time and I were pushed into home ownership. Renting was for losers, we were told: purchasing a home was the path to upper adulthood, and the bedrock of financial and marital stability. In the case of financial stability, the advice was sound. As for marital stability, my marriage was over before the eighties were.

My family and friends were not surprised about my divorce, but when they learned I was moving from Oakville to Hamilton, there was a collective intake of breath. "Hamilton? Are things that bad?"

Hamilton was the armpit of Canada; a dirty, industrial steel town of working-class grunts. In 1988, moving from ladies-who-lunch Oakville to gritty Hamilton was the British equivalent of moving from Chelsea to Wolverhampton, or the US equivalent of moving from Carmel-by-the-Sea to Buffalo. While life's vicissitudes do not always hand you address choices, in some corner of my mind I sensed that although my marriage had failed, my world was about to be reassembled in an exciting way in Hamilton.

I was completely unfamiliar with Hamilton, but my move there was dictated by a few factors, chief among them being that I had a part-time job at *The Hamilton Spectator*, my only source of income. (Out of pride and stubbornness, I flatly refused any form of social assistance offered to single mothers.) Being a single mother was about as low down the societal totem pole as you could get when I moved there. Drug dealers commanded more respect. Social demographers and their flurry of research and data were all over single moms like lice in a kindergarten class, declaring that being a divorced mom was the fast track to poverty and to all manner of social, educational, and intellectual disasters for one's children. They were so wrong. I thrived as a single mother. My kids thrived, too.

Another reason for moving to Hamilton was that it was shockingly affordable. The city was only fifteen minutes down the highway from my previous home in Oakville, but the difference in terms of cost of living was like night and day. In Hamilton, I was able to buy a house in a decent area and cover the mortgage, groceries, and bills and have money left over, all on a part-time wage. You are hard-pressed to achieve that nowadays, and certainly not in Hamilton, which has recently seen the biggest jump in house prices in all of Canada. It gladdens my heart that the city has shaken off its down-at-heels reputation. Since moving away, I have become even more appreciative of this lovely, unpretentious city, and hold it in higher esteem than my birthplace of Toronto.

Hamilton's new gloss is evident on this bright spring morning as I drive into the city ahead of my dental appointment. The air is warm, and the magnolia blossoms are out. As I cross the high-level bridge over Hamilton Harbour, the city's burgeoning skyline rises in greeting. On the horizon, ghostly silhouettes of factories and steel mills slip in and out of the haze. Thirty years ago, they were alive, belching out the last gasps of the city's industrial heritage. Now they slumber like hulking beasts brought to heel.

The drive-by visits to my previous homes follow the same route, in chronological order, like stations of my personal cross. At each house, I pause in the car and silently recite the gospel that pertains to that particular home. Sometimes I pray; sometimes I just let the memories out for a little run. A few times I have wept.

I drive past the historic cemetery on York Boulevard, where I taught my kids to ride their bikes on winding paths beneath a protective canopy of maples. Across the road, stately Dundurn Castle, as creamy white as a butter cake, sits in a verdant ganache of parkland.

At the first lights I turn right on to Woodbine Crescent. The scenery changes abruptly from the elegance of Dundurn Castle to small, plain houses, some in a state of untidiness and neglect. My old home looks a little worse for wear today, and there is no evidence of the peony bush my boyfriend planted as a housewarming gift.

When I first met this house, it took me all of five seconds to tell the real estate agent, "Draw up the papers. I'm buying this."

"But you haven't seen more than the front hall!" he said.

"Don't need to—I know it will be perfect."

It was a plain early twentieth-century reddish-brown brick house with steps leading up to a small veranda, and a green asphalt roof that was almost all dormer housing the main bedroom. Inside, on the main floor, a small living room with dark-wood pocket doors opened up to a large dining room with dark-wood trim and rose-pink chevron wallpaper. The kitchen, at the back of the house, was white and had a walkout to a small backyard. The basement was partially finished, and it is where I set up a play area for my little boys, a small writing area for me, and a laundry room. Upstairs there were three bedrooms, a bathroom, and a walkout to a spacious deck that benefited from the shade of the cemetery's trees. I have never been wary of living next to a cemetery: such places provide me with a sense of calm and an appreciation for life.

The house was hardly luxury, but to me I was living the dream. It was certainly the antithesis of what those social demographers characterized for the single-mother lifestyle: according to them I should have been some greasy-haired slattern injecting myself with heroin. Instead, one sweltering summer afternoon I found myself stretched out on a chaise lounge on the upper deck, pink lemonade in one hand, *Vogue* in the other. I felt utterly content, and with it bloomed the sentiment *If single motherhood is society's version of the road to ruin, bring it on.*

The other trope about young mothers—and single moms, for sure—is that their homes are disaster zones of dirty dishes teetering in the sink, disorganized kitchen counters, toys and clothes strewn everywhere. That was never my house. I kept a tidy place both for my sanity and to imprint a standard on my children, for I believe that the first step to raising responsible children begins with teaching them to keep their own space tidy, and to carry that practice outside the house by respecting the property of others and the environment in general.

My eyes now linger on the veranda where my boys played, and as one memory fades another sharply inserts itself: of them waiting eagerly for their father to pick them up for the weekends. They would run squealing joyfully into his arms on Friday, and on Monday he had to drag them kicking and screaming back into my house. Their father was the fun parent; I was the scolding, strict, eat-your-broccoli parent. That my boys preferred the company of their father hurt deeply, but it was something that had to be endured.

To this day, I am grateful that I took the plunge to buy a home when the more likely and perhaps more prudent scenario for someone in my situation would have been to rent. Owning my own home focused my responsibilities and gave me stability and control. Besides, I did not want my boys to think that a woman on her own, especially a mother, could not shift for herself; I wanted them to see that there should be no discrepancy between the resources of a single father and those of a single mother. There was definitely wage discrimination—still is—but the point of my example was that there was no excuse for inequality. It was important for them to see that mothers can work and earn a living. With the rare exception, my experience has been that single mothers do not receive support payments that roll in like a monthly lottery win.

Woodbine Avenue was kind to me, requiring little in the way of fixing up. I did not do much beyond a bit of wallpapering and touching up the painted woodwork.

I acquired a boyfriend at this time. He was handy and did small repairs on the house, and I repaid him with hearty home-cooked meals. That summer of 1988 was hot and sultry, a typical southern Ontario summer. On Friday nights, we slid into his big, black '79 Buick Park Avenue and cruised down the Queen Elizabeth Way, windows down, cooled by a humid breeze. We drove across the Skyway Bridge, then over the Garden City Bridge, past Niagara Falls, and across the forty-ninth parallel into Buffalo. Sometimes we went for dinner, sometimes just for a drive. Time was an open, unhurried road with no horizon. I felt so free then, so blissfully alive, so in love. Life felt settled, and easygoing. There was no past, no future, only the present. It was a great time to be thirty-four.

A year and a half later, our respective divorces finalized, we got engaged. We bought a home together to accommodate his two children and my two. That is the home to which I drive next.

Trepidation jangles me whenever I approach Hyde Park Avenue; I tend to mentally brace myself, never sure of the reaction the house will elicit. Hyde Park is where a new life began and where it ended, where I finally breathed easy and then suddenly started hyperventilating. There have been times when I have avoided the house entirely on my drive-bys, but today for some reason an inner strength governs me.

I do not spot the house as soon as I turn onto the street. The trees and shrubs on the other properties have matured in the intervening years and now obscure the approach slightly. But then I see it: a still-handsome two-and-a-half-storey coral-and-cream brick Edwardian; three chunky creamy pillars supporting a broad veranda; cream trim around the windows. Its current owners obviously care for it.

The house impressed me at first sight in the summer of 1989: it had the space for our blended brood; it had the location for good schools; and it was in a leafy, tranquil neighbourhood. My low-cost single-mom years had me worrying that such a home was beyond our means; however, my fiancé was smitten, and his enthusiasm carried away any misgivings.

Four months later we married on a snowy New Year's Day. Our reception was held in our new home. The twinkle of white lights strung across the veranda and wound around the pillars reflected in the freshly fallen snow and made everything look magical and clean. My two boys and stepson in their little suits and bow ties, my stepdaughter in a pink floral dress and little pink ballet shoes: we looked like a happily-ever-after family. By the end of that year, we had a daughter, the bridge in our blended family.

What with the five kids bouncing in and out of our house, people wondered how I kept it all together. But I did—we did. Hyde Park was my Tara, and I adored the life I had there. Our home was the locus for street-hockey games, for dinner parties and birthday celebrations; of big family Christmas dinners, and cozy weekends in front of the fire playing board games or watching TV. I was even fortunate with work: In addition to my part-time editing job at the newspaper, I became the Homes columnist and feature writer. I was now paid to nose around other people's homes.

Life was good, and a few years later, one Christmas, we took the kids to Disney World. My husband and I were not fans of theme parks, yet we had a truly wonderful time. Best vacation ever, it was agreed by one and all. We even talked about returning one day.

But you can never trust the Magic Kingdom. Shortly after we returned home, everything toppled. My husband inexplicably ceased speaking to me. At first, I thought it was a joke, a bit of game playing, but no amount of cajoling or begging on my part would convince him to talk. He just stopped communicating with all of us. Was he worried? Upset about something? He would not say. I had loved my husband deeply, and we had been an affectionate, playful couple, so this swift change of behaviour was a kind of torture. It was hard enough to maintain a brave face with the children, but my husband and I were by then working at the same Toronto newspaper, and our disintegrating marriage became office gossip.

As the silent treatment continued, and I agonized over what could have brought it on—another woman? a sudden drug habit? a mid-life crisis?—I walked around the neighbourhood in the late evenings, cloaked by darkness, embarrassed by the state of my marriage. This was my second, so it certainly felt like a curse was upon me. I walked up and down the streets, looking enviously at the light spilling from other people's houses, wondering what ingredient I lacked that they apparently had in abundance. Were they really happy, or did danger lurk behind their confident laughter and smiles as they sat around the dinner table or chatted across the kitchen island with wineglasses in hand?

Dreams were my salvation—day and night—and I began to confide them to a diary. Always present in these little fantasies was a

Victorian cottage with my children tucked snugly and safely inside. They were a balm, these musings, but they also struck me as outlandish: surely my marriage would, could, be salvaged. I could not imagine being separated from my husband; then again, I could not abide being treated so harshly.

Now as I sit in my car outside the Hyde Park house, my nose prickles as memories and emotions collide. Just then, a well-dressed woman emerges from the front door. She eyes me with curiosity as she waters pots of geraniums on the veranda. I wonder if she is pretending. I grab my mobile phone and pretend to take a call. I avert my eyes. I do not want to engage with her or anyone on the street.

Hanging up my pretend phone call, I stare straight ahead and move the gearshift to Drive. I proceed up the street, not making eye contact with the other houses, each with a story I could tell. Left at the first intersection, then left again.

The next house is the one I thought might save my marriage, which is why I bought it one morning on my way home from grocery shopping. It sounds like something my mother would do.

My cell phone had rung while I was steering my trolley through the supermarket aisles, wondering if there was a meal I could cook that would change my husband's heart toward me. The person calling me was a friend who happened to be a real estate agent.

"I've found the perfect home for you. It's a Victorian cottage!" she said excitedly. I could almost see her jumping up and down. "Just what you wanted."

I had not told her about my marital troubles, though in hindsight it was likely all over the neighbourhood by then. The house sounded intriguing; I said I would call her the next day.

"No, you have to see it right now. It's not going to last the day," she said.

Fifteen minutes later, my car was turning into its driveway.

Whereas the Hyde Park home sat high and proud, the house on Stanley Avenue cowered like a cornered animal. It was a small house whose brick exterior had been painted rusty red; nonetheless, it was definitely a Victorian workers' cottage, and it was most definitely the home that had always surfaced in my dreams, though I had never driven past it before. It had few rooms, but they were generous ones. On the ground floor were two bedrooms, a kitchen, a bathroom, and a spacious living room/dining room. A ramshackle addition off the kitchen opened to a roomy side yard, which in turn led to a large backyard overgrown with tall grass. Upstairs were two attic-type bedrooms with low, sloping ceilings, and a large, unfinished attic space behind one of the bedrooms. The basement was too dark and scary to merit closer inspection, but it looked to be high and dry.

To say the house needed work was an understatement. It was as close to being condemned by the city as a house could get. But it was cheap, and even after renovating it there would be more than enough money left over to retire our debts, which might help my husband feel less burdened.

I made a lowball offer and left it at that. If it was not meant to be, then it was not meant to be.

When I returned home with the groceries, my husband was in the kitchen. He had resumed speaking to me but only on an as-needed basis.

"Is there more?" He was asking if there were other bags to bring in from the car.

"Not in the car. But I did buy something else." I braced myself. "I bought a house."

"You did what!"

I told him about our mutual friend's phone call in the grocery store.

"It needs work, but it is cute and sound. Huge backyard. But don't worry. I made a lowball offer. There is no way it will be accepted."

Relief blew out of his tight-set lips.

And then the phone rang.

"You got it!" the agent squealed down the line. "Can you believe it?"

My husband liked the new house and shared my vision for it. He enjoyed gardening and drew exciting plans for the backyard. But the house could not save our marriage. A few weeks later it was over, and our Hyde Park home went up for sale. It sold (we lost money on it, the first and only home of mine that has), and we went our separate ways.

I do not blame my husband for leaving; we all do what we need to do to get the life we are destined to have. Relieved of our collective and individual aspirations within a marriage, we become the people we are meant to become rather than the people we perhaps wanted to become.

STANLEY AVENUE WAS ONLY FOUR BLOCKS from Hyde Park, which meant that my children did not have to change schools or sever friendships. What did change was that they were now conscripted into helping with the renovation. When I was younger, I had wanted to get as far from my parents' penchant for moving and renovating, but here I was, back at it, and dragging my kids into it.

It proved a good home. If Virginia Woolf pined for a room of one's own, one now had, once again, a home of one's own. Although I was inconsolable about the demise of my marriage, the house erected a kind of force field around my grief. It also became a refuge for teary friends who showed up on my doorstep, having been ditched by their husbands. This divorce thing was racing through the neighbourhood like influenza. We medicated with wine.

There was something spiritual and calming about the Stanley Avenue house. It seemed to understand and absorb sadness, as if overseen by a non-judgmental, compassionate caretaker who slipped in quietly to mop up the tears. In the evenings, when the children were in bed, and dark and silence descended, I lit candles, put on a CD of Gregorian chant, and knelt before a blazing fireplace, praying for strength and for the continued safety and health of my children and parents. It was also during this time that my prayers gave me the strength to make the tentative steps toward confronting the trauma of my rape, which had happened fifteen years earlier. Around me the walls pulsated with the orange reflection from the fire, like beating angel wings. I knew nothing of the previous owner aside from the fact that he had been a churchgoer, and that his pastor had been his executor, but those small details felt like a kind of blessing bestowed upon the house of which I was the grateful beneficiary.

I am not sure whether people sit down and consider how much sacrifice and labour go into making a home, especially one with children. The physical plant—heating, running water, electricity, ventilation—is definitely vital, but there are the additional comforts that are chosen to ensure the home's inhabitants feel safe and snuggled: the arrangement of furniture, the placement of art on the walls and knick-knacks and books on the shelves. These all tell the story of the family's history, roots, and become daily visual reminders of that history: acorns scattered on the windowsill tell of a recent walk to the park; a shell conjures up a trip to the beach; a blanket at the end of a bed or draped over a chair evokes a memory of being read a story while you cupped a mug of hot chocolate; a painting on the wall triggers emotions and distinct memories of where it came from, a grandparent's anecdote about it, the way it alters in different kinds of light; a simple photograph on a bedside table that you see the moment you open your eyes in the morning can bring a moment of joy, heartbreak, or wistfulness. There is the gathering of appropriate furniture—desks on which to do homework; closets and chests of drawers to protect clothes; bins and baskets in which to store playthings. A cherished stuffed toy placed against the bed pillow can convey messages of love, order, and security that register mightily in a child's psyche and imagination.

Making a home for my children at this wrenching time in their lives was stressful for all of us. They were on the cusp of their teen years, with their opinions and elastic boundaries; they compared their home life with the style and the material comforts of their friends' two-parented homes. Status was a marker for their generation, and I did not want them to feel less worthy than their peers for the sake of a pair of the latest style of running shoes, so I took whatever freelance work I could get to supplement my income. I worked extremely hard to keep everything afloat.

I was not always at my best—alcohol and cigarettes helped me cope with grief and lack of confidence—but when that period passed and I shook off my weepiness and addictive crutches, I stood tall and assured—assertive, even. Walking out the front door was like crossing a border into a new land. My well-being bounced back; my physical strength soared. When it came to outdoor maintenance, I was like a machine: lacing on steel-toed boots and lugging eight-foot railway sleepers to frame a vegetable patch. I did all the heavy lifting—physically, emotionally, and psychologically—as single mothers do—because there was no choice, no one to off-load the responsibility for even a moment.

And yet I am humbled and privileged by this phase, of having single-handedly made a home for my family. It is only now, decades after they have left and have built nests of their own, that I see the enormous trust that was given to me, not just to make a home for them but to care, nurture, and of course love them. It is no secret that raising children is tough, especially if you are a single parent, and the regret is that you do not have time to stop and marvel at your fortitude and courage while you are in the midst of it. Only after the major parenting has been done can you look back and exhale, wondering how you did it, and how well you did it.

Stanley Avenue was home for five years until an opportunity, disguised as a near-fatal car accident, prompted me to move with my young daughter to Pelee Island during the winter of 2001. It was a deliberate escape from the caffeine-fuelled rat race in order to recalibrate myself and concentrate on my desire to write. For a time, it worked: the national newspaper I was working for as an editor commissioned me to write a series of columns about the experience, and my columns turned out to be a success. But once I returned, refreshed, to the frantic world of journalism, I got scheduled back into my old job—copy editing on the news desk at nights. Around this time, the newspaper offered to pay my moving expenses if I moved from Hamilton to Toronto. The car accident still fresh in my mind, I decided to accept the offer, and I sold my Stanley Avenue home.

After Pelee Island, we lived with my mother for a few months while I searched for a new home in Toronto. In late August 2001, we moved into a house in the Beaches area of Toronto. Housing prices were much higher than Hamilton ones then, and I ended up with a huge mortgage that sat like a tumour in my chest.

Two weeks later—not yet out of boxes—the catastrophic horror of 9/11 changed everyone's world. The impact of the attack reverberated in me as intensely as if it had taken a member of my own family. I remember staring at the startling blueness of the sky and wondering whether it was the result of the power of collective communal shock among humanity and its ensuing outpouring of silent prayer, or (morbidly) whether the carbon released from all those who lost their lives in the attack that day had altered atmospheric conditions. Or whether it was a hopeful sign from God. As fear and chaos radiated around the globe, economies and businesses contracted; people were laid off work. The media business in which I was employed was not immune: a week after the attacks I found myself in a crowded room with colleagues and a stack of severance packages.

There was no stability in the world; there was no stability in the workplace. Even our new home felt unreliable, unstable, as if it were teetering on precarious foundations. Whenever I went upstairs, bouts of vertigo assailed me.

In the midst of devastation there are always miracles. Two months after being laid off I was offered my first book contract, from which blossomed my writing career. I also gained a new friend in the single mom next door: we shared a party wall and, as we discovered, the same birthday, and became forever friends.

Despite the political, social, and emotional aftershocks of that period, the one thing that seemed unshakable was the Toronto housing market. Knowing I would not be able to afford the mortgage on my home without a steady job—and full-time employment then was pretty much non-existent—I put the house up for sale eight months after we had moved in. It sold within twenty-four hours, sight unseen, to an Australian couple. I even made money on it.

Two months later, the kids and I were back in the familiar environs of Hamilton, where the offer of a full-time job materialized along with our next home.

THE HOUSE ON HERKIMER STREET was an elegant detached Victorian with deep frontage. It had been divided into two rented flats, and I converted it back to a single-family home as soon as I became its new owner.

By this time, I was adept at home renovation—or rather, adept at knowing who to call to do the work. I never paid more for a house than I could afford: not the amount the bank said I could afford, but the amount I worked out on paper myself, based on what my salary could handle while leaving enough to care for my children. There is nothing worse than the stress of owing money. I once borrowed money from my parents in the early 1980s, and it was an experience I never wanted to repeat. While far from being mortgage-free, I was grateful to my bank for having faith in me: single mothers did not always get approved for mortgages (thankfully that societal attitude has turned). I worked out the cost of necessary renovations and factored that into my mortgage application. After that, I set financial goals and timelines for the work on subsequent phases of renovation. I was no financial wizard—far from it—but I was fortunate to have decent-paying jobs and a quiet social life. I was not always sensible or practical—some things were paid on credit—but I knew my limit and never overreached it.

Herkimer Street was a large project. Inside and out the house needed attention. By now, I had come to expect that I was doomed to buy fixer-uppers. The terracotta brick had been painted a flat, rusty red; the window frames and fascia boards were coated in layer upon layer of dull green paint that was cracked and peeling. Shrubs, trees, and grass had grown wild and unkempt. It was the sort of house a kid would avoid on Halloween. Inside, the place had been architecturally cleansed. Stately double glass doors between the living room and dining room had been ripped out—frame and all—as had a walnut mantel. Glass transoms had been painted over and sealed shut with flat white paint. The pine and maple floors were covered throughout the house in beige carpet that smelled of cat pee. None of this concerned me: I had my trusty list of Hamilton tradesmen to call upon to remedy it all.

My neighbours to one side had an identical house to mine, except they had fixed theirs up to a stunning degree. They were interior designers who were only too happy to offer decorating advice. They suggested paint colours for the exterior woodwork—mustard, dark green, and aubergine—the same colours they had used on their home. I was happy to comply: what looked great on their place would look great on mine.

There was a little something inside my home, however, that no amount of interior design could change: a ghost.

People are reluctant to talk about house ghosts for fear of being considered crazy, but ghosts exist; of that I am certain.

The ghosts in the Henry Farm house were benign things, just pootling about looking for people to tease. Given the age of that house, you would be naive to think none existed. But ghosts linger in modern houses, too. In one suburban home I lived in, where my first marriage ended, the new owners ordered an exorcism to rid the house of that just-divorced smell. I thought it was a bit extreme: I can be a bitch, but I am no she-devil. And frankly, people would be lucky to have me as a ghost. I would be exceedingly respectful.

The ghost in the Herkimer Street house was the real business, though: a cantankerous, miserable fellow, who made his presence known before I was halfway through the first can of pale-sage paint in the master bedroom. A whiff of pipe tobacco had curled into the room while I rolled the walls with paint. I paid it no mind, but when I heard heavy footsteps in the hall, I figured someone had come into the house.

"Hello?"

I peeked out the bedroom door. No one was there. I would later come to understand that the burning pipe tobacco and heavy footfall up and down the hall was the ghost's calling card.

That first night in the house, I was awakened at three in the morning by the scream of the smoke alarm. I fumbled for a flashlight and ran panicking through the house looking for fire until I arrived at the basement door. As soon as I descended the stairs, the door slammed shut behind me, and I heard footsteps in hasty retreat on the floorboards overhead.

It did not take long for me to figure out that while this was a home crying out for TLC, it came with a ghost crying out for me not only to leave it all alone but to leave period.

At first, the ghost used the usual bag of tricks: knocking pictures off the wall, slamming doors, and breathing close to my ear. The middle-of-the-night smoke alarm was a particular favourite. My children looked at me for an explanation to this paranormal mayhem, but I feigned ignorance.

One day, as I dragged the cat-pee carpet out the back door, a grizzled, ponytailed fellow leaned over my back fence.

"So, what do you think of the third floor in your house?" he chuckled.

"You must be mistaken," I replied, wrestling with the carpet. "There is no third floor."

"Oh yes there is," he said. "The trap door in the ceiling of the closet in the small bedroom?"

Gosh, he was awfully specific.

"Poke your head through that. It was Karl's favourite room."

Karl. So the ghost had a name. But a third floor? How come my neighbours knew more about my home's layout than I did?

I went back indoors and climbed the stairs to the second floor. I peered up at the small trap door in the ceiling of the little bedroom. Then I went back downstairs and decided to hold off further exploration until someone with more nerve showed up.

A few days later, my ex-husband arrived to pick up our daughter.

As he waited by the front door, casually admiring the house—we had both shared an interest in old homes—he asked whether I had come across anything interesting. I relayed my conversation with the ponytailed neighbour.

The ex's eyes widened.

"And?"

"Well, I wasn't about to check it out. Not on my own."

"Can I?"

"Help yourself."

"Kids! Grab a ladder!"

Soon, the ex was storming up the stairs, trailed by three children and a stepladder. He disappeared into the loft, groped around for a light switch, and then—

"Holy. Shit."

"What!" we all shrieked.

His face appeared in the trap-door opening. "Get a camera."

By then we were all frantically climbing over one another to see inside the loft.

And what we saw was eerie. A huge plywood board stood in the middle of the attic like the monolith from *2001: A Space Odyssey*. Upon it was mounted all manner of switches, fuses, an old TV aerial, and a tangle of electrical wire, most of it dangerously frayed. Beside this master-control board was a little wooden bench upon which sat a conical-shaped hat made of tin foil. According to my ponytailed neighbour, Karl would climb to this attic perch each Friday to dial in Mars.

A month later, an electrician came over to dismantle the contraption. He entered the loft, switched on the light, and then—

"Holy. Shit."

His head poked through the loft hatch.

"Mind if I take a picture? I have never seen anything like this before."

Okay, so old Karl had been an eccentric. It was also clear that Karl had not quite left his earthly home. I could live with that. What I could not abide, however, was Karl's blatant irritation with my renovation plans. Whenever I started moving furniture, ripping down wallpaper, or tearing up carpets, Karl made his displeasure known.

When work began on the upstairs bathroom, Karl retreated to the back bedroom and kicked up an unholy racket similar to that wreaked by Marley's ghost in *A Christmas Carol*. It sounded as if Karl were pounding the walls and upending the furniture, yet when I opened the bedroom door nothing was amiss.

I was not the only one privy to this cacophony: Gord, the builder, heard it also. He was redoing the bathroom. Thank goodness he was not spooked by Karl. Not in the least.

"I had a ghost in one of my income properties," he told me in his matter-of-fact way. "It did everything to get me out of that house. One day, it unleashed a hideous smell. I swore at the ghost and took a sledgehammer to the walls. That took care of things. There are a lot of homes with ghosts who don't like their surroundings disturbed."

While Gord worked on the bathroom, I weeded the garden. I had decided to try to win over Karl, so I complimented him on his landscaping. "Nice garden, Karl. Such a variety of flowers!"

But since Karl was making it clear that he was not going to be buttered up, it was time for the gloves to come off. You can only take so much of a ghost's tantrums, and Karl was like having another teenager in the house. The few friends I dared to confide in about the ghost advised me to invoke the mantra "Go toward the light, Karl" and be done with him. But I never take the easy way out. This was war.

I started with mockery. "Fancied yourself a DIY guy, eh? One of those misguided morons who think he does better work than the pros. Well, you know what? You are shit at DIY, Karl. If I had not come along, this place would have got a yellow card from the fire department."

Karl paced loudly up and down the stairs.

When I scraped the paint off the glass transoms and finally jimmied them open, I sneered: "Was this intentional, or just sloppy paintwork on your part?" He sighed heavily next to my ear. I paid no heed, and blithely hummed "Highway to Hell" as I continued to scrape.

Whenever he let loose his fury, I flew at him unflinchingly: "If you were any kind of a man, you would not be trying to terrorize a poor single mother and her children—you would be protecting us and helping us. I am busting my ass all day at work so that I can pay to correct your crappy workmanship, while you live here free of charge and complain. You call that gratitude?"

One day, I returned home from work just as the floor refinishers were packing up their gear in the front hall. It became apparent that someone—I assumed it was one of the crew adding the final coat of Varathane—was still upstairs, so I stood with them making small talk.

After a too-long length of time, I asked the foreman, "What is taking your guy so long?"

"There is no one up there. We are all here," he said. He glanced at his mates.

We paused to listen to what sounded like someone beating their fists on the walls and jumping up and down on the floor.

"Do you hear that noise?" I asked the men.

"Yes. We heard it earlier, too," one of them said, "but we thought it was one of your kids."

"It is not my kids. One second."

Hands balled up into fists, I stormed up the stairs. When I reached the door of the room from which the sounds were coming, I yelled, "I have had it up to here with you. You are behaving like a child. Either you cut that out or you get the hell out of my home!"

With that, I stomped back downstairs, waving my arms in frustration.

"Sorry about that," I apologized to the floor refinishers, who by now had their backs pressed against the wall, eyes as wide as saucers. "We have a temperamental ghost living here. He gets pissed off with the renovations."

It was the last job they did for me.

I eventually gained the upper hand over Karl. I like to think that I gradually wore him out. Perhaps the laughter and boisterousness that percolated through the house softened him. Perhaps he figured that if he backed off, I would not play heavy metal music so loud.

The one bad memory I have of the home involves theft. One night, as the household slept, someone pried open the dining room window and stole my laptop. It had the draft manuscripts of two books on it. In my naïveté I had not made backup discs. Hard lesson, that. It is times like that when a ghost would come in handy: Karl had obviously been dozing on the job.

The rest is happy memories. This was a home of family celebrations, holiday get-togethers, and personal growth. My confidence blossomed, and I began to travel, gaining new female friends. Up till then, I had been shy and tentative about girlfriends, possibly from the fear of moving away and losing them, possibly from being unsure of my value to others; but new gal pals came from hiking groups, from those I met while walking the Camino de Santiago de Compostela, and through my writing. Of the few steady older friends I had, I paid better attention to them, appreciating more the comfort and familiarity of their warm companionship, and the kindness they had shown me over the years when I was too distracted or depressed to notice. Things had brightened now. We would sit in my garden late into a summer's evening beneath an umbrella of trees and flickering lanterns, sharing heartbreaks and dreams while fireflies zigzagged like fairies. I felt at my freest in this house: secure in my job; secure in my gradual transition into a writing life. Sometimes it takes a certain house to give you the space to grow and bloom.

My children were going through that rebellious stage that afflicts most teenagers, so our home was not immune to sharp arguments over curfews, homework, and, inevitably, overnight guests.

Early one beautiful summer's morning, I awoke to the sound of giggling coming from the bedroom of one of my sons. Was it the radio? I eased myself out of bed, tiptoed closer to his door, and listened. I discerned a female voice. I could hardly believe it. My son, my eighteen-year-old son, had brought home a girl to spend the night *in my house.*

I honestly did not know what to do. I turned around, tiptoed downstairs, made a pot of tea, and spent half an hour arguing with myself over the lessons I had apparently neglected to teach my children. They were, for the most part, respectful and obedient kids, so this was quite out of character. Surely they knew that bringing someone home for a one-night stand was up there on the not-done list.

After the second cup of tea, I gathered my courage, marched to the door of my son's bedroom, knocked politely, and asked in the sweetest voice I could muster, "Darling, may I see you for a moment?"

He emerged from his room wearing Donald Duck boxer shorts. I led him into my bedroom, closed the door, and addressed him, *sotto voce,* with a blend of incredulity and anger while I scanned his face for signs of substance abuse.

"What the hell are you thinking? Where did you ever get the idea that this is okay? I do not care who she is. Send her home now. I am calling a cab."

"Ah, Mom, not right now. It's early."

"Noooowww!" I drew out the word and held him with a "You are so in the shithouse, buddy" gaze.

The young lady presently came down the stairs. The cab was idling in the driveway. She introduced herself sheepishly to me, and said, "You have a lovely home."

"Thanks," I said with a tight smile, and opened the door. "Goodbye."

I marched back upstairs to confront my son, who was lolling in bed. I tried not to look too closely at the state of his room, particularly the bedclothes.

"Do you feel an apology might pass your lips?"

"It's not a big deal!"

"It is a big deal. That behaviour is not allowed in this house. Sending Sarah home early in the morning is embarrassing to her and to me."

"Sarah?" he said. "Her name is Sarah? Uh-oh. I thought it was Courtney!"

I sat down at my laptop and drew my line in the sand:

THE RULES OF THIS HOUSEHOLD

1. Absolutely NO sleepovers without prior (24-hour) notice and a really good reason.

2. Any sleepovers involving the opposite sex must receive prior verbal approval from me. Unless you are married or cohabitating, your partner cannot share your bedroom. They must sleep (alone) in the guest room.

3. Your friends are welcome in our home anytime, but they must leave by midnight (12 a.m.). There will be no extension to this rule. This rule is made out of consideration for our neighbours, as well as for my need of uninterrupted sleep.

4. You must immediately clean up after your guests, whether you have entertained them inside or outside. Smoking is forbidden in our home and is strongly discouraged outside our home. If your guests smoke, you must dispose of their refuse. Butts and other garbage are not to be tossed

in the garden or over the fence. Bottles are to be neatly placed in the outside recycling containers.

5. If your friends are drunk/depressed/fighting with their parents and they need a place to crash, this can be accommodated, BUT ONLY with prior verbal approval from me.

6. Those who live in this house must perform two chores per week. These chores will be determined by me and must be performed without pouting and/or protestations and within the time frame stipulated. It would be appreciated if you could anticipate the needs of this household from time to time and do a chore without being asked.

7. You are responsible for cleaning (vacuuming and dusting) your room and keeping it tidy and to my standards. Those standards may seem high, but as the owner of this house that is my prerogative. Beds are to be changed every second Thursday on the day the housecleaner arrives. Ditto for a thorough cleaning of your room.

8. As a writer with deadlines to meet, I require a tidy, non-chaotic space. Occupants of this home must respect that need and do their utmost to ensure it is met.

9. In return for your adherence to these rules and your day-to-day co-operation, you will receive my gratitude and respect, as well as free room and board and all the conveniences of this household.

10. Any deviation from the above will result in two warnings, followed by eviction.

Signed,
Jane Christmas,
Proprietor and Owner
July 14, 2007

Well, then, I hoped that made everything abundantly clear. I cannot believe I had to spell it out for them. Naturally, the children found the whole thing hilarious. They laughed at my list. They brought their friends over to laugh at it, too.

But this is the thing about homes: they need rules. The fabric of the building and the humans who live within its walls need care if both are to survive and thrive. Cohesion inside a home depends on a code of conduct, be it a tacit one or one that needs to be theatrically fixed to the refrigerator door with magnets. A home's peace is governed by its inhabitants, and the atmosphere, the warm and aromatic enveloping that you feel in the best homes, is often the result of co-operation and decorum. Aromatic oils do not hurt, either. Still, it is necessary to remember that a home does not make itself; its owners do, and the kindness you show a house is repaid tenfold. You can sense a well-loved home the moment you cross its threshold, and that intangible and ineffable something can be more important than how the house looks.

I loved this Hamilton house. I had always held the Hyde Park home as the gold standard of all my homes, but in fact it was this one, this Herkimer home, that is my favourite. It was the house in which I have lived the longest. It was a good family home, but it was also one that lent itself to a writer's life. It was rambling, but not too rambling; it was private, contained; the rooms spacious and airy, with the right amount of light at the right time of day.

The irony of home renovations is that just when you get it all done, just when you coax everything to your own level of comfort, it is time to move. At least, it was for me. The kids had grown and were off on their own adventures, and I was ready to scale down to a condo.

On moving day, I wandered through the empty house room by room, admiring the transformation, letting family memories off the leash. I stared out a window and watched the wind tickle the leaves of a tree my children and I had planted three summers earlier. Then I heard those familiar footsteps creeping toward me, softer and more considerate than in the past. The distinctive aroma of pipe tobacco, comforting now, wreathed nearby.

"I have really enjoyed living here, Karl," I said, turning my head toward the footsteps. "It has been a wonderful home. Truly. You could have a been a little less annoying, but there you go. Anyway, it's time for me to move on. A really nice young family is moving in. It would be best if you moved on, too. Go toward the light, Karl. Go toward the light."

HYDE PARK AVENUE

15

The Surprise Visitor

I return to England with renewed optimism for our renovation, but also with a nagging case of space envy. Everything in Canada seems bigger and wider, and I'm not talking Texas-sized; I mean just regular and comfortable proportions: broad, leafy streets; the square footage of houses, even those in high-density areas; wide front doors and spacious entranceways; big windows; built-in closets; roomy bathroom vanities; rarely do you see radiators sucking up wall space; large driveways and garages; in other words, your basic Canadian home. No one seems to have to measure their front door before ordering a sofa. In the UK, the compactness of the average home can make you feel as if you are living on an airplane, or in Toyland.

From inside our home, I regard the tight row of Victorian terraces on our street and calculate how many of them would fit on an average

Canadian lot: Three? Four? This is my new unit of measurement: VT. As in, The width of that little house is about two VTs; or, Wow, that house has to be six to eight VTs wide. And then there is the space between detached Canadian homes (on average between one and a half to two VTs), where you have to holler to get your neighbour's attention. Here in the UK, you can hear your neighbour sneeze through the walls; you can most definitely hear water rushing down the outside pipes when next door's loo is flushed or tub is emptied.

This is England, I remind myself sternly. Adapt. Roll with the punches, as my mother would say.

After a week away, I enter the house and step gingerly around building materials, buckets of plaster, dust-coated tools. I greet the trades and catch up on their progress during my absence. I chat, smile, and joke, hoping that my ever-present worry about the cost of this renovation is not showing up on my face.

At least the weather is co-operating. It is another gloriously hot, sunny day in Bristol. This southwest part of England has been enjoying an unusual heat wave. Good weather keeps up my spirits and those of my muscled, hammer-swinging troops. I am convinced that abundant sunshine makes a renovation go smoother and swifter.

Francis, the builder, is in the kitchen. Perspiration is already gathering on his upper lip and it is only half past nine. It is all good, he reassures me cheerfully. He has not hit any obstacles. The new windows arrive today, he adds, and the bifold patio doors will be installed tomorrow.

Things are moving quickly. The window in the second reception room has been enlarged to accommodate French doors, also arriving today. I am about to remind Francis that the bathroom is the priority—nothing has been done on that front—but decide that he has enough on his mind. Perhaps there is something I am missing in the way a British renovation has to proceed. As both builder and project manager on this job, he is the expert. I should just step back—like rich people do—and let him do his thing.

Besides, I have my own list of manual jobs. But before I crack on, a bit of brain candy is in order, in the form of mulling over paint swatches for the guest room.

I bound upstairs, walk into the guest room, and—Whoa!

My mother is standing by the window. Her round face turns slowly toward me, lips set in a tight line as she shakes her frothy ash-blond head. Her visit is not completely unexpected: Mom loves a renovation, especially when it gives her an opportunity to second-guess my plans or tut-tut how much I am spending. What is unusual is that she has been dead five years, so to see her standing there is, as you can well imagine, a bit of a surprise.

"You found us!"

"You should know better than to think you can hide from me."

I try not to appear shocked: she has a habit of reading shock as "You are concealing something from me." Since The Husband is not interested in discussing paint colours and decor schemes, and my mother was all about paint colours and decor schemes, I decide to enlist her help.

"I was thinking of taupe for this room, but I cannot seem to settle on the right shade." I bring the paint swatches nearer to her and to the light of the window.

She ignores the swatches. Her dark-brown eyes are narrowed on me, her mouth ready to spring open and unleash a torrent of recrimination. And then: "Is this really the sort of thing two elderly people should be doing?"

"P-P-Pardon?

"You and your husband."

"Who are you calling 'elderly'!"

"You're both senior citizens, and look at you, lugging floor tiles, stripping wallpaper, carrying buckets of rubble to the dumpster like someone half your age. This is not how a lady behaves. You're going to kill yourself. And that garden? When are you going to get around to that mess? It is ridiculous. I cannot believe what you paid for this dump. You have lost your mind, Jane. Honestly, you never learn, do you?"

"Me? What about you? You were moving and renovating up to the day you died. Don't think we didn't notice the notepad you left on your desk that showed you were planning two more moves. And might I just add, you were ninety-three—I am only sixty-three."

"Don't you dare bring my age into this," she snaps. She faces me full on, straightening every inch of her five-foot-two frame. As if that would intimidate my five-foot-six. She was always touchy about her age; it was as off limits as the crown jewels, and as heavily guarded. A few years before she died, I found proof that she had lied about her age, having managed at some early point in her life to alter her birth certificate. When I confronted her about this, she hit the roof, and then she swore me to secrecy. To be on the safe side, she hired a stone mason the next day to carve her fabricated birthdate into the headstone she would eventually share with my father. She justified this speedy action: "Now you only have to add the date of my death." She had said it like she had done me a favour. When she died, I was not sure whether she was eighty-four, eighty-nine, or ninety-three.

Returning to the issue at hand, she says, "Your father and I knew what we were doing when we took on a renovation. We certainly did not spend what you are spending." She pauses and tilts up her chin. "I can tell you that he is as disappointed as I am about this."

Ah, the dad card. Typical Mom. Whenever she wanted to drive home a point, she would throw my father into it, knowing that I took his advice to heart more than I did hers. I avoid the bait.

"That was a different time," I counter, drawing the conversation back to the cost. "Things were cheaper then."

"You have no idea," she says with a sigh of resignation and a slight change of subject. "We worked on those renovations with enthusiasm and a sense of fun. You two have not got a clue. You should be looking into retirement homes and taking it easy. Look at what you're doing to that poor man of yours."

From the guest room window, I observe The Husband in the backyard, sitting in a chair with *The Times* and a mug of coffee. He does not appear to be suffering. My mind swings back to memories of my father's suicide threats, his non-existent DIY skills, his obedience to my mother's whims and plans. I do not ever recall him sitting down with the paper and a coffee during their various renovations. So long as she was around, he was on his feet doing what strength and limited expertise would allow. In the end, it worked out for them: each renovation moved them up the property ladder and up the social scale. But at what personal cost?

During one of their moves—my father's last one, as it turned out—Dad was in the final stages of cancer treatment. He had wanted to move because he did not want to die leaving my mother alone in a country home. He wanted her settled in a town, close to everything. But the move overwhelmed his state of health and mind. The morning after that move, their belongings piled into their new home, my mother was on the phone to me:

"Will you please talk some sense into your father? Honestly, he does not know how to roll with the punches. He's in a state . . ."

And then my father had picked up the extension phone and started railing against "this woman who will not sit still. I have cancer and she moved me!"

"You wanted to move, John. This was your idea . . ."

"I'm sick, Valerie, and I need rest, but everything around me is in chaos, and now you want me to go and look at new bathrooms. I don't know how I'm going to get through this . . ."

"Oh, John, stop being dramatic."

I jumped into the conversation: "Look, I am going to come over right now, okay? See you in a few minutes."

When I arrived, my dad was standing by the front door, wearing his corduroy jacket and a hangdog expression. Poor guy. He put up with so much without hardly raising his voice, hardly a complaint. Now he was dying, and still there was not any rest for the man. My mother, meanwhile, was in the kitchen making a list. (Writing that sentence tells me exactly which parent I turned into.) I looked at the teetering piles of boxes and furniture piled to the ceiling. Gosh, so much stuff. My mother's idea of de-cluttering was to take a few things to a charity shop, and then hit the shops immediately to restock.

They left to do their various errands, and I stood amid the mountain of boxes and mess and wished I had a magic wand. I wanted to sprinkle serenity on their lives; I wanted to be the fixer so they would be proud of me; I wanted to cure my father's cancer.

Two hours later, seventy-five boxes of books had been sprung from their confines and decanted onto the bookshelves in the den, and most of the furniture had been arranged.

"Who helped you?" my parents asked with amazement when they returned home.

I felt a pinch of pride, but also of irritation: What else did they expect given all the times we moved house? Where else would I have learned the art of the quick unpack-and-organize?

To my friends, my mother was sweet, sharp, and a fascinating conversationalist. To me, she was all that plus talented and decisive. But she was also feisty and unforgiving. I feared her every day she was alive.

I desperately wanted to love her, but she made little room for me in her world. Instead, I was her never-ending renovation project. When her gaze landed on me, she would critique me like a room: "That hair needs to come up about four inches, just pooling around the shoulders. And it needs some colour, some brightening. That complexion—so dark. You must stay out of the sun or people will mistake you for a . . ." I refuse to write the word. "Those legs of yours—keep them straight or you'll end up looking like a Duncan Phyfe sofa." When her eyes fell on my bitten nails, "like chipped china," she would sigh and shake her head at the lost cause that was her daughter. "You better do well at school, because you will not get anywhere with those looks."

I was the one renovation project that never lived up to her abilities. When I was fifteen, she booked me in for a nose job. The kids at school had taken to calling me "Ringo" and "Jew girl," and my mother felt that surgery was the only way to stop the taunts. There were no words at home to soothe me; to tell me that the kids were idiots, and that my nose was just fine. No, I was the flaw that needed fixing. My mother made such a compelling case for the nose job that by then, even I wanted it. I prayed that the post-op transformation would finally make me acceptable and interesting to her, but once the bandages came off all it did was consign me to a life of fretting about my appearance and equating acceptance with attractiveness. Decades later, I saw the movie *The Hours*. The prosthetic nose Nicole Kidman wears in her portrayal of Virginia Woolf was exactly my old nose, and I desperately wished I had it back. It would have better suited my personality and face shape than did the streamlined version my mother drew for the surgeon.

I have come to understand that my mother's fixation with renovating was, in part, an effort to conceal defects that no amount of French polish could disguise. She disliked her appearance; complained about her weight while refusing to forgo the food, drink, and snacks that contributed to it. She deflected attention from her girth by turning a critical eye on others, mainly me. When she found her forte—old houses, the more decrepit the better—she discovered that it was easier to transform a wreck of a house than a wreck of a waistline. She could walk into a ruin and immediately envision its glorious restoration. She became a whiz at transforming property and decorating it to magazine standards.

I once enlisted her opinion of a condo I wanted to buy. It was the last property I owned in Hamilton. My youngest was in her last year of university and would be moving out soon. This was to be my scaled-down home after the Herkimer house.

The three of us walked into the flat. I was almost embarrassed to show it to them. It had been inhabited by an elderly couple for thirty years. The walls and ceilings were yellowed from decades of cigarette smoke; the dirty rose carpet in the living room had a black circular stain that looked like the result of spontaneous human combustion. Dated, chipped melamine cabinets hung from the kitchen wall. The bathroom had pink fixtures and a mobility frame over the toilet. But the windows in the main space were huge and lent themselves to the open-plan layout with a panoramic view of the city.

My mother took one look and said, "Buy it."

"Seriously?"

"Sure it's a dump right now, but you'll do wonders to it once you fix it up."

That she had faith in my renovation and decorating abilities was the biggest compliment she gave me. She was never fazed by my house moves or that I moved a lot. In fact, my moves allowed her to decant her excess furniture into my usually larger space without the finality of parting with her treasures. She would boast to friends, "Jane has so much of my stuff that I always feel at home when I visit her."

It is sad that she and I had such a thorny relationship. How wonderful it would have been had the two of us gone into some aspect of the design or property business together. I would have learned so much more from her. As it was, I gleaned some knowledge from her, but mostly I gained her restlessness, the striving for perfection, for "the right house."

I had a chance of ridding myself of that acquisitive lifestyle not so long ago when I considered becoming a nun. I had quit my day job, and sudden retirement had opened a field of glorious options. To be a nun, to devote myself mind, body, and soul to something much greater than moving, renovating, and decorating, was tantalizing. I moved from convent to convent in a gyratory state; seeking a place for my soul to settle, and a place to renounce my chattels and possessions. But I was not cut out to be a nun, and from the perspective of this current renovation, religious life would have been an almost unbearable freedom. I am not sure I could have coped.

I revisit my mother's remark about me and The Husband being "elderly." What a shitty thing to say. Granted, I can no longer clamber up a ladder as fearlessly as I once did, and yes, hauling porcelain tiles and bags of cement is hell on my knees. Whenever we help Francis unload tools and equipment from his van, I feel a lacerating pain in my shoulders and my back. Nor can I grip a screwdriver as firmly as I could once, or put enough strength behind the action to loosen a stubborn screw. I hate this ageing thing. But I can still wield a sledgehammer and strip wallpaper. What's more, my body feels stronger. At some point each day my quads, delts, blades, and pecs are on fire, in a good way. Eight months earlier an arthritis-like affliction crippled my knees and I could barely walk, but the pain has entirely disappeared. Was I now tempting fate? Was I pushing The Husband or myself toward injury? Or a heart attack? Was I endangering our lives? Our marriage? All for a stupid house?

"Well, I'm already committed to this," I say to Mom. "I can hardly bail out now."

Turning my gaze from the window toward her, I brace myself for her reply, but she is gone.

16

The Neighbours

"Wow! What did you have for breakfast?"

Francis and The Husband watch, slack jawed, as I shovel rubble from the kitchen floor into a bucket at a furious pace. I am like a machine. It takes me back to my steel-toe-boot days on Stanley Avenue. I wonder why I never thought to buy a pair for this job.

So to what do I owe this gratifying spurt of energy? Is it sheer determination? Or am I trying to make a point that I still have it; that I am not some weak old biddy, as my mother has suggested; that I am a force with which to be reckoned? I have already noticed, not with any amount of pride, that my biceps are bigger than my husband's. That said, I know he has physical strength: I have challenged him from time to time to an arm wrestle and he always wins. No, this is just one of those moments when I am overcome with an almost ferocious energy.

Francis has made quick work of gutting the kitchen and the interior walls that once held the utility room and bathroom. This is the last bit of wall to come down. He is a one-man operation, and we are his dogsbodies, working to save money and time. He demolishes—we clear. We shovel brick and concrete rubble into the plastic recycling boxes and a wheelie bin used for weekly garbage pickup, and drag or roll them out of the kitchen, down the hallway, out the front door, where we hoist them into the skip in front of our house and tip out the contents. As hard and dirty as the work is, I give thanks that at sixty-three I have the physical capability to do it.

I also give thanks that Francis is the type of worker who puts down his tools each day at 4:30. The noise level from our renovation makes me cringe with embarrassment each time a concrete saw or a power drill is turned on. I want to holler to the neighbourhood "SORRY!," but then, no one would hear me above the din. These Victorian terraces do not hold noise well.

Unless you know someone who already lives on the street you're moving to and can provide you with the local gossip, your new neighbourhood is a total crapshoot. Who knows what person lives behind number fifteen, or whether that unkempt house four doors down is home to a friendly pensioner or to a young family whose father just walked out the door and out of their lives the previous week? I remember a time—and surely it exists somewhere still—where a few neighbours would pop over on moving-in day, introduce themselves, offer assistance, or an invitation to supper. It is a different and more wary world now.

Before the renovation began, we put notes through the mail slots of our neighbours on either side of us to introduce ourselves and to apologize in advance for the disruption. So far, everyone is incredibly tolerant. No one seems to mind the bone-numbing noise inside our house, nor the rumble of lorries delivering tiles, windows, doors, bathroom fittings, and kitchen cabinets, nor the disruption of traffic it causes, nor the fact that our tradespeople take up at least two valuable parking spaces on a street that has only on-street parking. Instead, they smile and wave when they see us hauling another load to the skip. A few of them have wandered over to introduce themselves. No one mentions the noise and disruption except us: we raise the issue and apologize for it at every opportunity. They do not ask what we are doing, nor do they ask to see the work in progress. They usually ask where we are from, or if our plan is to fix up the house and sell it on. No, we assure them, this is to be our home. The Husband and I no longer look at one another for confirmation when we say it.

Cynthia, a Jamaican woman who lives in the house on one side of us, sees me weeding the courtyard in front of our home this morning and has come out to introduce herself.

I leap to my feet, stretch out my hand, and blurt apologies.

"Oh, don't you worry about the noise. It has to be done."

She has an aura of gentleness and kindness. She will be a good neighbour.

"The noisy stuff should be done in two weeks," I say with fingers crossed behind my back.

"However long it takes," she says in an unconcerned way. "Just don't worry."

I dig into the garden and pull out a few raggedy plants. I have already retrieved the small evergreens and replanted them in the backyard.

"You must be a good gardener," says Cynthia, eyeing my work.

"Actually, I do not know a thing about gardening, but I think I know weeds when I see them. Do you like to garden?"

She laughs. "I probably know less about it than you do. I have no interest in gardening, but I appreciate the gardens of other people."

Nodding at her neat front courtyard, I promise her that we will not be one of those people who keep a rubbishy front yard.

"Yes," she says, looking worriedly up the street. "I do not know how some people can be so untidy."

I long to ask her about the former owner of our house, but there is no gentle way into it without appearing nosy. I am keen to find out what sort of person he was—how old he was, if he had lived in the house a long time, whether he was a considerate neighbour. All we know is what the estate agent told us: that he had fallen ill and had been taken into care.

With the few plants I have salvaged from the front garden, I say cheerio to Cynthia and take the plants to the backyard for transplanting.

The Husband is already there, rake in hand, bravely attempting to make things look more presentable. Seeing me, he smiles and nods toward the opposite corner of the yard, where something unexpectedly lovely has cascaded into our patch. A jasmine bush. Its roots are in a neighbouring backyard—I cannot ascertain which one—but the plant has obviously grown to such a size that a considerable amount of it has flopped over the back fence, sinuous branches migrating across its breadth, star-shaped white blossoms standing out like constellations against a bottle-green galaxy. I make a beeline for it and plant my face in it. The scent is beyond heavenly. It is difficult to be upset about anything when you are surrounded by the scent of jasmine. The heady fragrance takes me back to when we encountered jasmine-lined streets during a holiday in Sorrento, before we were married, when the furthest thing from our thoughts (well, his, anyway) was renovating and moving. It seems like an eon, yet it was probably only four years ago. The Husband and I smile at one another, both of us for a moment connected to a pleasant shared memory.

Of all the plants we put into our garden back in Brixham the one we wished we had been able to bring with us was the jasmine tree, so this immense bush spilling over the fence is a gift: an unexpected housewarming; something to smooth our jagged dissatisfaction.

Together, we silently attack the brambles and tangle of vines in our new backyard. The two of us. A shared purpose, and one in which we have equal skill; that is to say, not much of it: neither of us has any expertise when it comes to gardening.

In the midst of our labours we hear the kitchen door open from the house on the other side of us, and a woman comes out. I look up to offer a neighbourly greeting, but she beats me to it, and comes bounding toward us with "Hi! It's transformed already."

All we have done is pull up weeds, shift the pile of debris into a somewhat neater pile, and placed two garden chairs in a corner. When that is all it takes to be called "transformed," it makes you wonder just how low the gardening bar is set in the neighbourhood.

We introduce ourselves and return the compliment. Her garden is a bohemian paradise. Apple, fig, pear, and cherry trees crammed into a small space, yet all of them thriving along with a couple of small raised garden beds that sprout rows of veg. A flea market table and chairs, a couple of garden ornaments; I would be entirely content with that.

"We love your garden," I say. "You must be a natural."

"Nah, I just putter and do what I can. I'm Ali, by the way. Are you getting rid of those old iron fences?"

I detect a New Zealand accent. I wonder if she and I will become friends.

"I am keeping the rusted ones, but you can have this gate."

"Sure," she enthuses.

The Husband and I carry it toward her. It weighs a ton, and we stumble and struggle to lift it over the boundary wall. Ali makes no attempt to help despite the fact that she is probably a good twenty years younger than either of us.

As if reading my mind, she says, "I have fibromyalgia. Very limited strength."

We manoeuvre it through her yard and position it where she wants it.

The Husband has a habit of gravitating toward people who are ill and weak. He loves a patient. He asks if there is anything else he can move for her. Suddenly, he is Mr. Handy.

"Yeah. Can you move that pot for me?"

While he does that, I apologize about the noise from the renovation.

"It's okay. Can imagine there's a lot to do."

"Yes, the house was in pretty bad condition."

Ali goes silent; looks at the ground.

Have I said something wrong? Have I inadvertently injected my standards into the conversation? After all, "bad condition" is a subjective term. I backpedal in an attempt to shift and restore the conversation away from any hint of insult: "It must be strange for you to have new neighbours. Shame about the former owner."

She raises her eyes; regards me warily.

"We understand," I continue cautiously, glancing at The Husband for support, "that he went into care. Had he been ill for long?"

Ali's eyes widen with incredulity. Her face goes scarlet; her voice rears up and explodes in an exhale of frustrated apoplexy as though it has been waiting an age to be released and has finally been granted permission: "Gone into care? Is that what they told you? That he went into care?"

We tense up and wait for the hammer to fall.

"He did not go into care. He went to prison!"

What?

"He was a nightmare!" Her words now gush forth in a waterfall of anger. "A major druggie. He'd have parties lasting three days. Loud music at all hours of the day and night. People coming and going. Police raids. It's been awful."

The Husband and I let that sink in as the dozen ephemeral pieces flutter into place: the imprint of a battering ram on the front door; the disturbed, careless atmosphere of the house; why nothing has been maintained; the strange locks on the windows.

It also explains the neighbourly goodwill. Like Dorothy, we have dispatched the Wicked Witch of the West without realizing it. A neighbourhood hellion can be a headache, bullying with their menacing attitude, putting everyone in a state of paralyzed annoyance. When our new neighbours venture over to shake our hands, it is as much a congratulation as it is a welcome. Who would not trade the havoc created by a pusher and a regular police presence for the temporary sound of power drills and nail guns?

17

The Wake-up Call

There is something startling, almost spiritual, when a book falls into your hands at the perfect moment, lifting your cares just when you feel your world is ending; materializing like a lighthouse beacon to shepherd you through that stormy patch to a new understanding or attitude. A book that patiently waits to present itself at precisely the right time, right place.

It is even more remarkable when the book in question is one you have avoided despite persistent recommendations from friends and strangers. I have had this experience with a few books. One of them was Ernest Hemingway's *A Moveable Feast*. Sure, I was intrigued by the book's title but not necessarily by Hemingway. Or by Paris. In fact, I held an almost hostile disdain for Paris, privately rolling my eyes when someone gushed about that city. My lack of interest in Hemingway and Paris were firmly intact when I agreed to go to Paris with a friend. She had once lived there, and she wanted to make a return visit but did not want to go alone. As soon as I told people that I was going to Paris, it was as if a concerted campaign had been organized to force a copy of *A Moveable Feast* into my hands. Everyone and their aunt from St. Denis were recommending it.

"You must read *A Moveable Feast*," they said.

My forced smile did not deter them.

"But you're a journalist and an author. You have to read it!"

Make me, I glared silently.

I endured this assault for months, right up to the day of departure. Strangers in the lineup to board the Eurostar to Paris urged it on me, practically shoved the thing down my throat as if under a financial obligation or incentive to do so. Each time I said that I had never read *A Moveable Feast*, they cried, "You must!" My private reply was *Je refuse*.

By the time my friend and I arrived at our Paris digs, an apartment lent to us by friends of hers, we were soaked to the skin from the rain, and in a thunderous temper to match. I threw off my wet clothes and, while trying to warm myself up, sulkily gravitated toward the living room bookshelves. There, sitting with Gallic insouciance, was *A Moveable Feast*.

"For crying out loud!" I petulantly grabbed the paperback off the shelf and opened it to the first page, muttering, "I hate you already." But within a minute it had me under its spell. From the remark about the rain (it was pouring at that very moment!) to the setting of the book (Hemingway was writing about the very neighbourhood in which we were staying!), it felt as if the book were meant for me. It did not leave my hands until I had gobbled up every sentence, and until I had conducted a pilgrimage to every place it referenced. My love for Paris has since become boundless.

During the renovation of this English home not one but two books land in my lap. I am desperate for my mind to be hijacked from decisions about budgets and floor tiles and relocating gas meters, boilers, and electrical panels. So, while grocery shopping in Sainsbury's, I impulsively pick up *Birdcage Walk* by Helen Dunmore. The book is set in Bristol, albeit in an earlier century, and Dunmore herself was a Bristolian, and I reason that it might acclimatize me to this new city that we will call home.

One of the novel's central characters, John Diner Tredevant, is a master builder who has invested all he has in the construction of a row of terraced homes. It is 1792, and his financial success is unexpectedly threatened by France's fomenting revolution and the political uncertainty it casts among British homebuyers. Shades of the Brexit landscape, I think. What anchors my attention is Tredevant's obsession with housing, and how home-buying and home-building fantasies can so easily lead to madness. I clearly see his folly, can even feel his folly, but I cannot decide if my sympathies are with him and his desire to realize his creative talents and reap the financial benefits for his family, or with his long-suffering wife, who has little option but to stand by passively and witness his self-destruction.

Where do I fit into this? Have I become as home obsessed as Tredevant? Like him, I have invested every dime I have renovating this English home. Is that prudent or foolish? If Tredevant had lived today would he, too, be trolling Rightmove and Zoopla?

BEFORE THE SECOND BOOK FALLS serendipitously into my hands, a devastation beyond belief occurs: The Husband and I wake up on the morning of June 14 to news that a fire has destroyed a twenty-four-storey apartment block in London. Much later, it will be reported that seventy-two people have died and more than two hundred families have lost their homes and belongings.

When the first pictures appear on the TV, I think terrorist attack. But then the cause is revealed, and it strikes me as equally horrific. Lives have been lost because someone cut corners on the procurement of materials; someone manufactured faulty, immensely flammable cladding; building standards and regulations were overlooked and ignored despite constant complaints and warnings by residents. That bright, energetic people have been the sacrificial victims on the altar of arrogance, have paid with their lives the price of snubbed advice, is almost too awful to believe. That the manufacturing of flammable building components is likely continuing and being applied to other buildings fills me with terror.

Hour after hour, night after night, the news blurts new horrors; points fingers at new suspects; defines the sharper, ever-widening parallel lines of distinction between race and class that exist in Britain. Confronting their leaders and demanding answers and restitution, survivors and supporters are rabid with accusations, frothing at the bureaucratically crafted key messages, baying and howling with their discomfiting grief. Politicians and royalty pay their respects, and the degree of their compassion and action is parsed and scrutinized. Everyone is a potential accessory to the crime. From every angle it is a catastrophe, but the question no one immediately homes in on is this: Who made the flammable material in the first place, and why are they not being held to account? Blame the council, yes, but is it not just as crucial to go after the manufacturers?

How much of a home is flammable? A large percentage. Lighter building materials, more petroleum-based products and materials, open-plan layouts—they all contribute to an efficient cocktail for destruction when fire strikes. It can take just three to five minutes for a room to get hot enough to burst into flames.

Why, in this post-millennial era, have we not developed safer materials? Or if they exist, why does no one see fit to apply them to new builds or to existing buildings being retrofitted? How does stuff like this escape building code when the relative safety of something like an electrical socket in a bathroom is deemed beyond the pale?

Of course, we know why. Cost.

What can be more terrifying than the loss of life in what is supposed to be a person's safest refuge—their home? What else but manslaughter can you call the negligence of a builder who installs dangerous materials in your home? Those who survived the Grenfell Tower fire have lost family, friends, neighbours, classmates. They have also lost their sanctuaries, along with all the totems and treasures, large and small, that animated their souls, their personalities.

When you think of it, humankind has not progressed much further than sticks and stones when it comes to building houses. We are more concerned with how the house looks, how streamlined its kitchen, how opulent and high-tech the fittings and fixtures. We are more focused on the visual design than on the safety of the fundamental building blocks. We tut-tut about life being cheap in so-called Third World countries, but First World countries are just as guilty.

The Grenfell Tower fire takes the air out of my ballooning aspirations. The petty things I am stressing over—how to surmount bureaucratic hoops and lingo to get our electric and gas meters moved, choosing bathroom fixtures, wondering how much the kitchen cabinets will cost—now feel like a guilty pleasure. None of it is as pressing as it was a few days ago. What replaces it is an awareness of how fortunate we are just to have a home. I suddenly feel as rich as if I belong to the 1 percent.

Walking through clouds of construction dust, I take a more practical, less materialistic, view of our home. I consider stopping the build, cleaning up the site, and moving in, adapting to what we have. At least the roof is watertight; we can make do. The words of *Birdcage Walk*'s narrator, Lizzie Fawkes, return to haunt me: "Our houses are palaces to those who have none."

A week later, I begin reading a second book, *The Forsyte Saga*. As with *A Moveable Feast*, I had no previous interest in this series of novels, nor did I watch the television adaptation. When I spied the slim, faded-green-leather volumes sitting in a curbside box, I dithered over whether to take them. I had, after all, committed myself to weeding our possessions, not adding to them. But books—ah, such a weakness. I picked up one of the volumes and thumbed its brittle, yellowed pages. The books were small; pocket sized, really. And free. Under such conditions it is easy to yield to temptation.

I always thought *The Forsyte Saga* was about a family, but it is actually about a house, about avaricious attitudes toward property (not just houses, but also art, women, and relationships), and about how possession warps and entangles in spite of our delusion that it does not. It is about the dreams we load into a home in the wishful belief that the home will transform our life, our marriage, our outlook on the world.

After reading a few chapters I shift uncomfortably in my chair. The snobby, ungracious, competitive Forsyte men, descended from farmers, have evolved into "men of property"; men whose whims and desires are sated with a flourish of their chequebook; men who are all about possession. As Young Jolyon says, "We are, of course, all of us the slaves of property, and I admit that it's a question of degree, but what I call a 'Forsyte' is a man who is decidedly more than less a slave of property. He knows a good thing, he knows a safe thing, and his grip on property—it doesn't matter whether it be wives, houses, money, or reputation—is his hallmark."

I wholly lacked the wealth and social stature of the fictional For-sytes, but I was as guilty of self-satisfaction and possession as them, as contemptuous of the overreaching lifestyles and pretensions of others while simultaneously courting them for myself. The Husband and I had bought a house in a middle-class, inner-city neighbourhood, and here I was dumping all my financial resources into a dream of trans-forming it, and by extension us, into a grander version. Was it right?

In the same way that I feel awkward sitting in a café with a cup of tea on the site where a horrific battle was fought, where hundreds were slaughtered in previous centuries, here I was, in a house for-merly occupied by poor working-class people, ordering a bathroom vanity that would have put food on their table for at least three years. Yes, times change and economics change, but I am nonetheless sensi-tive to how we blunder in and plaster over the lives of our ancestors.

Is there such a thing as a poor neighbourhood anymore or is it an abstraction? Today's lower-class neighbourhood is tomorrow's million-dollar des res.

This thought is slopping around my mind when I see next-door neighbour Ali puttering in her garden. I wave to her and call out hello. She turns on her heel and stomps back into her house, slam-ming her kitchen door.

Ouch. She had been so friendly up until now. Is our noisy renova-tion getting to her?

An hour later, The Husband comes in the front door, having returned from the umpteenth visit to the recycling centre. He looks at me accusingly.

"Did you say something to Ali?"

When something bad happens, The Husband tends to see me as

the instigator. He has a habit of saying, whenever I leave the house, even when I am going to church, "Don't start any fights." Now he thinks I have offended our neighbour.

"Why is it always my fault?" I ask.

"Well, she had the look of thunder about her. I said hello, and she ignored me."

"And that is somehow my doing?"

I am this close to snapping. Am I expected to carry this renovation as well as carry the blame for some stranger's change of mood? However, I draw back my indignation in case my words boomerang and hit me. The delicate mood that exists between The Husband and me has been hard won, and I do not want to upset it. Those renovation stats about divorce are never far from my thoughts.

Instead, I say, "Maybe the noise is getting to her." I suggest a modified Clooney manoeuvre. (George Clooney reportedly appeased neighbours during his home renovation with a £45,000 package that included a holiday in Corfu, a six-week stay in a luxury hotel, a whack of cash, and a new vacuum cleaner.) Our version would be a restaurant voucher.

"The offer of dinner might set a dangerous precedent," says The Husband.

We mull over other possible options of compensation as we trudge upstairs to continue painting the master bedroom.

The bedroom windows face the street, and they are open. As we pour paint into our trays and prime our rollers, Ali's voice reaches our ears. She is speaking angrily to someone out front. We edge closer to the window to listen.

"I'm being evicted," she announces bitterly to a neighbour who has sauntered by.

The Husband and I exchange looks of surprise and simultaneously mouth, Why?

Ali continues her rant: "Been living here for eight years, and now the owner tells me to look for someplace else to live, and to be out by October. She's decided to sell the house."

We look at one another again, nod and grimace understanding.

"There's no place to rent around here anymore," Ali continues. "This is what's changing the neighbourhood, and it's not good. Where will us renters live? These people next door [she cocks her thumb at our house, and our bodies reflexively reel back]—they move from nowhere and buy here, then tart it up. Wouldn't be surprised if they flipped it. It's just greed, you know? And now I'm being evicted because of gentrification."

So that explains the sudden coolness: we have gone from being the saviour Dorothy jettisoning the Wicked Neighbour of Easton to being the ugly face of gentrified boomers with indexed pension plans and cash inheritances.

At first, I feel guilty—we both do—but then my spine straightens. I am not having it. Blaming older people for the lack of affordable rental housing is a cheap, self-serving excuse. We are not the cause of the housing crisis; even the government is not directly to blame, though it absolutely needs to apply some teeth to stop developers from land banking on an industrial scale. What about those people who bank their homes: who purchase a home—or multiple homes—and leave them empty and derelict without developing them or fixing them up, figuring that if they wait long enough, they will double—maybe even triple—their money without lifting a finger? Those are the pariahs: the people who knowingly hold property in abeyance without the decency of at least tenanting the digs. What about the developers who promise to build three hundred homes but sit on the land, redraw the plans, scrimp on materials and fixtures, and fabricate delays by waiting for council to reapprove the changes and green-light the revised project?

We of the rank-and-file class are at the mercy of a minority of super wealthy people who are manipulating the housing market for their sole gain, and their actions, along with the general state of the world's economies and shifting power structures, have made it ridiculously difficult for young people and young families to buy a home. As the mother of young adults I am acutely aware of this. But it is also true that we have not put up a vigorous enough fight against consumerism and the ancillary cultural bullying that sees so many people spending their paycheques on two or three takeout coffees a day, gym memberships, cell phones and all manner of electronic gadgets that are upgraded with alarming regularity, luxury holidays, cars, expensive clothes, frequent dinners out, concerts, and sports tickets. Consumer-directed pressure and temptation have ensnared us, and the unfortunate victims of this are young people. Add the escalating costs of post-secondary education, and it's no wonder they are unable to save for a house. There should be laws against such aggressive and financially punitive marketing, because that is the only way we are going to help young people get on the property ladder.

But vilifying older people? Are we supposed to apologize for living longer? For being healthier? Are we supposed to stop being upwardly mobile and shuffle into some squalid flat? Screw that.

In the meantime, guilt stalks The Husband and me. When yet another delivery truck idles in front of our house, its high-pitched safety alarms alerting the neighbourhood, we cringe. When smart-dressed salesmen toting showroom sample cases show up at our house, we hustle them inside before they have time to knock on the door.

Renovation guilt is new to me, and it is hard not to take a defensive attitude. Neither The Husband nor I came to home ownership easily: we both worked from a young age and saved for a down payment. If we were now able to afford a crappy house in a poor neighbourhood—and bear in mind we have paid £300,000 plus for the privilege—then why should we not be allowed to fix it up to our comfort?

Were we supposed to live with dodgy electrical wiring? Inconvenient plumbing? With kitchen appliances that are old and possibly unsafe? It is not like we are digging out the basement and installing a cinema or swimming pool and gilding the window frames in gold leaf. I know I am part of a privileged class, but we have reached the point in our social history where the word *privileged* does not mean someone with a racing yacht or a Lamborghini; it simply means someone who can afford a home. I find that both humbling and frightening.

Despite Easton being considered a "deprived area" of Bristol, there are ample signs of change in the air. Every street, including ours, has at least one house encased in scaffolding for loft conversions, and there are skips outside dozens of homes as interior renovations are undertaken. Everyone is either renovating or capitalizing on the overheated housing market and selling up. But every neighbourhood with a social conscience should also make provisions for those unable to afford a home. There should be attractive affordable housing for people, and if not, then there should be more opportunities to help people get on the property ladder: schemes such as offering people of lesser means the chance to purchase derelict properties, with the proviso of additional grants or funds to enable them to renovate them in exchange for some sweat equity. It would be a step toward getting rid of areas of squalor and, more important, giving people pride of ownership.

Gentrification should not be looked upon as a crime; it is the bellwether of prosperity and aspiration. If a nation or a neighbourhood does not aspire to something higher than itself—whether materially or spiritually—then the economy flat-lines and takes everyone with it. If you are poor and your attitude is "Well, so what; let's all be poor," you do humanity a huge disservice by dousing ambition and advocating a cheerless baseline. A level playing field does not make everyone happy and leaves everyone miserable. Frankly, I do not want to be around lazy, unambitious people. There is nothing evil in trying to be better, in trying to do better. If Ali's landlord sees an opportunity to sell her house and turn a profit, then good on her. It frees up another house; gives someone else a toehold on the property ladder, someone who can begin to experience stability, reap equity.

Gosh, I sound like a proper Forsyte.

18

The Tea Station

When you hear of the British fondness for tea, it sounds like a charming, quaint cliché, until you actually live in England and witness the addiction—I mean, the affection—for tea. Everything stops for tea. Absolutely everything. You cannot go fifty feet in this country without encountering a café, and if you are undertaking renovations on your home, there is a tacit understanding that you will provide a tea station for your workers. No loos, thank you; just a tea station.

In North America, tradesmen show up with a Thermos, or nip out to Tim Horton's for their fix, but in Britain, workers expect tea to run like a continuous morphine drip.

It drives me crazy, and I refuse to be a party to it. I have enough on my mind what with the manual labour and stressing about the renovation costs.

The Husband stresses about the renovation costs, too, but being English he knows the crucial importance of tea in his homeland. He duly sets up a tea station and makes sure that we are completely equipped for service.

If the national grid does a forensic examination of our energy consumption during this period, it will reveal that our kettle is on virtually continuous boil. Grow-ops use less energy. It is one of the things that gets my goat about Britain, this apparently constant need for tea, especially among those in the building trades. I suppose that since we are on-site and therefore available to facilitate this tradition, the blame is ours. I know it is a gesture of hospitality, and indeed I greet each worker each morning with a steaming mug of java, but it is the covert expectation of follow-up injections of caffeine that brings my patience to a boil. If I hear one more time the phrase "This is thirsty work"—the backhanded cue for you to offer the person tea—I will scream. I do not begrudge workers who want to make a tea or coffee for themselves—the tea station has been set up for that purpose so they can perform their rituals whenever they want—but tea delivered every hour or so?

The Husband, however, is the kindest of men. He is a person of courtly hospitality, and this bugs me only because I am not. He is forever asking Francis and anyone who happens to walk through our door whether they want tea, or a top-up. I try to explain to him that we have no running water, no toilet; that our electrical system is but a rudimentary bar of sockets rigged up by Mark, the electrician. It does not deter him. I say that we have enough to do at the house without our time being sucked up by making tea. He ignores me and goes about his duties. I half expect him to don a pinny and a cap and wheel a small trolley from tradesman to tradesman. When he asks me

"Would you like a tea?" a bite of irritation accompanies my answer: "No, thanks. I am perfectly capable of getting through an entire day without one." Unlike your countrymen, my inner voice adds.

As the renovation progresses, I soften when the bigger picture looms into focus: The Husband has never strapped on a tool belt, never attempted a DIY project. He possesses no skill or aptitude for any trade, nor does he possess an inclination or desire to learn. He refuses to make a single decision about any aspect of a renovation. And that, I have surmised, is not due to truculence but to fear: he is fearful of making a mistake.

Whereas I will gamely blunder in with a stupid amount of confidence and the barest of knowledge to tackle a situation regardless of how foolish I might appear, The Husband is fully cognizant of his abilities and does not need to worry about looking foolish. What he can do, what he is good at and comfortable doing, is making tea, and that is the role he has created for himself.

Having sussed out his area of expertise, he takes on the task with diligence and proprietary attention: he is tea maker to the trades. He does make a lovely cuppa. Susie, an American friend, insists that The Husband makes the best cup of tea anywhere. As burly men stomp around in their steel-toed boots, thumbs hooked in the loops of tool belts slung low on their hips like cowboy holsters, The Husband— trim, genteel, always well groomed—clasps his hands and asks, "Would you like a cup of tea? A biscuit, perhaps?"

So far, we have gone through a giant box of tea bags, two big jars of instant coffee, and innumerable packages of chocolate digestives. When Francis arrived one morning with a jar of his own coffee, The Husband went to the shops to find the same brand, and now makes certain that it is always available at our house. He is that attentive a host. When we were courting and I would visit him in London, he always made sure my favourite foods were in the fridge and that there was peony-scented soap in the bathroom, remembering how much I love peonies.

While I have come around to The Husband's tea-making pro-clivities, and find them endearing, I am getting frustrated by his lack of heavy lifting. When lorries arrive and unload supplies, he always seems to be in the middle of making tea, so it falls to me to deal with delivery drivers, to help move the goods into our front garden, and to carry them into the house. Granted, I know this renovation territory—I have done this countless of times: I wear construction dust like a second skin. But I am feeling like the guy in our relationship, and that does not please me. I worry that the neighbours might think I am a bit butch, and who would blame them? My legs show muscular definition; my gait has turned from its usual bounce to a slight swagger; I have begun to check my jawline in the mirror for signs of five o'clock shadow.

Perhaps it is time to sit down and chill. Perhaps I need a cup of tea.

19

The Worrier-in-Chief

We begin to unravel, but damned if I can work out which of us is in worse condition. I have no sense of what psychosis is brewing in The Husband's head, but if it has any resemblance to what is going on in mine, it might very well need to be flushed through with a strong course of shock therapy.

My head currently exists in three different but parallel universes, careening from extended-version memories of my past homes, to thinking about this current one, to pretending that I am part of a reality TV version of a renovation project. If these three strands should overlap, they risk causing the sort of end-of-days disaster that figures in *Star Wars* when the beams from the lightsabres inadvertently cross. I most definitely do not feel like a Jedi knight, and the only Force that surrounds me is the one draining our bank account.

These strands must be harnessed before they collide and do me in, but they cannot be completely eliminated: all of them are competing for time right now, and I must respect their process. Memories and imagination have needs, too, and require an opportunity for healthy venting.

To manage them, I assign to each a specific time of the day or the undertaking of a specific task where they can go off leash. For instance, when I clear rubble or engage in an activity that requires cleaning, I give my mind over to revisiting past renovations and homes. When we are in the car driving back to our rental home at the end of the day I focus on this new home, on what has been accomplished during the day, what needs my attention for work to proceed tomorrow, and what needs to be ordered for the work ahead of that. It is all on copious notes stuffed into various labelled-by-room file slots of a red-leather portfolio I carry around. It sounds very organized, but in fact my most crucial notes are contained in a single notebook, while the file slots hold the easy stuff: paint and fabric swatches, along with rough pencil sketches of what each room is to look like when it is finished. If it ever gets finished.

The third strand, of pretending I am participating in a reality TV renovation, is saved for brief moments of downtime when I am at the house, wandering from room to room and talking to myself or explaining my grand plans to an imaginary camera. I must admit, my on-camera commentary is impressive. Once you set aside the wild, dust-streaked hair and the wardrobe that looks like it was fished from the bottom of a dumpster, my delivery has a calm, decisive assurance. I can smoothly articulate the methodical progress of what has been done and what needs to be done, and I can wax lyrical about the products and the design aesthetic I have chosen, but as soon as the metaphorical camera is turned off, chaotic reality rushes back in, and I am as articulate as Porky Pig: "Abedi, abedi, abedi, that's all folks!"

It is getting to me, this renovation. I feel swamped by its magnitude, and the way it incrementally diminishes the control I have of it. Or was that a fantasy?

Francis has the role of project manager, but my confidence in him is waning. He has made a couple of sloppy and costly blunders. The Velux skylights planned for the far end of the kitchen—the ones that were supposed to give the room the wow factor—have arrived, but they do not fit. Francis erred on his measurements. Norm from *This Old House* would not be impressed. Getting them to fit will mean taking the roof apart and reconstructing it at a cost of £15,000. No, thanks. Just plasterboard and paint the ceiling, I say. And since it was his mistake, I tell him he will have to swallow the cost of the Veluxes. (A few weeks later, he will try to sneak in an extra £4,000 on an invoice he sends me. When I catch this, he will be over-apologetic and blame his calculator.)

He has not made a move on the bathroom or indicated a schedule or time frame. With jocular confidence he says our house will be ready in plenty of time for our move-in date, which is five weeks away. I have already given notice to the landlord back at our Little Britain rental.

"All that's left is to plaster the kitchen, which will be done tomorrow, and then Pedro, the tiler, arrives Thursday to do the floor. After that it's a matter of installing the kitchen cabinets, which are being delivered today, and painting. You still want white, right?"

Yes, I say. White walls. White is the default choice of the undecided, but after the darkness in our Brixham house I want this home to be bright, and you do not get brighter than white.

"And the bathroom?" I ask.

"It'll get done," he says. "Paul [the plumber] is super busy right now and his wife's expecting, so we just have to wait till he's available. But after Pedro does the kitchen floor, I'll get him to do the bathroom tiles."

I move outside to take a call from Mark, the electrician. He has rewired the upstairs and roughed in the main floor. He is waiting for Francis to get the plasterer in to do his work so that the electrics can be finished. I can tell he is getting impatient.

The next day Mark drops by in the hope that a renovation fairy has flown in and magically done the plastering.

We still have not heard from the gas company about moving the gas panel, or from the energy utility about moving the electrical panel. Mark "knows a guy" who can move the electrical panel for half the cost of what the utility supplier will charge us. But The Husband, who reads the fine print on everything, who requires written and signed guarantees on company letterhead, and whose personal code does not stretch to anything that is done under the table, goes pale.

"We would save £400, not to mention time," I reason.

"And if we get caught, we could face a fine," he snaps.

"The last guy who used my mate was the chief of police," Mark pipes in.

That does not convince The Husband, and I am inclined to agree with him. We are the type of people who would get caught and bear the consequences.

"I will keep calling the utility and see if we can get a date," I say.

I make a note to call them as soon as I . . . what? My mind suddenly goes blank. I know there is someone else to call or to get after, or something to order. I look around. The place is strewn with bathroom fixtures, and kitchen appliances, packages of tiles stacked against every available wall along with lengths of pipe and wires, and tool bags. And dust. There is so much dust. It looks like Kabul after a bomb blast.

I consult my long, scribbled to-do list. The floor refinishers. And the kitchen worktops. Those are things I need to organize.

I check on The Husband. He has returned to his makeshift tea station, kettle on the boil, two coffees ready to go.

"Let me help," I say. "I will take this to Mark . . ."

"No, not that one, this one. Milk, no sugar. That other one is for Francis."

The Husband has assigned specific mugs to specific people. For instance, the blue mug is Francis's, always Francis's. The mug with the orange handle is Mark's. Anyone who is on the premises for longer than a day is assigned a mug by The Husband. This saves him from washing the mugs during the day, because, as you may recall, we still do not have running water. He has memorized everyone's coffee and tea preferences. In fact, he knows the trades first by their order—"one milk, no sugar" or "double sugar, one milk"—and second by their names.

I take the mug and, glancing up at his face, I notice how drawn he looks. He has not been sleeping well. In our rental home, he tosses angrily in bed, and then gets up in the middle of the night, wrenching his dressing gown from the hook on the back of the bedroom door and padding downstairs to flick on the kettle. The renovation has worried him beyond rationality. His dreams are likely populated with images of himself crawling on his belly through a storm of plaster dust, scrambling over rubble, falling down a shaft and emerging from it, catatonic with fear, only to be met with thugs who declare him bankrupt and destitute, and who turn him over to a maniacally laughing builder who threatens to put his balls in a claw-like vice.

Despite Francis being the picture of sunny optimism and assertions of "This is going better than expected" or "No problems at all. It's really straightforward," none of this is balm to The Husband's anxiety. And yet, he hides it well. When he talks with the trades or with people on the street, he is the picture of cheerfulness and easygoingness, a veritable Mr. Pleasant, but out of sight and with me he is the love child of Mr. Grumpy and Ms. Worry, and godson of Mr. Grumble.

Lately, he has fixated on house insurance and door locks, and has appointed himself security officer. He asks—as if I am supposed to know—whether the newly installed French doors in the second reception room have a locking mechanism that conforms to the rigorous code the insurers demand.

"There are certainly enough locks on them," I offer unhelpfully.

In England, windows have keyed locks on them. I have never seen this in any other country except Italy. England is almost as obsessive about door locks as it is about interior doors. Commandments eight and ten have evaded English culture. People exist about six feet from their neighbour, yet they trust no one.

My husband does not care about Italy or my views on English social behaviour.

"What if the house is broken into while renovations are taking place? Or a tradesman is injured, or if we are away for two weeks and something goes wrong?" he asks.

I throw up my hands: "What if the roof falls in, or a piece of flying rubble hits a neighbour two doors down? Why must you be so pessimistic?"

This infuriates him, my devil-may-care approach. It used to be what he found attractive about me; now he regards me like a walking four-alarm fire. His eyes say he wishes he could run as far as possible from this mess, and I daresay from me, too. Then he says, "I had my whole life planned out. My mortgage was paid off on my flat in London. I was ready to retire and travel. And suddenly you come along and put me on this, this grand tour into hell."

"Fine," I say. "We'll fix up the house and sell it, store our stuff and travel."

"No," he says. "You want a house. You're the one who says you need a place to put down roots. The problem is, you never do. You root and uproot."

I turn away with my best "you do not understand me" face, but deep down I know he is right. How can I explain that houses and renovations and moving are an addiction to me; that I desperately want to settle, but as hard as I try I just cannot? That despite the adrenalin rush from upping sticks, it also causes me great stress?

A week later it all finally gets to me. One night after supper, as we slump in front of the TV craving diversion from the bickering and from the thousand and one details that get served up daily, I swiftly double over with severe stomach pains. I hyperventilate. Nothing I do will regulate my breathing. Each attempt, each gasp for air, worsens my condition. The Husband dials 999.

The paramedics are swift in arriving. They look to be the same age as my kids, possibly younger, but they are efficient, cheerful, and professional. The Husband tells them, "She's renovating a house." *She*, not *we*.

Electrodes are stuck onto my upper body while I am asked questions, none of which have anything to do with appliance placements, the location of the boiler, or my preferred colour of Corian worktops. They take my blood pressure and run tests. They ask me the date and year. For a brief second, I consider giving a false answer. If I get sectioned, I will not have to face the rest of the renovation. It would be left to The Husband to complete. Hmm. Wouldn't that just do him in. At the same time, maybe being committed is the only cure for my restless obsession with homes. Still, I cannot lie. I answer honestly, and pass. My marbles are intact. Or so everyone assumes.

There is nothing amiss with my heart, the youngsters tell me.

"Take it easy," they say.

I smile, nod, and think: Yeah, I'll get right on that one.

Why is this renovation so much more difficult than the others?

Why the hyperstress? The answer, a little-known truism, is that renovations are best undertaken solo. I had considered sending The Husband off on a hiking expedition while I dealt with the house reno: he could enjoy his journey—I could enjoy mine. But he said we could not afford to do both. I think he felt guilty about leaving me behind to do it alone.

Augmenting the stress is the fact that I cannot seem to do anything. There was a time when I thought nothing of changing a toilet seat, or unscrewing curtain rods, or cutting a hole in a wall. Now, not only do I lack the strength, I have become petrified of incompetence. I am afraid of failing.

Things do lighten up. A few days later, while cleaning out the area under the stairs, I find a small silver ring that looks faintly masonic. I also find a small plastic baggie inside which is a multi-folded piece of tinfoil. I call over The Husband. I fold back each layer of foil, and it becomes obvious what it likely contains. Cocaine. However, it is such a small amount that it has turned yellow and dried up. Does cocaine have a best-before date? Does fossilized cocaine have more potency?

We show it to Mark, who is installing a smoke alarm upstairs.

"Rip up all the floorboards!" he jokes.

We show it to Francis.

"Don't snort it all in one place," I say.

He peers at the minuscule remnants and says with a laugh, "If you ask me one day to put marble flooring throughout the house, I'll know you've found the motherlode."

It beats what he found in the roof void above the kitchen: women's underwear and a nightie. Creepy.

On the way back to our rental home The Husband says, "If you actually found a pile of coke, how would you propose to convert it into money?"

"I would take it to the police."

"So you think the police would pay you for it?"

Okay, I had not thought of that.

"Well, then we would sell it. You know, privately."

"And then you would be arrested and sent to jail."

What a killjoy.

I had come across a story in a newspaper about a fellow who found a suitcase full of old cash in a house he had just purchased. He was acquainted with the home's previous owners, an elderly brother and sister, and alerted them to the stash. The notes were old and out of circulation, so he accompanied them to the bank to ensure that the money was converted properly and deposited into its owners' account. I thought that was awfully sweet.

You live in hope when you tear apart an old home. Has someone stashed cash under the floor? Is there a false wall hiding something? Has a family heirloom slipped between the floorboards? Is there a stone in the garden marking a safe full of gold?

No such windfall for us. In addition to the ring and the dried-up cocaine, I find an old nail, and a charming globe-shaped glass bottle that has since been filled with scented oil and placed in the bathroom. Oh, and there was an England's Glory match box with this joke on the back:

> *Wife: "How do you manage to stay out so late at night?"*
> *Husband: "Easy. I got into the habit when I was courting you."*

These are the spoils from our renovation.

20

The Project Tilts

It was bound to happen. After weeks of smooth sailing, the mast wobbles, and *The Good Ship Renovation* starts to list.

Francis has been a diligent worker. Has shown up every day at 8:00 a.m. and worked till 4:30 p.m., five days a week. He hardly takes a break, save for The Husband's frequent ministrations of tea. It is, therefore, not unreasonable when he asks for a few days off, especially given that work on the house is proceeding at such a pace that it looks to be completed ahead of schedule.

The kitchen is to be fitted next week, and the tiler is now at work on the floor. The bathroom still is not done but, or so Francis promises, the tiler will do that right after the kitchen. My mental calculations commence: three days to tile the kitchen floor, then three days to tile the bathroom, by which point the kitchen will be installed, and then three days, give or take, to install the fixtures in the bathroom. The painting—three days for that. In two weeks tops the house will be complete—two weeks ahead of schedule! The Husband and I will have the luxury of moving in gradually and placing our stuff into pristine new quarters. I am smoking from the renovator's crack pipe.

"Should we book the movers?" I ask The Husband.

He says nothing.

On one of his days off, Francis pops in unexpectantly.

"I've hired a kitchen fitter. I can't get the guy I wanted—everyone's on holidays at this time of year. But I found someone else who is brilliant. He'll be here on Monday."

"The bathroom?" I ask.

"Yeah, it will get done."

There is an edge to his voice that takes me aback. I have told him repeatedly that the bathroom is the priority. We have been good clients; paid invoices as soon as Francis has emailed them over. We have been helpful, courteous. Why the pissy attitude?

The following Monday, Jasper, the kitchen fitter, arrives. He is middle-aged and of medium build, with dark hair and dark-rimmed glasses. His tense smile and slight look of bewilderment tell me he is not quite sure what awaits him. In preparation for his arrival, The Husband and I have moved two dozen or so packages and boxes of cabinet components, along with the appliances, to the far end of the kitchen—the part that will be the dining area—so that Jasper will have all the pieces within reach.

"As you can see it's a basic galley kitchen," I explain while The Husband makes him a tea. "Nothing special or finicky. Here are the blueprints."

We leave him to it.

Halfway through the morning Jasper asks, "Do you have any plans?"

I look at the sheaf of schematics he holds in his hands.

"Like those?"

Jasper looks down at them: "Yeah, like these. Only better."

"That was all we have been given. Is there something wrong?"

He cannot make head nor tail of them. Furthermore, he is more than annoyed to learn that Francis is on holiday.

"I only agreed to do this job because he said he would help. I was to be the assistant, not the lead."

"He told us you were the kitchen fitter."

"No, I'm not! I'm a retired firefighter. I just do odd jobs, really."

We do not know what to say. I look at the boxes and flat-packed packages stacked to the ceiling. I look at The Husband for suggestions or reinforcement.

He smiles at Jasper and says, "Can I make you another cup of tea?"

Jasper manages to cobble a few pieces together, but he does not seem confident. He calls the kitchen designer, but she is of no help. In fact, the kitchen company proves totally useless. How they secured a Royal Warrant is a mystery. It will be a while before I trust that seal of approval again. What I did not know at the time of hiring them was that this particular kitchen company deals only with builders, not the general public.

Every so often we confer over the kitchen plans, our eyes boring into them, willing them to reveal their secrets, but they are not giving up anything.

Suddenly, there is a commotion at the front door. The floor sanders have arrived. I had hired them to start today, figuring that Jasper would be ensconced in the kitchen doing his thing, while the sanders worked on the rest of the house. They burst in like a Polish SWAT team. Six of them. It is madness. They are so focused and dedicated to their assignment that had the house been empty, they would have sanded and varnished the entire place in two days.

Then Mark, the electrician, arrives to check if the plastering is done so he can finish his work on the house.

Minutes later, Cyryl, the painter, shows up to quote for the job of painting the interior.

Then our cell phone rings: it is the utility company calling to say they finally have an opening; they can come tomorrow to relocate the electrical panel.

Then the people who are to deliver our shed phone to say they will be here this afternoon.

It is like an Italian comedy. The Husband is thrown into a complete state: he has only four mugs at his little tea station and there are eleven people on-site, with two more arriving shortly.

"Shall I go back to the rental and get more mugs?"

I shoot him a harsh look. "Seriously? You're thinking of mugs right now?"

He makes the rounds anyway, tentatively asking the Polish SWAT team for their order. They barely speak English but understand enough to politely decline his offer: they hold up their full water bottles to show that they have come prepared with their own hydration. A biscuit, perhaps, The Husband offers, brandishing a tube of chocolate digestives? They shake their heads and smile no, thanks. Bless them.

And then it begins. The sanders start their machines. A grinding, searing noise whines loudly through the house, rising to a crescendo. It sounds like the start of a motorcycle race when everyone is revving at the starting line, only this is two hundred thousand times louder. It fills the house and spills onto the street and spreads across the neighbourhood. It is ear-shatteringly loud. The house vibrates.

The noise is too much for Jasper, Mark, and Cyryl. They cannot work in such a din.

Jasper promises to be back the following day, and he will bring a mate to help him. I suggest he also bring noise-cancelling earphones.

Mark asks me to ring him once the sanders have finished.

Cyryl says he will be in touch with Francis about the quote.

They leave. A few minutes later, half the sanding team vamoose, having completed the prep work. They are picked up by their boss and driven to their next job.

In a matter of minutes, The Husband and I are left standing in the hallway with the most high-pitched whir screaming above us, like a convention of seagulls circling a chip wagon. I mouth to him that I am running out to the loo at the community centre three blocks away.

My ears stop ringing when I reach the community centre, but when I come back out to the street, I can hear the sanding machines from that distance. I slink round the back and take the long way home.

OF ALL THE DISCOMFORT one anticipates during a renovation, the one you least expect is xenophobia.

Britain has a trades shortage. It is impossible to find people to take on work because the British-born trades are either booked up or holidaying in the south of France. Immigrants are picking up the slack, taking a bit of heat off the shoulders of their British counterparts. But there is no gratitude among the British. No. They eye their brethren with contempt and suspicion.

As an immigrant myself, I am sensitive to xenophobia. Whenever people hear my North American voice, heads swivel, and I sense a stiffening of spines. I am not a tourist; I am a resident and a British homeowner, but still definitely a foreigner. Accents never meant much to me, nor did I get the sense that they mattered much to Canadians in general. If you encountered someone with an accent, you mentally registered that they were "from away," and then you got on with your business with them. But in Britain, accents are a kind of currency, a socio-economic determinant. The British media frequently opines that accents no longer matter, but it's a lie. Accents totally matter here. Your accent determines your class, how much you earn, how you are treated in a restaurant, a shop, over the phone, or in a meeting. Much fun is made of regional accents—Northern, West Country, East Yorkshire, the Borders, Welsh, to name a few—and of those deemed to be "cut-glass" accents. The media has been sniping about how Kate Middleton's accent has transformed since she married into the Royal family, but honestly, how could she avoid that when she is surrounded all day, every single day, by people with a certain way of speaking? We all adapt to our surroundings in various ways for the sake of our survival and to further our engagement with others. Aside from gauging where the speaker is from, what does a person's accent actually prove? Having a British husband spares me the brunt of British indignity, but there have been instances when my accent has been met with a swift and unkind change in attitude. At times, anticipating this reaction, I have asked The Husband to make a call, arrange a delivery, or get a quote because the price mysteriously inflates for non-British accents unless the person serving you is a foreigner, too.

I once mentioned to a young British man that I sometimes subsume my accent to avoid people suddenly staring at me. He replied, "That's because when we hear a North American accent, we assume you are all movie stars."

To which I replied, "Funnily enough, when North Americans hear a British accent, we assume you are all part of the Royal family."

We had a good laugh about that.

But seriously, accents are no laughing matter, as I discover on our worksite.

The Polish trades work diligently and quickly; the British cast them a look of disapproval. I try to soften the Brits by praising the work ethic and kindness of the Polish workers in the hope that a modicum of respect will rub off. But no. If anything, it makes matters worse. The British workers, even those I had marked as kind, tolerant types, react to my effusiveness by glowering: here is a pecking order that I am not respecting.

We have been blessed with the nicest men to have descended on a home renovation. I can say unequivocally that not one of them has been rude or disrespectful; all are amiable and show a complete diligence to their work and profession. Any of them would be welcome at our dinner table. But the chauvinism I witness disturbs me. These are Brexit days, emotions are running high, and the Poles and every other ethnic or cultural minority are getting an earful of "Go back to your own country." For a nation that never forgets the Second World War and marks with great celebration every single battle ever fought, it is surprising that it has forgotten what valuable allies the Poles were during the war.

Despite this being a sensitive time, I cannot help feeling churlish about the British attitude. The self-congratulatory blather about Britain's long tradition of fairness and openness is a hollow boast. After conquering half the world, why is it so surprised when half the world peacefully, for the most part, rocks up to its doorstep? At one time, Britain was the most culturally and racially diverse country in the world; what a shame that given that laudable reputation it could not transition from world superpower to world leader in racial and cultural harmony.

Part of this attitude has something to do with Britain being an island nation. Island people are a peculiar breed. It matters not that the island is eight miles long or eight hundred miles long. Island people are bred with intractable beliefs about independence and territory that run contrary to the more open, more collegial-minded spirit of non-islanders, people accustomed to sharing borders and engaging in political and cultural quid pro quo.

A common accusation about immigrants is their resistance to integrating into their adopted society, but Britons can be just as guilty of not reciprocating. Sure, agencies and centres have been set up to help immigrants to navigate the system and to learn English, but that does not facilitate integration in a meaningful way. We, and I speak as a Westerner, shy away from a deeper involvement with immigrants. We tend to stick with our own kind, so why do we pass judgment on those from other cultures who stick with their own kind?

I appreciate that this puts a burden on government to support the influx of immigrants, but surely that same government will have at some point anticipated this eventuality, so why has it been so slow in creating policies of accommodation? If, in the case of Britain, the concern is that the arrival of immigrants puts a strain on such social services as the National Health System, why not charge non-natives to use the system? Not all will be able to, but many will. Just come out and say it clearly: *If you cannot afford our health system, you cannot use it.* Or, *There is now a user fee for those who entered the country as of a particular year.* But the British mentality is ostrich-like, and not built for flexibility or adaptability or confrontation. It holds up institutions like its much-vaunted NHS as a birthright, but passive-aggressively refuses to accept that times and circumstances change. No one can afford to say: "This is how it has always been done."

The following week, a fellow named David shows up to make an adjustment to our shed. I join him outside.

"Interesting neighbourhood, innit," he remarks. His "interesting" is British speak for "unexpected," "not my cuppa."

David, who is white British, is telling me about the "interesting" sight he encountered as he drove to our home along St. Mark's Road.

"N'er been ta dis patch o' Bristle," he says.

"Have you lived in Bristol long?"

"Aye, all me life! But what I sawr on that road was no Bristle I know. Tot t'was in Morocco!"

For people like David, to travel down a street where some of the men are in robes and turbans, and some of the women are in chadors and niqabs, is to encounter a scene from *National Geographic*, not *Britain*. I am tempted to tell him that the sights he encountered are as alien to his eyes as his bewildering Bristol-accented lexicon is to my ears, which I am struggling to understand, and could he just speak proper English.

"Bristol is a multicultural city," I say.

"'Tis beyond multicultural," he says. "We're being overtaken."

"Well, I am as much an immigrant as they are," I counter.

"Are ye."

It is not said as a question but as a statement, indicating that because I am white with a Western accent, I am an acceptable immigrant. And yet, the truth is that no matter how much British history and culture I gobble up I will always be an outsider here. I will always be the Other.

David abruptly falls silent when Cyryl, the painter, who is now a daily fixture on-site, comes out for a smoke. I see David's posture straighten, his mind thinking: 'Nother furner.

I introduce them, both tradesmen, both of whom earn their living by the sweat of their brow, but the standoffishness is palpable. And Cyryl is white. Apparently, only certain shades of white are acceptable to people like David.

THE FOLLOWING DAY THE HUSBAND and I are on our way to the house when our mobile phone rings. It is 7:05 a.m. The company delivering the materials for the wardrobes being built in the master bedroom has arrived and its truck is idling outside the house. It is not due until after 7:30. It is the first time someone has arrived early. The Husband steps on the accelerator.

We open the house, and the two men unload their truck and carry the various pieces upstairs, though not before The Husband has taken their tea order.

The delivery is done quickly, and the men catch their breath in our narrow hallway, sipping from their mugs. I apologize for not having chairs and invite them to sit on the stairs, but they say they prefer to stand. They have been sitting in their truck for two hours, having left at 5 a.m. from Wolverhampton.

Long-distance drives are not uncommon for them, they say. They have done the journey from Wolverhampton to John O'Groats and then down to Land's End more times than they care to count.

Sandy, the driver, has been in the job for several years. His mate, Jeff, says he was laid off from his job in a shipyard, so he relocated inland, and now does this to earn his livelihood. He has a young family: a son was born three months ago. At the end of a long haul, he is eager to get home.

As the men chat, I am struck by all these small conversations we have had with strangers who have delivered goods and services to us during this renovation. Everyone brimming with stories and snippets of lives lived, of dreams dashed or redirected. Everyone arrives with a life lesson. When I enter into a small part of each life and just listen, it lifts me out of mine for a moment; allows the brain noise about budgets and my past to fade into the background, and to snap to the fact that there is not just my expectations and desires in the queue to be answered. These random chats with those who make the deliveries, whose lives briefly intersect with ours, remind me of the many hands, many of them unseen, who contribute to reshaping our home.

But now they must push off to their next drop: Plymouth, 120 miles away. Mugs drained, they climb back into their lorry and are off.

I look at my watch: 7:33. I pull out my list and tick off "wardrobe delivery."

For a moment, The Husband and I luxuriate in the rare silence. The morning sun scythes through the transom and finds us amid a towering puzzle of flat-packed boxes, fittings, and appliances. I want to ask him how he is doing, but I cannot bear to add his worries to my own. I am saved by a knock at the door.

Jasper, the "I'm not a kitchen fitter," has arrived with a mate. I leave them to grumble over the kitchen schematics while The Husband sets them up with coffee.

A few hours later they have managed to build the cabinet carcasses and fit some of them to the walls. By the end of the day the fridge is in, but it has been installed so high off the ground that I will need to wear platform stilettos to reach the upper shelves.

There are more useless calls to the kitchen design company but no further enlightenment. How can putting it together be so complicated?

"Maybe you could just construct the components and disregard the plan?" My suggestion is ignored.

The sanders arrive with their heavy machinery. The Husband stalls them with coffee, which they accept this time. One with one sugar; the other two with three sugars. I do not know how he manages to keep all the orders straight. The sanders take their mugs outside and sit on the low stone courtyard wall, smoking and chatting in their language.

Back inside they start up the machines. It's 8:16. The neighbourhood judders.

I consult my lists to look busy; The Husband bolts to the shed and assumes his position—seated on a camping chair with his face buried in his hands. My mouth tightens.

Looking down at my list, I tick off "floors refinished" just for the dopamine rush and to convince myself that things are moving forward. But who am I kidding? There are so many more key items that need to be ticked: working loo, running water. Many of the deadlines are seven days hence, so anything is possible. The guest room, the room that will be the least used in the entire house, will be done in two days. I study everything on my list, except the budget. My way of dealing with budgets is to ignore them.

I join The Husband in the backyard, but no sooner am I seated than Mark, the electrician, appears at the back door. We have not seen him in days. His appearance is like the return of the Prodigal Son. The Husband offers him a coffee. Mark declines.

"Who can make coffee or do anything with that noise! Look, I need to get into the front room and finish a few things, but the sanders are there, and the work I have to do requires cutting the power."

We decide to talk to the sanders. Mark and I walk into the front room. He raises a hand, like Jesus about to address the disciples, and the machine grinds to a miraculous halt.

Mark speaks to me, I speak to the youngest sander, and he translates to his older colleague. In the end, it is agreed. The sanders will down tools and return tomorrow to finish. They will also come Saturday morning to lacquer the floors.

Mark takes over in both energy and vocal volubility. He bounces around like he is jacked up on three coffees.

Jasper and his mate walk in from the hardware store as the sanders are packing up. "They're finished already?" asks Jasper.

"No, they are coming back tomorrow because the electrician needs to finish up in the same room the sanders are in. I think he also wants to finish wiring the kitchen."

The Husband and I fuss with the sanders, offering apologies. They are the hardest of workers, and they not only work quickly but they do fine work.

"No problem," says the young one, smiling.

I realize I have not bothered to ask their names. "He's Victor. I'm Patrick."

We shake hands.

They turn to leave, and I mouth to The Husband, "We need to give them a tip at the end of this."

Mark is in the kitchen, hands on his hips. I hope he is not going to jettison Jasper and his mate, as well.

"Right. Let's look at what's going on here."

Mark pirouettes from one side of the galley to the other. "So, the extractor hood is going here, right? The hob here?"

No, the microwave goes there.

"Right. So, I'm going to run a spur . . . how many mills is this backing?"

"Eight mills," says Jasper.

"Great, so I'll run that into this box. And here . . ." He drops to the floor like he is ready to do push-ups, and peers under the cabinets. "I'm going to wire into that outlet . . ."

And then he is off with his electrician's lingo. The Husband heads back into his safe place, the shed. I stay nearby in case I am asked a question.

Satisfied, Mark moves off to the front room, and Jasper and his pal return to staring at the incomprehensible kitchen schematics.

Both Mark and Jasper have radios blaring on different channels. I am wondering how that will shake out when Mark bounces into the hall and hollers to Jasper, "What are you listening to, mate? I've got Radio One."

"Mine's on Radio Two," Jasper calls back.

"I'm more than happy to have Radio Two on," says Mark. "I'll switch mine over."

If only the bigger problems of the world could be sorted so amicably.

THE FOLLOWING MONDAY, when Francis finally returns to the site, all jolly and upbeat from his holiday, we show him what Jasper has managed.

"He did quite well," he says, striding proprietarily through the room, though almost nothing has been done.

"Um, he was really pissed off," I say. "He is not a kitchen fitter. He told us. And he said you were supposed to help him."

Francis shrugs.

"And this fridge," I continue, trying not to sound like a whining five-year-old. "It should not be this high. I cannot reach the shelves, and it's not like I'm short."

Francis puts his fingertips together like a Delphic oracle. "Sometimes we have to make adjustments to the plans."

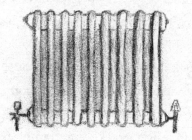

21

The Mind Tilts

It is mid-August. In less than two weeks we move in. We are still without running water, and the kitchen appliances are not yet hooked up. The bathroom walls and floor have been tiled; the shower tray is fixed in place, ditto the tub; but nothing is connected, and the room is strewn with lengths of pipe and opened boxes of fixtures and fittings.

I have taken to dreaming about our new home. At night, in bed, I think about what the house looks like in the dark, about how it reacts to the silence without workers banging and reshaping it, how it rests with the stars blinking above it against the bruised sky.

The following morning, I arrive with a plate of chocolate-chip oatmeal cookies that I baked the night before as a way to blow off stress. I bring them into the kitchen to offer to Francis.

He announces triumphantly that the toilets are now working.

Great! My shoulders relax. Two days later I point out the not-insignificant fact that there are no doors on the bathrooms.

"Absolutely," he replies, and walks away.

My simple galley kitchen that I thought would take three days to install is into its second week. Francis has brought in a helper named Mick. I hope it means twice the work will now get done. Mick, all tattoos, swagger, and long metal chains trailing from the pockets of his dusty black trousers, wears a flinty expression that taunts with intimidation. He looks at me as if I am the enemy.

I am not having it. I walk toward intimidation to show that I am fearless. Buddy better notice my biceps. I am so wired on stress that I am ready for a fight. I might not be able to hold a screwdriver without my bifocals, but damn if someone thinks they can scare me. When I am four feet from him, I look him square in the eye, and lift my chin, and a mug, to him.

"Coffee? Tea?"

"Tea would be lovely. Thank you."

The unexpected politeness takes me aback.

The tea lady—I mean, The Husband—is rearranging the shed, so I do the honours. I return to the kitchen with filled mugs, and a readiness to chat. I want to know why the kitchen is taking so bloody long. Did the kitchen company mess up on the calculations? Did Francis? Whatever it is, something has definitely gone wrong, because both Francis and Mick look uneasy. When I ask the question aloud, I receive puffed cheeks blowing out air, shaking heads, shrugging shoulders. What I do discover is that beneath Mr. McFlinty-Look's tattoos and chains is a soft soul. He is curious, intelligent, articulate. Easy with conversation. The hubris is an act. Wonder what he is hiding.

He asks me about myself, what I do, where I am from, how I got here. The attention makes me uncomfortable. None of the others have asked anything about my life. When I tell him that I am a writer, he says he is working for another client who is also a writer.

"She just got some big advance for her book, and so she and her husband have taken off to travel. Left instructions on the renovations they want done to their house—massive project with all sorts of audio technology involved."

I hate this woman immediately, but I smile magnanimously. Who is this writer who has hijacked my life? Why can't that be me? Then I realize it has been five years since I had a book published because I have been spending too much time thinking about houses and moving. The frittered life.

By afternoon, the kitchen takes shape, but no one is rejoicing.

Mick leaves to go to another job. I wonder if it is to the writer's house. Lucky bitch.

I bring Francis another coffee and continue the small talk. He had mentioned at the start of the project that his wife is expecting. The baby is due in a few months. I ask how she is. From what I've gleaned by observing his urgent, concerned phone calls, and from what he has told me, not all is well. Episodes of perinatal depression have resulted in more than one dash to the hospital emergency ward.

His wife, he mentions, is a psychotherapist.

"Then she must know how to deal with things such as perinatal depression."

As soon as the words pass my lips, I realize my stupidity. It does not matter what profession you are in: mental illness does not discriminate when it attacks its victims. I know that from experience. And just because you can diagnose and treat others does not mean you can diagnose and treat yourself. You lose all perspective when you are the patient. I apologize to Francis.

"It's okay. I get it. You automatically assume that psychotherapists would know better, or be better prepared, or look for warning signs in their own behaviour given that they diagnose it in others all the time, and they work in that field. But it's not like that."

He takes a long sip of his coffee. "You know Mick? The guy who was just here? His wife was a psychotherapist and had the same problem during her pregnancy."

"How bizarre. Two women in the same profession with the same problem. Is she doing better—Mick's wife?"

Francis looks away. "No, she killed herself. He's now a single dad to two girls."

My hand flies to my mouth. The sleeve of tattoos, the bravado—they explain a lot.

I do not quite know what to say except "Mental illness is everywhere now. It is frightening because it comes with no warning. I have been there. A few times."

Francis takes a big breath. "I had a mental illness."

Ah yes, the builder who had recommended Francis had mentioned this. "What happened?"

"It came out of the blue, about two years ago. At the time, I had my own company, and one day I just could not leave my house. I wasn't bedridden or anything, but for some inexplicable reason my brain would not let me leave the house. It went on for about a month or so. I lost my business. Relationships went down the tubes. And then just as quickly I became really bold. You know? Kind of fearless. And my brain, whoa, it became hyperaware. Everything I saw—every insect, flower, no matter how minute—grabbed my attention, fascinated me. I would study a single drop of rain forever, examine it like it was a miracle meant only for me. My brain spun like crazy, felt like it was running at a hundred times its normal speed. I became both paranoid and ultraconfident. Saw myself as a kind of master, a god, seeing the world from a heightened vantage point."

"That must have felt very strange."

"Oh, it was. But when you have this fearlessness, you feel invincible, like you can do anything."

He stops, gives an embarrassed laugh. "Hey, I better get back to work here."

"Are you okay now?" I ask, hoping he has not regretted being so candid.

"Yup. No more meds, no alcohol."

"But it can come back," I caution. "It is important to know that so you can pace yourself."

"I'm cool now," he says. Another nervous laugh.

I smile, too, but his words sit with me. His work ethic has become erratic of late, and probably explains the delays, why things have inexplicably gone off schedule, and why the kitchen measurements do not add up. He has a child from another relationship, and now a new wife is expecting a baby, and he is juggling our renovation while getting over a rather significant breakdown. It is a lot to carry.

It is now seven days before we move in. I feel on the verge of a breakdown: my bones and organs are functioning, but my emotions are slopping like lava inside Vesuvius. If I can just keep breathing and adopt a Zen-like attitude, we can hold off calling the paramedics again.

The detailed, orderly spreadsheet I created looks like it has been handled by a preschooler.

Worse, the itemized costs and expenditures show we will be over budget. I cannot ignore it anymore. I do the sums and subtractions again and again. No change. It is not a massive amount, but still. How were my calculations so off? The windows. I had not factored in new windows; had only agreed to them when Francis suggested replacing all of them, rather than just the new ones we were installing.

I look at my spreadsheet to see where there might be savings, but at this late stage there is nothing that can give. Trades have been scheduled; certain non-negotiables, such as moving the gas meter, boiler, and the electrical panel, were booked months in advance. I had so wanted to have at least a few thousand left over for some new furnishings. And bookshelves. I must have bookshelves. I go online to check out Ikea.

The real worry is The Husband. How do I tell him that we will be over budget? All this was riding on my shoulders: I was the one with the grand vision; the one who said we could get it all done, loft extension and landscaping included, within our £70,000 budget. But now I must concede defeat. We cannot afford to do the loft or the landscaping. Failure weighs on me.

Things have cost a lot more than I thought—or rather, more than what I remembered them costing from previous renovations. We have not made excessive purchases aside from the bathroom vanity and the Corian kitchen worktops. I can blame the new windows, though I am glad we had them done. But there, too, I acted rashly. I did not ask Francis what they would look like; did not bother getting a second quote. I was too proud, did not want to appear like a novice; was keen to show I was decisive and savvy so others would not take advantage of me. But they have anyway.

And then there is Cyryl, the painter, to consider. When Francis gives me his quote, I almost have a seizure: £2,500 to paint three rooms and the upper and lower hallways.

"How is that possible?"

He shrugs, smiles sheepishly. He assures me that Cyryl's work is excellent, and that he works fast.

I say "Fine" only because I have run out of energy to say no, and we are desperate for things to get done. Who knows when the painting will start? The living room and hallways have yet to be plastered. How will they get plastered, and dried, and painted in the space of a week?

✦ ✦ ✦

THERE IS AN EDGE TO MY VOICE, as biting and tight as the scream of a circular saw. It rises only in conversation with The Husband. He goes off to run, or to find a quiet café where he can have a cappuccino or two and read the paper. I am at the house, on my knees, finessing paint strokes on the skirting boards and trying not to get oil-based paint on the newly sanded floors or the newly painted walls. I am trying desperately to make it look as if I do not mind my husband's absences or his lack of interest in fashioning our home. But I do. A renovation demands its participants be present, enthusiastic, and willing to learn.

I pretend that someone asks me, "Would you do this again—renovate another home?" And my answer is "I would love to, but not with this husband." I could not do this to him or with him again. If there is anything I have learned, it is that he is truly uncomfortable with just about every aspect of it. If someone tells me, "Oh, I could never do that," I think: Sure you can! Let me show you! Because I see renovating as a thrilling act of courage, not something to fear. Courage, they say, is fear that has said its prayers. Renovating is not skydiving. But who knows? Maybe the idea of jumping out of a plane at ten thousand feet is more preferable to some people than stick-handling a house renovation. What has become glaringly obvious is that this is more than a renovation: this is a marriage, and I suppose smarter people know enough when to step away from the challenge, even when that challenge beckons like a siren's call, when you would just as soon jab a needle into your vein as say "Yes!" to that challenge.

I was raised on renovation; The Husband was not. He has been generous enough to give me the space and opportunity to have my fun, but it was always going to be a one-off project, not a lifestyle. Unfortunately.

✦ ✦ ✦

When the utility company arrives to move the electrical panel, we are sitting outside. I say to The Husband, "I am going inside to see what I can learn."

The Husband stays planted in his chair with the newspaper. I can feel his eyes follow me, wondering why I bother "to learn" or thinking: What can she possibly learn?

My attitude is to lean in; his is to stand back. Each can be seen as a strength and as a weakness. Plenty has been written about who we choose as partners, and how when differences rear up it should not be taken as a sign of failure or that we chose incorrectly; rather, it should be seen as a signal that this person, this creature who is so different from us, is teaching us to grow. The Husband and I are different. That is why we married.

I have not forgotten about Cheryll. In the evenings, once we are back in Little Britain, showered, fed, and exhausted, I spend a good hour online trying to find my childhood friend. The fact that she continues to bob into my head is, for me, a sign. I have long regarded my inner sense of urgency as a cosmic nudge that needs to be attended to *tout de suite*. It is time to find Cheryll. Besides, the stress of the house work is so all-consuming, so close to pushing me over the edge, that I need something to focus on other than hammers and nail guns.

Finding Cheryll, however, is not as easy as I thought, despite my having applied journalistic skills to the task. I have tried various cities where she might live. I have tried the names of her parents and siblings. But the search leads nowhere. I have even scoured the obituaries, and so far it has proven a dead end, no pun intended. There is always Facebook, but social media and I are not acquainted. I often think that it is only me and Wilma Flintstone who have not signed up on Facebook, Twitter, Instagram, whatever.

Weeks of fruitless online searching begins to add to my anxiety. Finding Cheryll clings to my brain like a wet shirt. Finally, I swallow my pride and surrender my virginity to Facebook. Within seconds, I find her. Hooray! She lives! There is a picture of her sitting with friends in a restaurant. She looks happy, carefree, like I suspect she has been all her life.

I figure out how to post a message (yes, I am that ignorant of this kind of thing) and ask her to get in touch. It occurs to me that she could have got in touch with me, but all my moving and marriages would not have made that easy. After three marriages and four name changes, even I have forgotten who I am. Maybe my name means nothing to her now; I am just a blip in her past. Maybe she will think it creepy that I want to get in touch after such a long stretch. Maybe not. Who truly understands you but the friends you had as a child?

Move, settle, make friends, lose friends, repeat. That pattern is the only continuity I have known.

THREE DAYS BEFORE WE ARE to move in there is still no bathroom.

22

The Move

"You need to roll with the punches." My mother's words roll back at me.

It feels as if I have rolled enough, and gone extra rounds to boot, like some glutton for punishment who allows everyone to take a swipe at her.

It is the day before our move, and work on the bathroom has picked up with the arrival of Paul, the plumber. The kitchen still is not done. In fact, when I walk in, I find Francis and Mick dismantling the kitchen and starting again.

"What the hell?"

"Now, don't worry," says Francis. He is clearly worried. "We want—I want—to get it perfect. Don't worry. It will be done."

But Francis's "It will be done" mantra has lost its calming power. It sounds more like a desperate prayer.

I climb the stairs and retreat into the corner of the master bedroom, where I cry as quietly as I can without anyone hearing me. I am so fed up, I feel utterly pummelled and defeated. Nothing has turned out the way I had hoped. When I hear a sound at the foot of the stairs, I turn to the doorway of the bedroom to close the door, but this brings on another squirt of tears: the door still has not been put on. In fact, none of the doors, including those for the bathrooms, has been put on. How many times do I have to ask? I now hear someone coming up the stairs. Sounds like The Husband. I quickly daub my eyes on a corner of my dusty T-shirt and try to pull myself together. I cannot let him see me like this.

They say communication is key in a renovation, especially between builder and homeowner. But everyone's definition of communication is different. You, the homeowner, can be present and receptive and cheerful and helpful all you want, but if the builder is not explaining the detail stuff or not doing what he says he will do, if he is just forging ahead under his own steam, lost in his own world of worry, then communication is moot.

The Husband tiptoes in. "You okay?"

My chin quivers; tears tumble in fat drops down my cheeks. "I am so sorry this has not worked out the way I had hoped and you had hoped. This is not how I envisioned it."

He puts his arms around me and draws me to his chest.

"Don't worry. We'll get through it. The bathroom looks nice."

"Yes," I say, blinking away tears. "But there is no door."

I draw the sleeve of my shirt under my nose. The Husband winces and hands me his handkerchief. I daub my eyes with it; hand it back to him.

When he goes downstairs, I pick up the broom and dustpan.

And then I pause in the room, and in a ragged whisper I plead with the house, "Please accept us as your new owners. Shelter us, keep us warm, and we will look after you so that you can live another 125 years."

I have to make friends with this place, whether I love it or not. I have never moved into a home about which I was so ambivalent.

THE HUSBAND AND I WORK ALL DAY and long into the night, sweeping and washing down surfaces, only for them to accumulate another layer of dust. The house seems resistant to cleanliness. So much of its life has been spent in a state of despair that it needs to be coaxed out of it.

Meanwhile, the feverish work of Francis and Mick does not let up. The sun sets, night draws in, and still the persistent sound of nail guns and power drills come across like a frantic attempt to save a life.

Midnight rolls around and it still is not done. None of us are on speaking terms. Francis and Mick plead exhaustion and leave. The Husband and I, covered in dust and grime from head to toe, stand in a house that looks as if sacks of flour have been detonated.

Tears and anger are out of the question at this stage. It will only open the floodgates to recrimination. I pluck a tired mantra from the ether and repeat it: "It will get done." What saves me from totally imploding is a sight we came across the previous day.

We had taken a walk around the leafy streets of our neighbourhood, to get away from the dust and noise. As we crested a rise near Greenbank Cemetery, we saw the perimeter road lined with horse boxes and vans. At first, we thought it might be an event of some sort, but the closer we got the more apparent the situation. This collection of panelled trucks, caravans, campers, and horse boxes were in fact people's homes; a veritable colony of them, at least forty vehicles.

These are the van dwellers, the people priced not only out of the housing market but out of the rental market, too. One of the vehicles labelled Horses has had the *r* crossed out and replaced with a *u*: it is that easy—a simple transposition of a letter—to slip from one social reality to another; it is that easy go from Horse to House. Outside one of the caravans, a dreadlocked mother in orange-striped harem pants and a stained T-shirt bearing the words "The Good Life" held her infant in one arm and checked her cell phone with the other. I cannot imagine raising a child in such conditions: no running water, no bathing or toileting facilities. It is August, but would they still be here in December? Yes, they would. What would they do for heat?

It was awful for them, and awful for the neighbourhood. Easton is liberal territory, but even liberals have limits. I am not complaining in a NIMBY way, but homelessness is something that cities are not dealing with quickly enough, not just politically but civically and corporately. Why the lack of action? Why is there no office to take control of the situation and to look at ways of handling this and ferreting out options for accommodation? A city is a money-making engine, but it also has a duty of care and hospitality to its residents. Of all the empty houses, warehouses, and office buildings that exist in this city, why is it so difficult for someone to figure out an inexpensive remedy to house people and get them off the streets? Previous eras had no difficulty in forcibly requisitioning buildings and supplies for wartime and emergencies. What does it take to declare this an emergency? People will complain that they do not want empty office blocks being turned into favelas, but what is the alternative? Is it not better to adapt empty office space for housing?

We had walked back home, to our dusty, partially finished two-storey home. In the scheme of things, in the current climate, our situation is more a brag than a complaint.

✦ ✦ ✦

Predictably, the house move of my dreams, of having the work finished two weeks before the movers arrive and of gradually and leisurely moving our stuff in, does not happen. What we get, instead, has all the calmness of a riot.

The casualty of the day was our gorgeous grey, curved-backed sofa, bought when we lived in Walthamstow. It would not fit through our Bristol door. Every possible angle was tried, but in the end, it was reloaded onto the van and taken into storage, where it will await flogging on eBay.

Our two-hundred-year-old pine dining table, salvaged by my parents from the basement of the Henry Farm house, fared better, but only just. The movers squeezed it through the doorway with no more than a quarter of an inch of allowance.

"I can live with the sofa not fitting through," The Husband says later, "but if your pine table hadn't made it . . ."

We shudder and shake our heads. Of all the furniture I own this is the one piece I want to pass on to one of my children. That table is more than a place where we eat our meals. So many of my childhood memories of home, good and bad, are etched into it. Literally, in one respect: One night during supper—this was around 1965—I was deep in discussion with my parents when our eyes pivoted toward my brother (a year younger than me), for no apparent reason except that he was unusually silent. There he was, idly carving his initials into the table with his dinner knife. It was a brazen act of vandalism that ended in a heap of punishment. The initials remained.

Memories are shoved into the far corner of my brain for now. It is the present that commands my complete attention; more precisely, how to sort through all our chattels. When I was packing up my Canadian home to move to England, a friend asked why I was not selling everything and buying new stuff in England. I thought the idea was outrageous; how could I part with things that have travelled with me for so many years? In hindsight, it was a more sensible suggestion than I gave it credit. I was certain I could fit my old life into my new life, but that rarely works well.

Our furniture is roughly sorted according to room. Towers of boxes are everywhere: I know exactly what I will be doing for the next month. In the room earmarked as my office there is a flash-mob of boxes broken only by a narrow path leading to the French doors opening into the side return leading to the backyard.

A single memory, like a stray thread, inches forward as if apologizing for the intrusion in my thoughts but certain that it might be helpful to me right about now: It is the memory of me standing in my parents' home the day after their own house move—when I offered to sort out their things while they went off to look at bathroom fittings, and in which I managed to pull off a little miracle of organization in just two hours. Could I achieve the same miracle here? Not likely. For one thing, there is simply no room—not an empty space to decant things to or rearrange. It is like a Rubik's cube: to shift one box or one chair you have to move six other pieces. We still have too much stuff, and this after I had done a major cull at our previous home . . . and the home prior to that. How much stuff have I accumulated in a lifetime? So no, that memory is not helpful. I banish it to the back of my brain.

Despite the state of things, it does not break me. What grounds me is the image of the caravans arranged like covered wagons around Greenbank Cemetery. And always, in my peripheral vision, is the blackened shell of Grenfell Tower.

The Husband and I are still struggling with the reality that neither of us loves our home; we lack the necessary sense of pride about it. I wonder whether we will ever get over that hurdle. Still, the fact remains: whatever the state of our minds or the chaos before us, we are still far, far better off. We have a home.

✦ ✦ ✦

THE DAY AFTER THE MOVE, Francis shows up. I fling open the door and glower.

"Look, I can come back tomorrow, or another day to finish up," he says, wisely interpreting my expression.

"Not today, not tomorrow. We will call you next week." I try not to snarl before closing the door. I do not want to see that man again. But I have to.

The following week he returns.

We have no water in the kitchen; no shelves in the pantry—food lies in boxes on the floor. No gas for the hob, so everything is cooked in the electric oven. We cannot figure out the microwave.

"The interior doors? Can you please put them on? Not even the bathrooms have doors." How many times do I have to ask him?

"Sure, I can do that."

He hooks up the water in the kitchen, and then goes outside to start repairing the pebble dash around the windows. It is as if his avoidance in putting up the doors is meant to make a point. I resort to following him around like a terrier, barking, "Could you please do the doors?"

Finally, he spends an afternoon putting up the doors. He says he will be back in two days.

When I go and check his work, I find that he has put on all the doors except two: the bathroom doors.

Three days later, the bathroom doors are up, but he forgets to install the jambs. Or he puts a catch plate on one door and neglects to install its lock. He calls out that he is running to the hardware store to get supplies, but when he returns, he never has what he set out to pick up.

✦ ✦ ✦

We are not the only ones frustrated by Francis. As each trade trickles back to put the finishing touches on their work, we discover that everyone to a man is fed up with Francis. A support group might be needed to deal with their complaints.

A few days after we have moved in, Cyryl, the painter, arrives. He had already painted the kitchen before we moved in, but given that Francis was rejigging the cabinets up until the final hour, Cyryl offers to do touch-ups. "In normal procedure you put up kitchen then paint," he grumbles.

Elsewhere, we clear small areas, shuffling piles of boxes and stacking furniture from one corner to another or moving stuff into the backyard so that he can paint the living room. We repeat this, multiple times, in every room in the house, though Cyryl tells us not to, that he is happy to move things. But we cannot help helping. He has a number of other clients scheduled, and the delay on our project has put them all into backed-up mode.

Today, he and I are sitting on the hall steps sipping coffee, commiserating about the work ahead for both of us.

"How much you pay for this?"

At first, I think he is asking how much we paid for the house. Or does he mean the renovations? Then I get it: he means how much did we pay for his services.

I tell him what Francis quoted me. I want to ask him to justify his fee, but at the mention of the quote he nearly chokes on his coffee.

"Two thousand five hundred?"

"Isn't that what you charge?"

"I tell Francis fifteen hundred. For entire house!"

"He told us two thousand five hundred for two rooms and the hall."

"I never work for him again," harrumphs Cyryl. "Next time you need painter you call me direct. No Francis."

Francis was right about Cyryl's work, though. It is nothing short of astonishing. It is not so much what he does to the walls, it is the magic he applies to the woodwork and the cornice mouldings. I thought I would have to bring in a plasterer to smooth the battered mouldings, but Cyryl has a bag of tricks that fills in missing bits and makes everything look new.

I am embarrassed by the painting The Husband and I have done in the bedrooms, particularly on the master bedroom ceiling. Cyryl has noticed it. I have caught him peeking into the room and grimacing at the sight of it. I tell him we were trying to save money, so it was one of the rooms we did not have plastered. But now the flaws in the ceiling have revealed themselves, especially on a patch that is resistant to paint because the old plaster has lost its key.

"When you lie in bed, you will see bad ceiling and it will make you angry. Let me fix."

Within the hour he has smoothed the rough edges and cured the paint-resistant section. It looks amazing.

Cyryl is not the only one who feels screwed by Francis.

Paul, the plumber, is furious, too. He arrives one evening to fix the bathroom sink and ends up having to take apart Francis's work. I sit on the toilet and chat with him while he works.

Paul, lying on his side on the floor, a free hand wrapped around a J trap, finally says, "May I ask why you waited so long for the bathroom to be done?"

The question startles me.

"Us? We were waiting for *you*. Francis said you were away, or that you did not have time because you had just had a baby."

Paul's head bangs against the bathroom vanity. "That's not true!" he says. "We were all set to do the bathroom in July, but Francis said you guys were not ready."

"What? The bathroom was the first thing we wanted done! We had all the pieces here by the end of June, waiting to be installed. He kept saying that people were away."

"Bullshit. We were ready. We begged him to let us get on with it, but he said you didn't want anyone back for a while. It didn't make sense. There's something wrong with that guy. I'm never working with him again."

"He mentioned that he had had a breakdown."

"He can't handle a full project on his own. Seriously, he does good work, but he needs people directing him."

"He told us that he was a project manager, that he still does it on the side."

"Don't believe a word of it. The guy can't organize breakfast, let alone a full-scale project."

"But he did your house."

"He did not do our house."

"He took us to your house and showed us your kitchen. He said he had done it. We hired him on the basis of how your house looked."

Paul forces himself to put down his tools calmly. He looks me straight in the eye.

"Are you serious? He took you into *our home?*"

Yup.

He takes a slow breath through his nose. "He did the demolition at the back of our kitchen. That is all."

"He took us up to your bathroom and said he did that, too."

Another deep breath. "Nope, he didn't do that, either. I did that with my brother-in-law and my dad."

We are very familiar with Paul's brother-in-law and father: his brother-in-law is Charlie, our plasterer; his father is Jasper, the retired firefighter who Francis told us was the kitchen fitter.

If Paul's anger is rising, so is mine, but who would I blame?

We hired someone who had shown us work he insisted he had done.

"We only kept coming back because of you and your husband," says Paul. "We like you guys, and we saw that Francis was screwing you over."

Cyryl has said the same thing to us, and it is humbling. All that tea making The Husband did has paid huge dividends.

As we adapt to our new home, a glaring flaw presents itself: The Husband cannot find a café in our neighbourhood that opens before nine o'clock in the morning.

"There has to be one close by," I say. There are three within a five-minute walk of our house.

"Nope. Checked them all. None of them open before nine."

He takes his cappuccino at seven—seven thirty tops. This is a man with a routine. He has taken to leaving the house and making the fifteen-minute drive back to Longwell Green so he can go to Costa or Caffè Nero in the retail park. We did not move to an urban area so that we could drive to cafés in suburbia.

The poor guy looks on the verge of a breakdown, and it is not due to the lack of an early-morning café. The stress of the reno and the move, my fessing up about going over budget, has sent him to the brink. I try to show enthusiasm for what has been done so that he can find pleasure in all the pain, but he only sees dust and debt.

The project has sapped me, too. There is no better indicator than a renovation to show how much the body ages between forty and sixty. Agility and foresight are on a downward trajectory.

It has been nearly twenty years since I last did any hard work on a home. I can plan and envision and make decisions, but in terms of physical work, well, I am shocked at how unsteady I have become on a ladder (I will not even touch on the matter of bravery and heights). How do we change so incrementally and yet so fulsomely? Then again, I must also acknowledge my ignorance: I have not kept pace with the tools of the trade. Everyone uses cordless tools; I am still using Jurassic-period screwdrivers and hammers. I should ask for a nail gun for Christmas. But then, it is not solely about the tools; it is about my ability.

This renovation has not improved my confidence about doing even small jobs. I need to put up a curtain rod in the guest room: I have everything for the job—tools and materials—but the metal curtain rod I want to use has to be cut. In my previous life I would have measured, marked the cutline with a pencil, then taken a saw to it without a second thought. Now I am scared of fucking it up. I have fucked up enough decisions and small jobs already. I cannot even budget correctly.

I stand staring at the curtain rod I hold in one hand, the hacksaw in the other, as if I do not know what to do with each of them.

The Husband appears.

"You need that cut?" he asks matter-of-factly.

He takes it from me, lays the rod on the edge of a step, and saws it perfectly.

I look up at him as if he has parted the Red Sea.

OUR SIXTH ANNIVERSARY ARRIVES, and we spend the day as far from wedded bliss as possible. I imagine him rueing the day we ever met. We have come close to a massive fight. I offer to leave the marriage, and let The Husband return to the quiet, orderly life he had before I came along and threw it all into a vortex of magazine dreams and renovation mania. But he says no, that my departure would leave him worse off financially. No mention of love, then.

The flaws and shortcomings in our home stick out as if marked in fluorescent paint. We cannot see beyond them. We grumble like spoiled children on the verge of a tantrum when the evidence of a beautiful home stares back at us.

This dissatisfaction wears me out. I am exhausted from keeping The Husband's spirits up; from keeping Team Renovation cheerful, on track, and paid. This project has been more emotional than physical.

Eventually, it sinks in that our grumbling and dissatisfaction are not about the house per se or any perceived or unperceived flaw but more about our expectations of one another and our individual and private failures. My upbringing put a premium on impulsivity, on the person with the brilliant snap decision, the decisive pronouncement. Where did that get me? Privately, I wish that we had the funds to do everything we wanted; I also wish I could do it again and do it right, and better. And within budget. I so wanted to be the saviour and the deliverer of dreams; to prove myself, so that The Husband's faith in me might grow. Right now, we exist as stubborn residents of Limbo, unable to name—much less get rid of—this acrid smell of defeat. It is just easier to blame Francis for it all.

23

The Flaws

Three months later, Francis arrives on a rainy Saturday morning to finish the remaining bits. He had asked us to hold back £500 until all the work was completed. At least I was not naive enough to do that: I held back £1,200.

In the interim, other trades have finished their work or have popped in to undertake new work for us. Jasper was a godsend helping us hang a large mirror, and install a radiator cover, towel racks, and shower caddies. Mark, the electrician, returned to hang two ceilings fixtures and install a Datapoint computer outlet in the study, which I still do not understand, even though he must have explained it to me half a dozen times.

In the past, I have been sad to see my builders leave. I had developed a rapport and rhythm with them, a sense of security and fraternity in their presence. Or maybe it was because I was on my own that it was nice to have a man in the house, if only for the day.

But Francis—I am not overjoyed to see him. I just want to see the back of him. I had considered paying him what was owed and telling him not to bother finishing up, but that is no way to complete a renovation. As much as you might grow to dislike your builder, he has probably grown to dislike you, too, and so the unspoken protocol is that you both uphold your respective ends of the bargain. It is one thing for you to call your builder "unprofessional," but he has every right to label you the same if you do not see things through to the end. Just as there are cowboy builders, there are also cowgirl clients.

I wonder whether I expected too much of Francis. That I wanted him to do more than renovate this house: that I wanted him to make it a home. But with the clarity of time I realize that only The Husband and I can do this.

When Francis appears that December day, he strides confidently through our home, as if this has all been his magic. He gloats about how fine it looks. I want to kick his ass. I want to tell him what a bastard he has been, screwing us financially, telling lies about us to the other trades, doing a shit job with the kitchen finishing, causing us grief. But I do not want to set him off. I just want him to get the final bits done and then get the hell out of my life.

He runs his hand across the white Corian countertops. Self-congratulation erupts on his face like a case of measles. He had nothing to do with selecting, ordering, or installing the countertops.

"Wow. They look great."

"Don't they, though," I say tersely. "The company I hired to fabricate and install them did a really fine job."

But there is no telling Francis that. As far as he is concerned, he did it all.

I let him get on with his work because I want him gone by noon, but when I happen to walk back into the kitchen fifteen minutes later, he has his phone out and is taking pictures of the room.

"It's for my website. You don't mind?"

"Sure," I say through clenched teeth. "But under no circumstances are you to identify us or our address."

"No problem." He continues to snap away. Soon, he is going through the entire house, taking photos in every room.

"Okay, that is quite enough." I say it like a schoolteacher.

When he finishes his work, he asks me for a testimonial. I give him a look that says: Are you on drugs? After scamming me on the painting quote? After trying to scam me on an invoice? After showing us a house in which you claimed to do the work? After the crap refinishing of the kitchen? Don't think so.

Francis's last task in our home is to install a small shelf in the kitchen. It is only when I am dusting it a few weeks later that I discover he has installed it upside down.

Guests arrive for dinner one drizzly Sunday. They had seen the house shortly after we bought it, and it is fair to say they thought we were crazy for buying it. Today is the big reveal. They are astonished by the transformation. The Husband beams and graciously directs all credit at me. "This was all Jane's work."

A friend who is a real estate agent in Toronto and shares my renovation mania has been my long-distance sounding board. I send him before and after photos of the kitchen. He responds via email: "My heart literally stopped when I saw the photos. I cannot wait to see it in person."

Everyone who comes through marvels at how bright our house is, how tranquil, how perfectly designed and organized it is. When we point out a flaw, people give it a half-second's notice and then return to praising the whole. And that is when I realize that that is how we should be looking at our home, too: not for what it is not but for what it is and has become.

The Husband and I slowly gain confidence in living here, and the imperfections recede like scudding storm clouds. As they do, we draw a bit closer to one another, until we are gushing with pride about what we have accomplished. Yes. *We.*

And still, my fingers itch as I continue to rattle around on Rightmove.

I HAVE NOT HEARD FROM CHERYLL since I posted the Facebook message. It troubles me. Does she not want to hear from me? Maybe she does not check Facebook. Maybe she has decided too much time has elapsed; that reviving our friendship is more trouble than it is worth. I worry that I might never reconnect with her.

I used to scorn those who never moved out of the neighbourhoods into which they were born, whose childhood and teenage friendships flowed effortlessly into adulthood, whose idea of adventure was to try out a new grocery store in another part of their city. I am grateful for my varied and somewhat free-spirited life, but such a life comes at a cost, and I fear that cost, later in life, will be disconnection and loneliness.

I sink into a kind of mourning, angered and perplexed over why, after forty years, these childhood memories are flaring up, scratching my heart, wielding so much power over me. This grief feels as if it has resided in me a long time. It is not just about missing a person I once knew; it is grieving the loss of a once-carefree existence. My life was constructed with orderly perfection in mind, but life has instead delivered a jerky quality of starts and stops.

I cannot entirely blame my parents for this: in adulthood I was always distracted by my career, by my family dramas and divorces, by bouts of trauma-related depression. Each house I moved into was to be a fresh start, and it was going to be where I got organized and settled once and for all. Except, it never works out quite that way.

It is naive to see a new home as a fresh start, a clean slate. Clean slates are constructs of delusion; a clean slate is what we call it when we fool ourselves into thinking we have control over our lives. There is no such thing as a clean slate. Even people in a witness protection program do not believe in clean slates.

In marriage there are no clean slates. Reports say that 12 percent of couples consider divorce when renovating a home. I would think that statistic is higher. A home renovation sharpens and deepens the cracks in a marriage like nothing else: two people viewing the same project from opposite perspectives and experiences, and projecting on to it their greatest fears, be they fears concerning money or creative expression. It is the rare couple who share a vision equally and faultlessly. We toss onto it our beliefs that once the construction dust has been swept away it will augur a new beginning. What actually happens is that a new tension arises, between one person desiring that fresh start and exploring a new setting, and the other desiring to turn back the clock to that period of stable familiarity.

All is not lost. I came across a study from the University of Edinburgh showing that moving house is a sign that a couple have a strong relationship, the proof being that the couple value one another more than the social network they will leave behind. Turns out that social ties, and not squawking seagulls or those annoying thirty-three steps up to the garden, are what prevent people from moving. According to the study—and validating what my mother told me sixty years ago—movers (people like my mother) value their overall life satisfaction more than they do their social circle. Furthermore, the study says, "Movers seem to value their spouses or partners more highly than stayers."

WEEKS PASS AND THE HOUSE gradually comes together. Our shed holds fifteen boxes of uselessness marked "charity box/boot sale." I draw up a short list of things that we need: a sofa that can fit through our front door, a few rugs, a deck out back, a new front door, window shutters, some light fixtures; the usual bits and bobs, but nothing critical.

We have hung paintings, arranged our familiar belongings into the five rooms and two loos that make up this English home, and yet it feels oddly strange, as if we are not meant to be here. In previous homes it has taken me all of twenty minutes to make a new place feel like home, but not this one. Not yet. Perhaps once the books are unpacked and onto shelves (still to buy) and my desk is set up and arranged with its totems. Maybe when a friend comes to stay.

There is no spiritual force in the house that has caused this lack of affection; it is just—I do not know—a sense of something missing, or something wanting. I am reluctant to form an attachment to the house. I wonder whether this means that this place is meant to be temporary.

Both The Husband and I acknowledge this. This house does not feel like home. It looks clean, finally, and modern. The natural light is wonderful, and this alone has immeasurably improved my well-being and mood. The kitchen is my favourite room. It is light, airy; it is possibly the best kitchen I have ever had. Being able to look out from it to the backyard, the greenery in the garden, the changing colours and mood of the sky—rain, snow, sunshine—has been worth the aggravation of the past year. We watch a few seagulls high above our house but cannot hear them: the wonders of double glazing.

✦ ✦ ✦

BOOKSHELVES ARRIVE FROM IKEA. The Husband rolls his eyes. It is possible that his dislike for Ikea exceeds his dislike for renovation.

At first, he shows no interest in helping me put them together, but guilt forces a change of heart. He ends up enjoying the process so much that he assembles them all. I have a theory that if you can put together Ikea furniture, you still have brain cells, and the will and capacity to learn.

Fifty remaining boxes of books, stacked along the wall in what is to be our study/library, have sat there so long that they look like a permanent piece of furniture or sculpture. Now it is time to empty them. Every single box gets emptied—every last one. Joy of joys, there is room to spare on the shelves so that I can intersperse among the neat rows of books, arranged by subject matter, a small painting, a few African statues collected by The Husband's parents, a majolica jug from my mother's collection, a few Royal commemorative mugs, my PEZ collection. It is such a relief to stand back and admire my little library that I call out to The Husband, "We have no more boxes to empty!"

"Except the fifteen in the shed," he calls back.

"Those don't count."

He sighs.

By December, however, things shift a little. Our lovely sofa that would not fit through our front door suddenly sells online. We order a new one. Comfort and style are important in this new sofa, but its dimensions must supersede all criteria. It has to fit through the front door. I have obsessed over the dimensions of door and sofa, hoping that the sizing provided on the website is truthful. Why did those Victorians make their entranceways so narrow? Two weeks before Christmas, the sofa is delivered—and makes it through the front door with barely an inch to spare.

The Husband lights the wood stove in the living room; heat and the amber glow envelop us as we snuggle on our new sofa. We watch the flames crackle and spit. It is good that our own crackling and spitting is over. We survived the renovation with our marriage intact. *Phew.* Now the house begins to feel like home.

BRISTOL

24

The Cost

I awake from a bad dream, heart pounding, face damp. Once I reassure myself that it was just that—a bad dream—my heart beat returns to normal. Eyes swivel to the clock on the bedside table: 12:35.

I ease out of bed so as not to disturb The Husband. The yellow glow from the streetlight illuminates my way out of the bedroom. I softly pull the bedroom door behind me until it almost closes but not quite. Everything returns to dark, the house silent and pitch-black. I stand in the hall to give my eyes time to adjust, but it truly is dark. I grope for the smooth wood of the banister and allow it to guide me down the hall. My hand bumps up against the edge of the first newel, and it is my cue to step down—one, two. When I touch the second newel, I turn the corner and prepare to descend the long stretch of stairs. Light from the street lamp floods through the transom above the front door, aiding my progress. I tread carefully down each step, willing it not to creak. At the newel post at the bottom of the stairs, I turn right, and right again, padding along the floorboards that do not creak. I stretch out one foot slightly to feel the edge of where the floorboards end and where I know there is a step down into the kitchen.

But I do not step down. My left hand grazes the wall, searching for the two light switches. I press them in unison. A dozen pot lights ignite, and their white brilliance bounces off the white Corian worktops, the glossy oversized grey-taupe porcelain floor tiles, and the sheen of the graphite cabinetry. The graphite metal frames of the windows and patio doors contrast nicely with the white walls, and I notice for the first time how well it echoes the black frames of the pictures that hang on the walls. The old pine table anchors the far end of the room and beckons me over, to pull up a chair, but I do not want to disturb a single thing. I just want to look and take it all in. Just for a moment. In silence. Without anyone around.

In the bad dream that had awoken me, the kitchen had been completed, or so I had thought, until a wind blew through it and I realized that Francis, the builder, had taken the bifold patio doors with him, and now there were no doors, no protection for the house. To top it off, the building inspector was coming round, and one of the suppliers we had used during the renovation had mixed us up with another client who had not paid, and now they were about to arrive to repossess the kitchen cabinets, and . . .

A bad dream. Still, it was so vivid that I briefly consider opening the laptop and consulting my renovation spreadsheet to ensure all the boxes under the "Invoices Paid" column have been ticked. But I am tired. It was just a dream. Besides, I feel as if I have paid everyone twice. And anyway, there is no money left. I refuse to let this bother me, and I give my head a shake to dislodge the negativity. Our pensions and the occasional royalty cheque will see us through. Maybe I can find part-time work. Things will sort themselves out. They always do.

Regrets and what-ifs are pointless after a renovation, though it is easy enough to wallow in them. But right now, at this moment, I am all smiles. The house, this kitchen, looks beautiful. I could hunt down imperfection—I know where it lurks—but all that does is engender a level of obsessive pickiness that will kill you. You have to make a pact with contentment.

Our street is a good one. We have kind neighbours on either side of us. I chat with Cynthia over tea and over the fence; on the other side where Ali used to live, two thirty-somethings, a brother and sister, have bought the house and are fixing it up. They are having their floors sanded as I write this. We have exchanged veggies and fruit over the fence from the bounty of our respective gardens.

Someone on the other side of the back-fence line keeps chickens and a rooster, and the clucks and crows are delightful and comforting. I have joined the Pilates class at the community centre, and there is a church around the corner where I offer thanks for my good fortune. The Husband has yet to find the perfect café to patronize, so he patronizes three or four. We have choice here.

Seagulls are a blessedly rare sight above our backyard, but a magpie frequently flies into our yard to test its authority. I will be seeing to him in due course.

There are still things that need doing on the house, but those will come when time and bank balance afford. It is not a house to boast about: it is not grand in size or distinctive in architecture, and what we have done to it will not win awards or merit magazine interest;

but its history, the tumultuous social and political periods it survived, its neglect and restoration, has earned my respect and appreciation. The fact that nowadays so many struggle financially to find a home makes me feel almost guilty about having one.

That said, hand on heart, if I was not married, I would be buying, renovating, and selling property all the time. I love it. I love the thrill of the hunt, the pulse-quickening chaos of the move, the settling in and discovering if, finally, this is the right place. The words "in need of improvement" are clickbait to me. Sometimes I just love peeking inside someone else's home to see how they live, and what they have envisioned for their home. I might have momentarily reached peak renovation, but not peak move.

Satisfied that my bad dream was just that, and that nothing has been stolen or repossessed, I turn off the kitchen lights, and retrace on tiptoe the route back to bed.

"What's wrong," The Husband mumbles sleepily.

"Nothing," I say. But before I fall back to a contented sleep, I think: Yes, I could—I would—do it all again.

THERE IS A COST TO ALL THIS, but it is one that cannot be tallied up in pounds and pence. The sense of displacement and dislocation cannot be overstated. Not just for me but for my family.

The day I left Canada and moved permanently to England, my eldest son, Adam, drove me to the airport. I had repeatedly asked my children if they minded me moving away, and they were swift in their replies: Of course not. Don't worry about it. Please go! As I mentioned earlier, they were all living in different parts of the country. Adam, however, is the only one of us who continues to live close to the area where he was raised. At the time, he was in his late twenties, had finished school, was working, volunteering, and enjoying his friends. When the day came for him to drive me to the airport, I kept my emotions in check so that I would not be some desperate, wailing mother. But I did tell him I would miss him very much, that I would be back at least twice a year to visit, and that I hoped he would visit us at some point. He waved away my concern for him and his siblings: "Mom, I'm nearly twenty-eight. Don't worry." So I shut up and kept the chin trembling to a minimum.

Two years later, we brought Adam to England to celebrate his thirtieth birthday. It was thrilling to have one of my children in my new home in my newly adopted country. As he and I caught up with one another, our conversation rotated back to that day he drove me to the airport. I congratulated him on his stoicism, and confessed how sad I was about leaving but that I had not wanted to break down in front of him. His reply was unexpected:

"After I dropped you at the airport that day and began to drive home, it all hit me. On the highway I finally had to pull over onto the shoulder because I was crying so hard. You were gone, Matt and Zoë had moved away, and I realized that I was the only one left. It was like my entire family had vanished. I had no idea where home was. Sure, I had my own place, but where was the family home?"

And that is the biggest cost of all. My embracing a shallow nomadism has left my children without any sense of Family HQ; of where everyone will gather for Christmas, birthdays, and anniversaries; or where they will go to locate that birth certificate or social insurance card that mothers are so good at filing and retrieving; or where remnants of school artwork and childhood toys can be found; where they can drop in and be corralled into some eye-rolling chore; where, when life goes tits up for them, they can regroup, fall onto their old bed, and be comforted by the familiar smell of their bedding, the cozy fug of their room, and the aroma of cookies or a favourite meal coming out of the oven. As it has turned out, home for my family is a moral construct that requires rigid internal scaffolding to support something achingly familiar and desired but entirely intangible.

It is a fact of life that children leave home and seek their future, and that they create their own nests. And it is a fact of modern life that they often move far away from home, sometimes halfway around the planet, when opportunities arise. But they never truly leave home, because "home" is a fixed place in their heads and their reality. It is also a fact of life that some of them never leave home, period; or they are forced through economic necessity to boomerang to the parental home.

I have encountered a stark contrast between British offspring and North American offspring when it comes to home and parental devotion. North American children seldom think twice when circumstances move them across the country or across the world. But young British adults actually turn down jobs if it means living far—and that can mean across town—from their parents. On Friday evenings, a radio station takes calls from listeners sharing how they are spending their weekend, and almost all of them are doing something with their parents or families, whether it is driving to Scotland to visit Mum, or heading to the West Country for Granny's birthday, or braving bumper-to-bumper traffic through the Midlands to join the clan for a get-together. No one is hanging out with friends; everyone is going home. This strong, passionate tie is curious and unusual to me, with my less family-oriented North American experience. An hour or three with Sis or Dad or Granny, yes, but an entire weekend? That's how murders start. I would venture so far as to deem the behaviour among adult Britons as a form of arrested development, but then, maybe that's my envy speaking.

Of all the homes I have lived in, working on this English home has made me think most deeply about what home is; where I belong, and whether I even have a need to belong anywhere. Maybe belonging is an old-fashioned sentiment designed to anchor us permanently; that the "new belonging" is where we are and with whom we are at that moment in time, and that to cut anchor releases us to explore the world and expand our understanding of it, as is our birthright.

Having never been the type to make five- or ten-year plans, I have let Life take the lead, and carry me on its current of surprise, chance, and opportunity. Experience has taught that a random encounter, a fleeting comment, or a tragic event can flip everything.

It does leave me in a bit of a quandary. On one level, all my house moves have made me a little bloodless, without allegiance to country or kin. The past is not meant to be revisited or idealized; it is merely a series of loose chapters that, out of necessity, are scattered to the four winds. It is easy for me to feel that I belong nowhere and to no one. Moving a lot and having people enter and exit my life have muted sentimentality. On another level, however, I work very hard to resist that attitude. I *do* want to feel rooted. I *do* want to belong. To feel otherwise does not sit well with me. Still, at this stage I feel stuck somewhere in the middle, and I wonder what it would take for me to topple fully into one camp or the other.

Despite their obsessive moves and renovations, my parents gave me a foundation upon which to construct a life. It has taken me this long, and with this English home, to understand that our loved ones—partners, children, dear friends—are the vital joists that underpin our lives. Careers and experiences—good and bad—are the interior framework that, like any interior framework, can be altered if you have the vision and desire to do so. Given all my homes and moves, it surprises me that I have only recently recognized the similarity between building a home and building a life. Brick by brick. Experience by experience. We are all individual homes built upon the remains of a previous home, previous settlement, some previous generation. We are all little ruins trying to rebuild and renovate ourselves.

IT TAKES SEVERAL MONTHS, but I finally locate my long-lost childhood friend Cheryll. It was not via Facebook. Turns out she does not like using it, either, and almost never checks it. I find her online, in a city outside Toronto, her name linked to a charity that raises money for mental health. A phone number and email address are provided on the charity's website.

Assuming that the phone number is the organization's general number, I dial it. My hands tremble as I punch in the long-distance coding for Canada and then the phone number. I rehearse in my head what I will say when I am asked to leave a message. But the female voice that answers does not announce the name of the organization. Instead, she answers with a simple "Hello?" It takes a moment before I cotton on that it is not the charity's general phone number; it is Cheryll's direct number. I ask if this is to whom I am speaking. She hesitates before answering, then asks who is calling. I tell her who I am. In seconds we are both sobbing into our phones.

She has been trying to find me, too, she says, but since I have had so many different surnames it has proven impossible. I am likely harder to find than Jimmy Hoffa or Lord Lucan. We exchange email addresses and send summaries of our lives. I send her mine; she sends me hers. It is wonderful and at the same time painful: we discover that both of us have experienced rape and continue to be haunted by its sustaining trauma.

Still, the relief of reconnecting with her, with an integral piece of my past, turns up like the welcome arrival of spring after a hard winter.

Cheryll mentions in an email that she is coming to England in a few months.

"You have to stay with us," I email back. "We have a new home." But I cannot help myself: without dropping a beat, my inner voice whispers, "For now."

ACKNOWLEDGEMENTS

Just as it takes many hands to renovate a home, so too does it take many hearts to write a book.

I would like to thank my family—The Husband, my children and their partners—who provide endless love and encouragement. It is a privilege to make a home with and for them.

On frequent visits to Canada, Rik and Jeannette Emmett and Paul Maranger and Robert Brown have been the most generous of hosts by opening their homes to me. Each visit reminds me how lucky I am to have them in my life.

Friends can be unwitting casualties in a house move, and only if you are fortunate do you get the chance to recover that loss. A thread in this book concerns the search for an old friend, and I am grateful to Cheryll Drew for allowing me to recount our subsequent reunion.

Finally, huge thanks to Patrick Crean for his advice and unstinting enthusiasm, to the folks at HarperCollins for shepherding this book to publication, and to the indefatigable Samantha Haywood and company at Transatlantic Literary Agency for doing what they do so well.